THE POLITICS AND POETICS OF IRISH CHILDREN'S LITERATURE

The Politics and Poetics of Irish Children's Literature

NANCY WATSON

IRISH ACADEMIC PRESS
DUBLIN • PORTLAND, OR

First published in 2009 by Irish Academic Press

2 Brookside, Dundrum Road, Dublin 4, Ireland	920 NE 58th Avenue, Suite 300 Portland, Oregon, 97213-3786

www.iap.ie

British Library Cataloguing in Publication Data
An entry can be found on request

ISBN 978 0 7165 3003 9 (cloth)

Library of Congress Cataloging-in-Publication Data
An entry can be found on request

Printed in Great Britain by the MPG Books Group Bodmin and King's Lynn

Contents

Foreword

A paradox underlies Nancy Watson's unusual and unprecedented book. In colonial times, an equation was often made between childhood and the mentality of spontaneous and unself-conscious Irish subjects: but after independence it was children, sooner than adults, who achieved a genuine independence of spirit. While many grown-ups still tended to act 'dependent' and refer all their judgements back to Britain as an epitome of human norms, children often seemed astonishingly self-possessed and more at home in the given environment.

One consequence was that the invisible republic of childhood became a sort of tribunal to which adult authors could appeal with any new or challenging idea. Nancy Watson is not exaggerating when she suggests that the re-examination by our younger contemporary historians of painful themes in Irish history, from the Great Famine to the Easter Rebellion, was rehearsed first of all in books by authors as different as Eilís Dillon and Marita Conlon-McKenna. If Lewis Carroll was able to explore being and nothingness in the crazy world of Alice down a rabbit-hole decades before Sartre and the existentialists, then Dillon could offer a mocking, occluded portrayal of Éamon de Valera well before most of the current deconstructions.

This book is based on the first doctoral dissertation to be submitted on the subject of children's literature at University College Dublin. Drawing as it does on the critical thought of the Frankfurt school and on post-colonial theory, it shows that the chosen texts are as richly responsive to deep analysis as works which are the subject of more traditional and conventional academic study. Watson also investigates works by Mark O'Sullivan, Siobhán Parkinson, Cormac MacRaois and Matthew Sweeney. These commentaries are, in the words of Robert Dunbar, 'characterized by clarity of expression and evidence of original thought'.

If a book is worth reading when we are 10 years old, it is worth reading (or re-reading) when we are 50. Watson sees as one of her main themes 'the reciprocal relationship between the adult writer and the child reader'. Equally important is the fact that many contemporary authors in their 50s have quite literally chosen to become children again, in order to evoke the ecstasies and terrors of their own earliest years. Many of these memoirists have written coming-of-age narratives which have been best-sellers as well as works of literary value.

Since nothing seems as remote as our own distant pasts, these books provide a priceless perspective on a time when childhood seemed a lot more protected than it does now. Yet at the heart of many of these memoirs of youth is that same sense of terror which has led so many, in some desperation, to evoke that lost earlier time. If childhood offers no final escape from the complications of the adult world, that is because children have always known more than they were supposed to. It is their destiny to be mute but feeling witnesses to the foolishness of the older generation.

Nancy Watson is alert to all these ironies – and to the fact that any children's book, however popular among the young (as all her chosen texts surely are), is ultimately produced by adults with very specific agendas of their own. However, she is also keenly aware that many difficult challenges posed by intrepid authors are deflected by adults, who sometimes believe that they can take the harm out of a text by re-categorizing it as an example of 'children's literature'. The great value of her study is that it subjects such works to exactly the kind of criticism normally reserved for books aimed at adult readers.

In helping to open up the academic study of children's literature in Ireland, she has, in a series of audacious analyses, thrown the very distinction between it and adult literature into question.

Declan Kiberd
May 2008

Introduction

There are few people who would argue that the successful and highly respected writers discussed in this book do not have a value within the category of children's literature. However, although the work of the six writers examined here in some detail is complex and sophisticated, there is currently very little critical analysis to do it justice. Their work has not, to my knowledge, figured in any discussion of post-colonialism, revisionism or post-modernism, either in literary articles or magazines. I started out on this project determined to show that the best literature for children was no less complex or well written than the best adult fiction, and determined to place these novels in a general hierarchy of Anglo-Irish literature as a whole. Intent on demonstrating the necessity of integrating children's literature with mainstream literature by applying and testing theory on a range of Irish children's books, I hoped to show that there was little or no difference; that these writers showed a concern for contemporary problems and offered a critique of contemporary society that was at least as valuable as that of adult literature. But, of course, there *is* a difference. It is not a difference in the complexity of the subject matter or the quality of the writing. The difference lies with the subject position of the child reader and the ability of the writer to allow us to see things from this new perspective; a perspective that allows us to see our unquestioned cultural assumptions through new eyes.

Deborah Thacker argues that 'While critics of children's literature *use* theory to argue the case for children's literature, theoreticians in general seem slow to *use* children's literature despite its relevance.'[1] Thacker goes on to say that theory *'needs'* children's literature if it is to properly examine the interplay between reader and text and the social and political forces that mediate this interplay. Without a consideration of child readers and the ways of reading available to them the picture must always be incomplete. I want to show that the best writing for children offers plenty of material for theoreticians.

Critics have pointed to problems in the concept of children's literature. For example, Jacqueline Rose has written about the impossibility of children's fiction, 'not in the sense that it cannot be written (that would be nonsense), but in that it hangs on an impossibility, one which it rarely ventures to speak. This is the impossible relation between adult and child.'[2] It is undoubtedly true, as Rose says, that there is 'an acknowledged difference, a rupture almost, between writer and addressee'.[3] But, this difference can be one of the advantages of children's literature. It is not necessary that the child be *used* as 'a concept to buttress different arguments and positions in the establishment of our relationship to changing cultural forms'.[4] It can be a more inclusive process; a two-way thing where children can be challenged to become involved in and grasp the complexity and multiplicity of the world in a way that encourages them to recognize ambiguities and difficulties and to understand them. While on the other hand, the attempt to view events from the different time and place of the child reader brings a new energy and optimism to our adult vision of the future, because the view from the child's position is generally more flexible and forward thinking than that of the adult.

Francis Spufford in his memoir of childhood and reading says that 'the book in the hand is a tool of growth'.[5] He believes that:

> The books you read as a child brought you sights you hadn't seen yourself, scents you hadn't smelled, sounds you hadn't heard. They introduced you to people you hadn't met, and helped you to sample ways of being that would never have occurred to you. And the result was, if not an 'intellectual and rational being', then somebody who was enriched by the knowledge that their own particular life only occupied one little space in a much bigger world of possibilities.[6]

Of course, these are the things that make reading worthwhile for all of us and not just children. On the other hand, the impact of children's literature on adults comes from the different perspective available to child readers which may be shared with adults. Viewed in this way, the phrase 'a good book for children is a good book for adults' takes on added meaning.

While all of the following chapters could probably be read in isolation, I hope that they each contribute to the main theme – the reciprocal relationship between adult writers and child readers. Although the different chapters may range from historical fiction to fantasy and poetry, in each case the different style of writing favours a particular perspective and provides a new context for the main theme. Each writer is aware of the different time and place occupied by the child reader, thus contributing to the emerging argument and giving shape to the complete work.

What the authors have in common is that they are all Irish, writing in the latter half of the twentieth century or the beginning of the twenty-first. Beginning with the Ireland of the 1940s and 1950s, between them they document the changes and highlight important trends evolving in Irish society up to the present day. I have made no attempt to give an overall view of Irish children's literature in this period, or even a comprehensive coverage of the works of each writer discussed. Rather, I have chosen the most appropriate texts to illustrate my line of argument.

The opening chapter begins by exploring some of the debates surrounding the concept of childhood, its changing meaning and most defining aspects. By looking at some Irish stories of childhood, particularly Eilís Ní Dhuibhne's *The Dancers Dancing,* it also examines the relative success – or failure – of some Irish writers who have attempted to bridge the gap and reach back to their former child-selves through literature. Ní Dhuibhne's novel is a particularly good illustration of the fact that, although bridging the gap between childhood and adulthood may be difficult, the world of childhood is not closed to us completely.

Chapters Two and Three deal with historical dilemmas and the way in which seemingly insurmountable problems can be solved by a child's eye view. In Chapter Two, Eilís Dillon shows how a child's perspective can help to connect old traditions to the present and future and bring new life to Irish identity in the post-colonial period. In Chapter Three, Marita Conlon-McKenna illustrates how the different subject position occupied by the child reader offers a way out of the impasses of Irish history constructed from the problems of 800 years of colonization.

In Chapter Four Cormac MacRaois' Giltspur Trilogy uses Irish mythology and legend as a contrast to the meaninglessness and emptiness of contemporary life. He highlights the important role of children both in questioning the kind of society they will inherit and as mediators in producing change.

In Chapter Five, Mark O'Sullivan concerns himself with the development of subjectivity in a social and cultural context. In the two novels discussed here, problems are solved through the development of dialogic relationships. A new vision of the future is constructed based on communication, understanding and cooperation between the different generations, showing that it is through intersubjectivity that each subject comes into its own.

Chapter Six brings a shift from dealing with the content of stories to a focus on the actual function of storytelling as a way for young people to learn how to share different life experiences and support each other.

In the two novels discussed in this chapter, the power of storytelling transforms the lives of the protagonists by shaping their experiences into recognizable forms and expanding their understanding of each other. Siobhán Parkinson shows that an exchange of narratives is an intersubjective thing that benefits both teller and listener.

Chapter Seven features the poetry of Matthew Sweeney. This chapter is included because the way we understand stories depends on our ability to use what Ted Hughes describes as 'the brain's fundamental genius for metaphor'.[7] Metaphor can be used in a variety of ways both to understand something that might otherwise be incomprehensible and as a way of expressing the inexpressible. It also enables us to better judge the meaning behind what we read or hear and poetry is seen as the most effective way of exercising this inbuilt and essential faculty. The intensity of Sweeney's recall of childhood emotions is also further proof that we *can* reach across the gap to our former child-selves.

While I hope that readers of this book will find new and convincing arguments that reflect the findings of literary theory, I also hope that they will be interested in the intersubjective nature of literature written for children and the way in which children's books can shape future political and social attitudes for both adults and children.

NOTES

1. Deborah Thacker, 'Disdain or Ignorance? Literary Theory and the Absence of Children's Literature', *The Lion and the Unicorn*, 24, 1 (January 2000), p.1.
2. Jacqueline Rose, *The Case of Peter Pan or the Impossibility of Children's Fiction* (London: Macmillan Press, 1984), p.1.
3. Ibid., p.2.
4. Ibid., p.142.
5. Francis Spufford, *The Child that Books Built* (London: Faber & Faber, 2002), p.9.
6. Ibid., p.10.
7. Ted Hughes, 'Myth and Education', in Geoff Fox and Graham Hammond (eds), *Writers, Critics and Children* (London: Heinemann Educational Press, 1976), p.94 .

Do You Believe in Children?

Every new child is nature's chance to correct culture's error.
Ted Hughes[1]

In *The Disappearance of Childhood* Neil Postman, an American sociologist, explains the construction of childhood following the invention of the printing press and its subsequent erosion in the present expanding information age.[2] He believes that childhood is a social artefact, not a biological category, and that the kind of 'adult' information that children are receiving is undermining the construct. It could be argued that this is true to a certain extent. We can hardly deny that children today have access to much more information than in previous years and that this has changed the meaning of childhood. But, just because today's young people do not fit into the same mould as previous generations of children does not lead anyone to suggest that they are not real children. In the same way, just because the meaning of childhood may change from one generation to the next does not mean that childhood dis-appears. The 'social artefact' that Postman talks of may indeed disappear, but, as the phrase indicates, and as Postman comprehensively documents in his book, this is something imposed from without and as such is always liable to change. I do not believe that what constitutes the spirit of childhood is the amount of forbidden information that children do or do not have access to. I believe that the most defining aspect of childhood is an inbuilt, natural and irrepressible curiosity. Curiosity is surely the essence of childhood and what renders it anarchic and subversive and, I would suggest, less easily disposed of than Postman would lead us to suppose.

For Postman, what is undermining the state of childhood is the acquiring of adult secrets; secrets that are to do with sexual relations, money, violence and death. There is nothing new about children's exposure to this kind of knowledge. For example, as Marina Warner has said, there was never anything in the least childlike about fairytales. They had always explored sexual experience and fantasy and had also often equated fame and fortune with happiness. Warner quotes John Updike, who described a collection of Italian folk tales as 'the tele-vision and pornography of their day',[3] and it is true that the example of most fairytales and folklore would seem to tell us that children already know the secrets of adult life.

Alison Lurie also would agree that children are well able to cope with so-called 'adult' knowledge. In *Don't Tell the Grown-ups* she points out that in the original ending of 'Sleeping Beauty', 'the heroine gives birth to two children as a result of the prince's passionate awakening of her'.[4] She argues that well-meaning adults who are horrified by the original versions of fairytales and consider them unsuitable for children are mistaken. They are, she says, a much better preparation for life than the pleasant 'realistic' tales that adults favour and which most school texts are based on:

> After we grew up, of course, we found out how un-realistic these stories had been. The simple, pleasant adult society they had prepared for us did not exist. As we had suspected, the fairy tales had been right all along – the world was full of hostile, stupid giants and perilous castles and people who abandoned their children in the nearest forest. To succeed in this world you needed some special skill or patronage, plus remarkable luck; and it didn't hurt to be very good-looking.[5]

Lurie points out that the illusion that children should or could be protected from adult knowledge would soon be dispelled if we listened to school-yard rhymes. Testing her theory, I enquired of one ten-year-old friend what skipping rhymes she and her friends were currently using in the school playground. This was one example:

> Cinderella dressed in yella
> Went upstairs to kiss a fella
> She kissed a snake
> By mistake
> How many doctors did it take?
> One, Two, Three ...

The rhyme was familiar. I remember my own children singing the same rhyme almost twenty years ago and of course even then it wasn't new. I also remember a hand-clapping game which included the lines:

> When Susie was a teenager, a teenager, a teenager,
> When Susie was a teenager, she went like this:
> Ooh, ah, I lost my bra
> I left my knickers in my boyfriend's car.

Iona and Peter Opie found that this game was played all over England from the late 1960s, with verses that varied only slightly from place to place and by little girls of eight or nine who were delighted by the audacity of the words. They point out the obvious derivation from another hand clapping game, 'When I Was a Young Gel', which is more than a hundred years old.[6] The survival of these games and rhymes would suggest that they have always been, and still are, passed from one generation of children to the next and are a way of expressing 'adult' knowledge. As the character Tom Crick, in Graham Swift's novel *Waterland,* told his pupils:

> I wish to point out that (despite the availability and variety of con-traception – despite the lowering age for the incidence of preg-nancy amongst schoolgirls – and despite the apparent quicker maturation, physically, sexually and ... even mentally, of today's juveniles) your present generation has no monopoly.[7]

According to Crick's 'impromptu theory', previous generations of children may have had less access to information but that didn't stop their natural impulses and curiosity. He believes that curiosity is what drives sexuality, science and story-telling. Although his younger self had lived in a time when 'there were no TV sets or tower blocks, no rockets to the moon, no contraceptive pills, no tranquillisers or pock-et calculators, no supermarkets or comprehensive schools, no nuclear missiles',[8] it didn't stop him and Mary from sexual desire and experi-mentation. 'Mary itched', Crick explained, 'And this itch of Mary's was the itch of curiosity ... Curiosity drove her beyond all restraint, to want to touch, witness, experience whatever was unknown and hid-den from her.'[9]

In spite of this, it would be disingenuous of me to suggest that the surfeit of soaps and sitcoms on television, the easy internet access and the violent computer games to which both children and adults are exposed, makes no difference. Unfortunately, Postman's portrayal of moral decline was essentially correct. The evidence is all around us in statistics on crime, violence and broken families. But, it is not simply a problem of children being exposed to adult knowledge. History shows that children are quite capable of dealing with this. The mind-numbing effect of overexposure to sexually explicit and violent images that erode one's sensibilities, along with bland sitcoms and soaps whose simplified plot lines encourage polarization and reduce one's ability to think rationally, is indeed worrying. But this is something that affects adults no less than children. It may even be the case that children are better equipped to cope with it than adults because children are, by their very nature, constantly asking 'Why?' A question which implies 'dissatisfaction, disquiet, a sense that all is not well'.[10]

Francis Fukuyama in *The Great Disruption* points out that the disruption of social order by the progress of technology is not a new thing. The pattern is there, he says, in the change from hunter-gatherer to agricultural societies, from agricultural to industrial societies and in the present change from the industrial to the information era. He identifies the breakdown in values that has accompanied the information age with a culture of intense individualism that 'corroded virtually all forms of authority and weakened the bonds holding families, neighborhoods, and nations together'.[11] What began as an era of freedom and equality has fast become the destruction of the system of customs and values that underpins a stable society; what Fukuyama refers to as 'social capital'. Fukuyama's thesis is that 'social order, once disrupted, tends to get remade once again, and there are many indications that this is happening today'.[12] He is convinced that the present phase of disruption is ending and that 'the process of renorming has already begun. Rates of increase in crime, divorce, illegitimacy and distrust have slowed substantially and have even reversed in the 1990s in many of the countries that earlier experienced an explosion of disorder.'[13] An article in *The Irish Times* in 2003 where the front-page headline announced: 'Serious crime figures for first quarter this year down by 9%' would seem to back-up his statistics.[14] The reason we can expect this to continue, he says, is that human beings are, by nature, social and rational creatures whose natural state is to live in an orderly society governed by moral rules.

Whether you agree with Fukuyama or not, there is no doubt that he makes a very strong case for his view that great disruptions in the social order occur periodically and are always restored to a rational normality. But he may be mistaken in his belief that change comes from the top down. He believes that social order will be reconstructed through public policies of policing and education. There is, however, another idea that refutes the notion of children as the passive subjects of socializing processes; a suggestion that 'the socialising process comes from below, not from above'; that 'values are not being transmitted, they are being created'.[15] It may be true, as Fukuyama says, that nature can be relied on to reconstitute the social order, but, as Ted Hughes' statement that 'every new child is nature's chance to correct culture's error'[16] suggests, nature's instrument for bringing about change in the social order may very well be childhood.

Hughes believes that children have a 'double motive' in their attempt to restore an inner, more spiritual world: 'they want to escape the ugliness of the despiritualized world in which they see their parents imprisoned'. They are aware that 'down there, mixed up among all the madness, is everything that once made life worth living. All the lost awareness and powers and allegiances of our biological and spiritual being.'[17] In a new preface to the republication of *The Disappearance of Childhood* in 1994, Postman added comments that he had received in letters from young pupils in Year 5 and 6 in response to the earlier edition. These children did not agree with Postman's theory. They offered comments such as: 'I think your essay wasn't very good. Childhood doesn't disappear – snap! – like that.'; 'Childhood doesn't disappear because you watch TV.'; 'Most kids who watch TV shows know they are not real.'[18] Their comments prompted Postman to conclude 'that children themselves are a force in preserving childhood. Not a political force, certainly. But a kind of moral force.'[19]

Bryan Appleyard takes this idea further and suggests that, contrary to how it might seem, it is young people who are resisting the spirit of the age and it is young people who have a sane understanding of the world, while their parents struggle with broken marriages, drugs, drink and depravity. Appleyard believes that 'the social goods on which the previous generation expended so much energy – anti-racism, feminism, environmentalism, peace – are taken for granted. A deep conservatism, a longing for stability, is the new, powerful force.'[20] Writing in the Culture Section of *The Sunday Times*, Appleyard, using the example of the popular TV series 'Buffy the Vampire Slayer', puts forward a theory that it is teenagers who 'become the authentic Americans, struggling like their settler ancestors, to build order amid the chaotic wilderness'.[21] The series is set in a high school in California and the vampires who persistently invade the school and who must be constantly struggled against are, he says, a sustained metaphor for every kind of teenage trauma. 'The demons', Appleyard believes, 'are metaphorical expressions of the way that life, to the teenager, seems more frightening and more significant than it does to anybody else'. This theory is confirmed by Joss Whedon, the creator of the show, who says: 'when we remember the sort of human relationships that people have that are really twisted and scary, and sort of extend those into horror stories, rather than just have a monster show up. That's where the stuff really disturbs me, when it's somebody's parent or somebody's friend who is turning into something horrible.'[22]

It is not just their own demons of sexual and social anxieties that these teenagers are fighting. Appleyard also sees popular culture as saying that 'the dislocation of values embraced by the 1960s generation must now be reversed and order must be restored'.[23] He sees teenage protagonists, such as Buffy, as fighting the dysfunctional adulthood of their parents and the breakdown in values and moral certainties that began in the 1960s. One of the characters from the series refers to the vampires as 'the Old Ones'. Appleyard equates them with 1960s liberals or, as he calls them, 'the wreckers from Woodstock' and says that it is they, not their children, who are being manipulated by demons. He also refers to the British sitcom *Absolutely Fabulous* and the Hollywood movies *The Faculty* and *Clueless* as examples of teenagers trying to reverse the 'dislocation of values' begun by the 1960s generation. He identifies a deep conservatism and a longing for stability as the new force driving the young, with stability being of the highest value. Appleyard concludes by saying:

> The fundamentalists, therefore, should not be alarmed. All of these works – and Buffy in particular – may be unorthodox, but they are extraordinarily moral. This is not the easy, ineffective moralism of political correctness. Rather, it is based on the genuine moral impulse to confront disorder and injustice. It is also more realistic than the liberal morality of the 1960s. Whereas the 1960s liberals believed in technological or political fixes that would put things right once and for all ... Buffy's struggle is eternal: the vampires keep coming.[24]

It would seem from the above that the so-called disappearance of childhood may in fact be an adult predicament and that when adults talk about the disappearance of childhood, very often they are talking about the disappearance of their own childhood or perhaps their own belief in the future. When they look back, it is not so much childhood that has changed as the person they once were. It has always been the case that, while the substance of childhood is for adults a fixed and unchanging thing, for the children in it, the present has 'more than one face' and can bring 'both joy and terror',[25] because even the smallest incident can play a large part in our destiny. No one can tell what outcome the events of the present moment will have on the future, because the 'here and now' is not a concrete time and place. It is a fluid phase of both the past and of a future succession of present moments. This means that children are looking forward with a mixture of curiosity and trepidation to a future of infinite, unexpected possibilities rather than backwards in the vain hope of a new beginning; a second chance. On the other hand, in a purely historical sense, 'any childhood revisited bears upon it the stigma of fatality'.[26] It is undeniable that 'what has happened, *has* happened: certain circumstances prevailing, certain decisions taken, have produced certain results, and there is no going back in time to change any one of them'.[27] One reviewer of Graham Swift's novel, *Waterland,* compared the situation to a forlorn fantasy about rewinding a film in order to dislodge settled facts. He had a friend who taught modern German history and who confessed to an annual depression as he reached the events of 1933: unalterably, every year, like a doom which does away with all our faith in freedom, the Nazis came to power again. In other words, the potential that adults are searching in vain to retrieve has not yet been lost by children. For adults then, identity is often contained in memory, for children it is in projection. This does not necessarily mean that adult identity has to be a stagnant and determined thing. Richard Kearney identifies narrativity as a means of resisting stagnation and a way of imagining oneself otherwise in the face of what seems like an unchangeable past. He says:

> along with every culture's sense of *constancy* over time goes an attendant imperative of *innovation* ... For once one recognises that one's identity is fundamentally narrative in character, one discovers an ineradicable openness and indeterminancy at the root of collective memory. Each nation discovers that it is at heart an 'imagined community' ... that is, a narrative construction to be reinvented and reconstructed again and again. The benefit of such discovery is that it becomes more difficult to make the mistake of taking oneself *literally,* of assuming that one's inherited identity *goes without saying.*[28]

All stories of childhood written by adults are narrative reconstructions and as such they contain a certain amount of innovation. It is difficult to get beyond memory to the actual consciousness of what it was like to experience remembered events as a child, and so these stories are often woven around factors that are important to their authors at the time of writing. In some cases the actual autobiographical events are of minor importance. Richard Coe, in his analysis of autobiographies of childhood, uses Jean Genet as an extreme example of a writer imposing his own pattern on the past, thereby taking charge of his own destiny. Of Genet's *Miracle de la rose,* which recounts his experiences in the reform school of Mettray, Coe says: 'If those characters for whom he is God are modeled on real, living beings, and particularly on beings who, in the past, controlled *his* fate, then does he now retrospectively control theirs?' The answer is 'Yes' because:

> even if he allows them to act as in fact they acted in reality, dur-
> ing his own childhood, these same actions *now* serve a lucid and
> coherent purpose – *his* purpose ... If 'they' – the staff at Mettray
> – thought that they were controlling Genet's destiny, they were
> right – but only because, in the pattern of the book, Genet him-
> self shows that it was necessary that they should do so.[29]

In this way, Genet has not only imposed his own pattern on the past, he has also created for the characters in his story 'a significance which they could not conceivably have possessed without his cooperation'.[30]

Coe has pointed out that, in the second half of the twentieth century, 'childhood autobiographies have proliferated on an unpre-
cedented scale'.[31] He attributes this to the upsurge in an obsession with questions of identity that has accompanied the nostalgia for lost tra-
ditions and cultures in the face of globalization. An obsession with identity, related to their history, may explain why Irish literature over the past century is rich in stories of childhood. Yeats, Joyce, Elizabeth Bowen, Louis MacNeice, and Frank O'Connor have all written memorably about their Irish childhoods and all of them tend to be associated with the questions of identity which plague a colonized country. Roy Foster describes 'The elision of the personal and the national, the way history becomes a kind of scaled-up biography, and biography a microcosmic history' as 'a particularly Irish phenomenon'.[32] And, as with any history, selections are made. As Coe says, 'At best, the outcome is a compromise. Childhood revisited is a childhood *re-
created,* and re-created in terms of art.'[33] Coe goes on to say that 'the truth ... will be relative to the fact and the manner of writing; it will also be relative to whatever scale of values happens to be uppermost in the writer's mind on the day he sits down at his desk'.[34] Stories of childhood may claim to relay only the child-self's formative influences, but they also disclose the adult's attitude and beliefs at the moment in which they are told. Looking at the experience of Irish childhoods through a small but representative selection of texts on the subject, it is possible to distinguish some different methods of writing about childhood and adolescence for adult readers. These examples would suggest that the connection between adult and child *can* be recovered but adult desire is often an issue in the construct of childhood. When dis-
cussing the writing of autobiography and the unreliability of memory, Elizabeth Bowen comments that, 'Almost no experience, however

much simplified by the distance of time, is to be vouched for as being wholly my own – did I live through that, or was I told that it happened, or did I read it? When I write, I am re-creating what was created for me … The past is veiled from us by illusion over illusion. It is that which we seek, it is not the past but the idea of the past which draws us.'[35]

Yeats called his account of childhood a reverie. He realized that while, in theory, one might have the best of intentions of telling the whole truth, in practice it is easier said than done because of the difficulty of translating imperfectly recalled thoughts and feelings into language, and so he wrote in the Preface:

> I have changed nothing to my knowledge; and yet it must be that I have changed many things without my knowledge; for I am writing after many years and have consulted neither friend, nor letter, nor old newspaper, and describe what comes oftenest into my memory.[36]

In *Reveries Over Childhood and Youth* it is possible to recognize the development of Yeats' later interests. The tone is one of wonder and fantasy where stories of death coaches, ghosts and other supernatural happenings are accepted rather than rationalized. At the time of writing he was interested in mysticism and was attending séances, and in his childhood recollections he tells matter-of-factly of his prophetic dream about his grandfather's steamer being wrecked, or about hearing very distinctly the signal of some dead smuggler who had lived a hundred years earlier in a house where he was spending the night. He heard, he says, three loud raps, adding that his 'cousins often heard them and later on [his] sister'.[37]

Denis Donoghue has described *Reveries Over Childhood and Youth* as 'a book of persons and places',[38] and it is true that many significant events are related to family and country. Yeats' ancestors are picturesque and, he implies, noble and passionate. He is delighted, he says, 'with all that joins [his] life to those who had power in Ireland or with those anywhere that were good servants and poor bargainers'.[39] Despite the fact that a lot of his childhood was spent in England, Ireland is the centre of interest and many of the events that he relates are formed into evidence of his Irishness. He tells of being a child in London and 'some old race instinct like that of a savage'[40] making him long to hold a sod of earth from Sligo in his hand. Features of the landscape and portraits of his kinsmen feature heavily because they gave him the notion of a distinct Irish identity.

The tone of Yeats' narrative is what Coe refers to as a complex mixture 'of poetic meditation and plain reminiscence'.[41] George Moore declared that it wasn't an autobiography at all because the memories are 'pure externalities',[42] but the concentration on external forces is important only in so far as they bear on Yeats' own personality development. It is clear that Yeats believed that the narrated events were all true to the spirit of his development even if they were not entirely factually correct. It is also clear that incidents are chosen and described according to their emotional or imaginative significance to his Irishness and his art.

Although first published in 1916, the same year as Yeats' *Reveries Over Childhood and Youth*, the hero of Joyce's autobiographical novel, *A Portrait of the Artist as a Young Man*, belongs to a completely different culture and the major themes are very different. It was his efforts to 'fly by' the nets of nationality and religion that preoccupied Stephen Dedalus and it is in his rejection of these themes that the young Stephen's identity finally emerges.

By giving the name of the Greek mythological hero, Dedalus, to the protagonist of his autobiographical novel, Joyce has not only drawn attention to the symbolic truth of his nature and destiny, he has also distanced himself and has thus enabled himself to structure his own past self. Everything is retrospectively interpreted and has significance. Richard Coe sees the absence of trivialities or meaningless events as one of the flaws in Joyce's *Portrait*. He cites as an example the infant song 'O, the green wothe botheth':

> Nothing, in the *Portrait of the Artist as a Young Man,* could seem less likely to escape from the domain of intimate triviality than the infant song 'O, the green wothe botheth'; yet later when, at the age of ten, Stephen Dedalus makes his first attempt to elaborate an aesthetic, the seemingly pointless 'green wothe' suddenly sharpens into focus and, pointless, makes the point: 'But you could not have a green rose. But perhaps somewhere in the world you could' ... The trouble is that all this is too neat; *everything* fits in, everything is part of a pattern.[43]

Coe believes that a true narrative of childhood must contain an element of randomness because that, more than anything else, is what constitutes the experience of a child.

As has been suggested by Richard Ellmann, *A Portrait of the Artist as a Young Man* is about the growth of a soul.[44] The succession of events that Joyce chooses to write about makes up the structure of the growth of that soul and its subsequent escape from the restrictions of

Irish nationality and Irish Catholicism. Everything leads up to the event of Stephen's conversation with the Director in Part 4. When the Director issues an invitation to him to join the order of Jesuits, Stephen's soul had already escaped and the pattern is complete: 'His soul was not there to hear and greet it … His destiny was to be elusive of social or religious orders … He was destined to learn his own wisdom apart from others or to learn the wisdom of others himself wandering among the snares of the world.'[45]

Although both Yeats and Joyce do offer a sense of their present selves being rooted in their childhood, there is also a great distance between the writer and the child each is writing about. This is, after all, what makes it possible to write about childhood in a detached way. Yeats wrote in a letter to his father: 'When I was immature I was a different person and I can stand apart and judge.'[46] However, especially in Joyce, there is a sense in which the recollections chosen have been selected as relevant to the subsequent identity of the artist and retrospectively interpreted so that events may have acquired a meaning or produced a feeling that was absent or different in the lived experience. Yeats himself pointed to the difference between the present moment and our memory of it when he said: 'As I look backward, I seem to discover that my passions, my loves and my despairs, instead of being my enemies, a disturbance and an attack, became so beautiful'.[47] He also said that in his youth he had as many ideas as he had years later at the time of writing but that in his youth he 'did not know how to choose from among them those that belonged to [his] life'.[48] In their stories of childhood, both Yeats and Joyce have translated life into art by arranging the pattern of events in a way that defines the meaning of their life at the time of writing.

There are other more recent and less distinguished examples of childhood memories, such as Frank McCourt's *Angela's Ashes* or Alice Taylor's *To School Through the Fields*. The concept of childhood in these more recent childhood stories often has more to do with the implied reader than with any real attempt to recover the fears and hopes of the child in the story and this plays a large part in their commercial success. McCourt's story of a miserable Irish Catholic childhood may appeal to Americans with a particular view of what it was to be an Irish Catholic in the 1930s. Alice Taylor's *To School Through The Fields* is, by contrast, an engaging memoir, but it lacks any authentic sense of childhood recalled. It is less a book about childhood than an adult's nostalgic dream of childhood which allows her readers to return to the pleasures of their youth without any of the pain. In a sense, both

McCourt and Taylor's stories of childhood are myths in that they reflect perceptions of the two main strands of Irish childhoods at the time – either a miserable state of poverty that is only relieved by emigration, preferably to America, or, de Valera's vision of a frugal rural idyll. R.F. Foster makes the acerbic observation that while, due to extreme poverty, the young Frank McCourt and his siblings saw 'the remnants of the family end up living with a repulsive cousin, whom the passive and exhausted mother is forced to sleep with ... Simultaneously, in a parallel universe, little Alice Taylor is out there in the countryside saving the hay and milking the cows and quenching the lamp'.[49]

The truth is that childhood was probably always difficult; a mixture of misery and magic, embarrassment and excitement. Eilís Ní Dhuibhne's *The Dancers Dancing* captures all of these things by getting close to the actual consciousness of its young teenage protagonists. Although it explores sex, class, politics and cultural identity like other Irish stories of its kind, it differs in that its basic element is that of recreating the different world that is childhood. Consequently, it is surely one of the most direct realizations of those themes which remain virtually the same for each succeeding generation of teenage girls; namely the social and sexual highs and lows as experienced in their raw state rather than transformed by memory.

Orla is one of a group of Dublin girls from a convent school who are sent to the Donegal Gaeltacht in the summer of 1972 to increase their knowledge of Irish language and culture. In effect, just like the protagonists of the six writers to be considered in the following chapters, the rite-of-passage experience of the young adolescent protagonist of this novel is paralleled by the development of Irish identity. In this case, at the beginning of a time that R.F. Foster describes as 'the exact period which saw the final abandonment of the introverted, autarchical national view in culture and economics inherited from early Sinn Fein'.[50] Foster sees this 'aggressive modernization' of the early 1970s as being linked to Ireland's joining the European Union in 1972, the date in which *The Dancers Dancing* is set. This time of change is very closely interwoven with 13-year-old Orla's experiences of growing up. On one level the novel is about the Education Act of 1967, the escalation of the Northern troubles and other issues related to Irish language and cultural identity. But, on a different level, all of these events merely form the backdrop to this artist's portrait of a young girl.

For example, it was the introduction of free education at secondary level in Southern Ireland in 1967, enabling the less well-off to continue their education, that caused Orla's social anxieties. For her mother,

Elizabeth, it means taking in lodgers to earn enough money to ensure that her daughter can attend a convent school and be better educated than her parents. With the extra money they can afford the uniform and the bus fares and the books. For Orla it means that she can never invite her friends home. Her house was a house of lodgers and consequently 'the inferiority of Orla's family to the families of Orla's friends is immense. It is an ocean that no bridge or ship or airplane or seagull or albatross or anything could ever cross ... If the friends got wind of it ... she'd be done for.'[51]

As far as the North was concerned it was like a foreign country to the Dublin girls. When asked whether she is in favour of a united Ireland, Orla replied: 'Not really ... I think it's more fun having the North ... it's like having a foreign country sort of on your doorstep.'[52] For Orla and her friends the North meant 'Opal fruits and Mars Bars ... Chewy tangy lemon and lime. Thick rich chocolate peanuts. Walls ice cream.'[53] For the children on the bus on the way to Donegal, the taste and the names of unfamiliar sweets conjures up an exotic image. Even the young British soldier who steps on to the bus at Aughnacloy is 'thrilling' rather than the depressing evidence of an occupying army.

Similarly, the ending of the IRA ceasefire in 1972 is memorable not because of the consequences for the North but because one of their house mates, Jacqueline, decides to return home to Derry. Not, as her friends originally think, simply because she is upset at the bad news on the political front, although she is. But when she gives her reasons for going home the ending of the ceasefire is just one of many:

> she complains bitterly to Headmaster Joe about the Doherty's primitive household, about her enforced starvation, about the lack of hygiene in the preparation of food, about her disenchantment with the Irish language and with the climate of Donegal, about her loneliness for her family, about internment, about William Craig, Whitelaw, Ian Paisley, and about several other things.[54]

The title of this chapter, 'The Truce is over (but not to worry it's 1972)', underlines the notion that 'an event as we imagine it hasn't much to do with the same event as it *is* when it happens'.[55] The reality of the present moment contains all the banal, ordinary and random things that are forgotten when we look back over momentous events. Even for Jacqueline, who comes from the Bogside in Derry, the disastrous events that are occurring in Derry even at that moment have an annoyance value somewhere between the lack of chips for dinner and the fact that she has just found a slug in her salad. It is not that she sees the ending of the ceasefire as trivial. It is more the fact that, in Jacqueline's adolescent mind, none of these things are trivial. In her small, egocentric world, they are all catastrophes.

In the end, *The Dancers Dancing* has less to do with the historical moment than with an adolescent girl's inner excitement and anxieties. The emphasis is always on the confusion of Orla's inner thoughts and emotions. In an interview Ní Dhuibhne said that she 'wanted to write about the wildness of young girls on the brink of adulthood, on their attraction to risk and danger, and about their affinity with the natural world'.[56] For young girls on the brink of adulthood the initial discovery of sex is what is described by Richard Coe as 'one of the "magical" experiences of childhood'.[57] The situation may be different now, but in 1972 it is probable that many Irish adolescents first discovered the *possibility* of sexual contact at Irish college. It is unlikely that sex was discussed with either parents or teachers or even between themselves. Ní Dhuibhne's narrator says that Orla and Aisling 'seldom discuss boys' bodies, or boys. Their sexual talk ... is all focused firmly on themselves. To be attractive, to learn how to present the perfect Orla or Aisling, with gleaming hair and glossy, slender limbs enclosed in the most alluring and correct garment, is such a huge preoccupation that it is as yet an end in itself.'[58] Their talk of marriage and honeymoons too is an end in itself and the 'dream man' is in no way connected to the boys that they know. When an image of Micheál does cross Orla's mind she pushes it away. It never occurs to either of them that what they are talking about has any connection whatever with sexual experience. Aisling advises Orla: 'You should do medicine then, if you want to marry a doctor. You know what Sister Veronica says: on your honeymoon you have to be able to talk about what he's interested in, otherwise he'll get bored with you. And you know, not like you anymore.'[59]

When Orla does feel the first stirrings of adolescent sexual desire it is towards Micheál and because of this his image is forever imprinted on her memory so that when she sees him years later:

> every curl on his head and every line on his body are as well-known to me as my own ... I have not looked at him for years. But he is in my head, he is in my dreams, he is in my body ... Micheál is more active in my dreams ... than anyone else, perhaps because he featured in my reality for such a short time.[60]

The adult Orla's emotion when she sees Micheál many years later has little to do with love. It is nostalgia for the intensity of the emotion he generated all those years ago. As her *first experience* of falling in love, Micheál is more active in her dreams and still has the power to excite her because he is associated with a unique feeling from that period of her life. A feeling that, although sought after, can never be replicated in later life because it has no equivalent in adulthood. The exalted sensation of such experiences is what constitutes the 'magic' of childhood and it is the loss of that magic that ensures that the image of Micheál will never be replaced in Orla's mind.

According to Richard Coe, 'it is significant that it is at moments such as these, when the grip of the "magic" is at its strongest, that ... prose gives way to poetry'.[61] When she follows the burn through the Doherty's garden and out into the surrounding countryside Orla's inner and outer worlds seem to correspond. She finds herself in an enclosed green area – 'a verdant tunnel' – which seems, like the future, to be dangerous and magical at one and the same time. In this place and at this time, pure sensation and imagination combine and the wild raspberries that she finds growing there are a taste of things to come:

> Sweet, tangy, cool, fresh, wild, tinged with an exotic flavour, like Turkish Delight, attar of roses, some flavour that is a perfume from a golden-covered volume of fantastic stories, a flavour that is a confirmation, for her, of the jewel-studded world that awaits exploration, that in all its richness is waiting for her to step into, to experience sometime soon, when she grows up. That is what the berries seem to be: a taste of a wonderful future.[62]

The poetic prose with which Ní Dhuibhne invokes the sensation of wonder and enchantment that Orla experiences with her first taste of the raspberries is the result of her effort to recapture the authentic sensation and the emotion of that moment for the child in it. There is no rational explanation for the effect that the few wild raspberries have, but the poetic language is almost certainly the outcome of a sudden flash of recognition in the writer's consciousness. It allows for infinite possibilities and the episode suggests a magical moment; magical 'in the sense that pure existence in itself is magical and miraculous'.[63] The process of growing into adolescence, the being-in-between, can be difficult to describe in ordinary language. For Julia Kristeva, poetic language is distinct from language used for ordinary communication. It is a writing practice 'that parallels the logic of the unconscious, drive-ridden and dark as it might be; such a practice thus assumes the privilege of communicating regression and jouissance'.[64]

If *The Dancers Dancing* will produce a shock of recognition in many of Ní Dhuibhne's readers, it also seems to have produced a shock of recognition in the adult Orla. In the final short chapter entitled 'Now', the narrative voice makes one of its many shifts in style so that Orla is speaking directly to the reader. In this short ending, she seems to realize that the child she is writing about is a stranger with vastly different experiences to the adult she has become. She is looking back across the gap, almost in a daze, at that recreated young girl who has become someone from another world with a different angle of vision and at a way of being that has no parallel in her present adult world. In relating her story, Orla is not simply revealing her childhood-self to her readers. In the process, she is rediscovering that other person for herself. As she comes to realize, 'You dig and dig and sometimes you don't recognise what you find'.[65]

I have no doubt that the six writers discussed in the following chapters believe in children. Like the character of Tom Crick, they believe in the 'comforting marker-buoys and trail-signs of stories'.[66] But the evidence would suggest that they see stories written for children, not only as a means of connecting children to their world, but also as a way of expanding those stories by bringing a child's-eye perspective and the experience of the child reader's own time and place to them. They know that the natural, inborn curiosity of childhood is the 'true and rightful subverter'.[67]

Writing about childhood can, of necessity, only be done from a distance and bringing a child's-eye perspective and the experience of the child reader's time and place is not easy. Picasso understood the difficulty when he responded to a comment on one of his paintings that 'a child could have done that'. He is reputed to have replied, 'Yes, but could a forty-year-old child have done it?' However, despite the difficulties, the episode of the wild raspberries in Ní Dhuibhne's novel is proof that it *is* still possible for an adult to catch momentary flashes of the magic of childhood and to reconstruct it in poetry. With *The Dancers Dancing* Eilís Ní Dhuibhne has brilliantly demonstrated that an adult writer can bridge that gap, if not in actual experience then at least in terms of openness to its different dimension, and it is this different dimension that makes children's literature an important element in academic study.

NOTES

1. Ted Hughes, 'Myth and Education', in Geoff Fox and Graham Hammond (eds), *Writers, Critics and Children* (London: Heinemann Educational Press, 1976), p.91.
2. Neil Postman, *The Disappearance of Childhood* (New York: Vintage, 1994 [1983]).
3. Marina Warner, *From the Beast to the Blonde* (London: Vintage, 1990), p.xiv.
4. Alison Lurie, *Don't Tell the Grown-ups: Subversive Children's Literature* (London: Bloomsbury Publishing, 1990), p.21.
5. Ibid., p.18.
6. Iona and Peter Opie, *The Singing Game* (Oxford: Oxford University Press, 1985), p.461.
7. Graham Swift, *Waterland* (London: Heinemann, 1983), p.158.
8. Ibid., p.55.
9. Ibid., p.44.
10. Ibid., p.92.
11. Francis Fukuyama, *The Great Disruption* (New York: Touchstone, 2000), p.6.
12. Ibid., p.6.
13. Ibid., p.271.
14. Carol Coulter, *The Irish Times*, 19 May 2003.
15. Bryan Appleyard, 'Welcome to Teen World', *The Sunday Times*, Culture Section, 18 April 1999.
16. Ted Hughes, 'Myth and Education', p.91.
17. Ibid.
18. Postman, 'Preface', in *The Disappearance of Childhood*, p.viii.
19. Ibid.
20. Appleyard, 'Welcome to Teen World'.
21. Bryan Appleyard, 'A Teenager to get your Teeth into', *The Sunday Times*, Culture Section, 10 December 2000.
22. Quoted by Appleyard in ibid.
23. Ibid.
24. Ibid.
25. Swift, *Waterland*, p.52.
26. Richard Coe, *When the Grass was Taller* (New Haven, CT: Yale University Press, 1984), p.109.
27. Ibid.
28. Richard Kearney, *On Stories* (London: Routledge, 2002), p.81 (emphases in original).
29. Coe, *When the Grass was Taller*, p.110.
30. Ibid., p.111.
31. Ibid., p.274.
32. Roy Foster, *The Irish Story: Telling Tales and Making it up in Ireland* (London: Penguin, 2001), p.xi.
33. Coe, *When the Grass was Taller*, p.84.
34. Ibid., p.85.
35. Elizabeth Bowen, *The Mulberry Tree: Writings of Elizabeth Bowen*, ed. Hermione Lee (London: Virago, 1986), pp.53, 58.
36. W.B. Yeats, Preface, *Reveries over Childhood and Youth*, in *Autobiographies* (Dublin: Gill & Macmillan Ltd, 1955), p.3.
37. Yeats, *Autobiographies*, p.16
38. W.B. Yeats, *Memoirs*, ed. Denis Donoghue (London: Macmillan Press, 1972), p.12.
39. Yeats, *Autobiographies*, p.22.
40. Ibid., p.31.
41. Coe, *When the Grass was Taller*, p.284.
42. George Moore in Richard Ellmann, *Yeats The Man and the Masks* (London: Penguin, 1987 [1948]), p.23.
43 Coe, *When the Grass was Taller*, p.213.
44. Richard Ellmann, *James Joyce* (Oxford: Oxford University Press, 1982), p.296.
45. Ibid., p.165.
46. Allen Wade (ed.), *The Letters of W.B. Yeats* (London: Rupert Hart-Davies, 1954), p.589.
47. Yeats, *Autobiographies*, p.62.
48. Ibid., p.83.
49. Foster, *The Irish Story*, p.168.

50. Ibid., p.xiii.
51. Eilís Ní Dhuibhne, *The Dancers Dancing* (Belfast: The Blackstaff Press, 1999), p.30.
52. Ibid., p.100.
53. Ibid., p.15.
54. Ibid., p.101.
55. Milan Kundera, *Testaments Betrayed* (London: Faber & Faber, 1996 [1995]), p.139.
56. Eilís Ní Dhuibhne, interview with Nicola Warwick via e-mail.
57. Coe, *When the Grass was Taller*, p.180.
58. Ní Dhuibhne, *The Dancers Dancing*, p.134.
59. Ibid., p.148.
60. Ibid., p.240.
61. Coe, *When the Grass was Taller*, p.35.
62. Ní Dhuibhne, *The Dancers Dancing*, p.72.
63 . Coe, *When the Grass was Taller*, p.113.
64. Leon S. Roudiez, 'Introduction', in Julia Kristeva, *Revolution in Poetic Language* (New York: Columbia University Press, 1984), p.3. 'Jouissance' can be defined as total joy or ecstasy.
65. Ní Dhuibhne, *The Dancers Dancing*, p.185.
66. Swift, *Waterland*, p.52.
67. Ibid., p.168.

2

Post-Independent Ireland: Eilís Dillon

> We – all of us – have come along either too early or too late.
> We'll have done the most difficult and the least glamorous
> job: making the transition.
>
> Flaubert[1]

I begin with Eilís Dillon because I see her work as 'foundational' in the
field of Irish children's literature in the same way that Seamus Deane
refers to Burke's *Reflections on the Revolution in France* as being a
foundational text in the contest between tradition and modernity.
Deane explains that:

> A foundational text is one that allows or has allowed for a read-
> ing of a national literature in such a manner that even chrono-
> logically prior texts can be annexed by it into a narrative that
> will ascribe to them a preparatory role in the ultimate completion
> of that narrative's plot.[2]

Like Deane in his view of Burke, I am not claiming that Dillon is the first
Irish writer from whom the whole tradition derived. She is not the first
successful Irish children's author, or even the most successful one, but
her children's stories are such that those which have gone before can be
seen as preparatory while those which come after show an evolutionary
or narrative progression. If previous Irish writers for children, such as
Patricia Lynch, had drawn the attention of the outside world to the separate national existence of Ireland, Dillon expanded that representation
for Irish children to include them as European and world citizens too.

Although the stories dealt with in this chapter are written retrospectively they are set in the period of Dillon's own childhood. They
are all set back in the early days of the new Irish state and explore
its growth in progress through the eyes of the young. Writing back in
the moment brings home just how profoundly colonialism seeps into

the minds of a people and how difficult some of the challenges they struggled with were. Because Ireland was one of the first colonies to gain independence, much of that which was condemned, and rightly so, by a writer like Sean O'Faolain, such as censorship, provincialism and political stagnation, can now be seen as problems that are common to every emerging nation and not just pertaining to Ireland. Writers such as Frantz Fanon and Edward Said have shown that some of the problems dealt with in Dillon's stories, such as internalized subjection, nationalist closure and an obsession with land, are part of the process of de-colonization and occur in varying degrees in all the countries which have freed themselves from colonizers. They are in fact symptoms of a sort of post-colonial sickness. The stories dealt with in this chapter show the movement from internalized subjection to the first growth of a confidence that is now reaching fulfilment; they show the necessity of keeping national cultures alive while at the same time allowing for multi-culturalism; and they deal with the dangers of the relationship between culture and imperialism. It is Dillon's treatment of these issues that this chapter will focus on.

It is important to remember that just as most of the child protagonists in Eilís Dillon's stories are on the threshold between childhood and adulthood, so the new Irish state at the time in which these stories are set is learning how to move from dependence to independence, from nationalism to true liberty. The nation too is growing up. To explore this growth through the medium of children's literature seems particularly appropriate for two reasons. Firstly, the fact that the period of learning and growth of the protagonist coincides with the period of learning and growth of the nation gives the choices and decisions facing the children of the stories a political slant. Secondly, if it is the case that it is 'when the children (in both senses) of the colonies read [such] texts and internalize their own subjection that the true work of colonial textuality is done',[3] then what better way to reverse the process of internalized subjection than by portraying the young (in both senses) as growing in stature and confidence.

'The first stage of a process of de-scribing Empire is to analyse where and how our view of things is inflected (or infected) by colonialism.'[4] In a speech made to the Parliament and Senate of the Czech Republic on 9 December 1998, Vaclav Havel says that the life of a society has two faces. One consists of the things people do in their daily life, the other is the relationship of citizens to their state, to the social system, to the climate of public life, to politics.[5] After long centuries of foreign dominance, the newly freed people have difficulty dealing with their relationship to the state. There is slowness to change, fear of innovation and a mistrust which comes from the old fear of those in charge. They find the responsibility that comes with their new freedom unbearable. Havel compares this odd state to 'the psychosis that follows imprisonment, when a prisoner used to living for years in a narrow corridor of carefully devised rules suddenly finds himself in the strange landscape of freedom, where he must feel that everything is permitted and at the same time is overwhelmed by the immense need to make decisions every day and take responsibility for them'.[6] He also says that it is easier to effect changes through young people because they are growing up after the collapse of communism and are free of this fear.

This of course also applies to those growing up after the collapse of colonialism and this is the theme of Eilís Dillon's *The Sea Wall*, a story in which old Sally MacDonagh tries hard to persuade the men of Inisharcain to bring in an engineer to mend the old broken sea wall. Sally remembers the damage done by the last big wave which engulfed the island and she fears that unless the wall is mended the same thing will happen again. But the people have a fear of officialdom left over from the days of oppression. They have transferred to the Irish government institutions the attitudes they once had towards the imperial government, so that the civic guards are looked upon as outsiders interfering in their community. They say that if they had men from the county council out 'the next thing would be that we'd have inspectors looking at everything and counting everything'.[7] Colonialism has become so ingrained that they have difficulty adapting to a new way of living and are prepared to put their island at risk rather than make a responsible decision.

Frantz Fanon says: 'It is not only necessary to fight for the liberty of the people. You must also teach that people once again, and first learn again yourself, what is the full stature of a man.'[8] Liberation, in Fanon's view, involves a movement beyond national consciousness to social consciousness. It is not simply a matter of recovery of the land; the new nation must learn how to take control in other ways. In *The Sea Wall* John points out the need to be able to take responsibility before you can become a man. Watching the small children who did not understand the gravity of 'the big wave', he 'tried to remember what it had been like to be five or six years old and to leave every trouble to the big people'. Now he is growing up and must learn how to make responsible decisions for himself. He recalls an incident when he was eight years old and he had to stay up half the night with a cow he was responsible for because she had slipped and fallen into a drain by the bog road. 'The morning after this experience he was a man.'[9] In the time in which these stories are set, this is not the case with most of the adults. After centuries of foreign domination the people were faced with the necessity to think for themselves and they were having difficulty adjusting to it. Sally has to get the two boys, John and Pat, to help her in her efforts because she says 'boys had to interfere when men wouldn't do what they ought'.[10] These formerly marginalized subjects have not yet learned 'what is the full stature of a man'. Only Sally and the children see and admit that nothing remains static. Either they must watch their island being slowly eroded or they must have the courage to move forward.

While they have a fear of outside controls and structures, paradoxically the people allow them to remain, in the shape of their councillor, Andy Phelan. He is typical of the colonial bourgeoisie, the new Catholic middle class who has taken over from the colonizer in that they have transferred the power and privilege to themselves, and his patronizing attitude enrages the islanders. As Pat remarks, 'Though he represented several of the islands at the County Council, it was well known that he cared little or nothing for the people that lived on them.'[11] The people are also still defensive in their attitudes and are not yet liberated enough or 'grown up' enough to ignore what they perceive as insults from Phelan, or even to refuse to re-elect him. He manages to insult the island people as soon as he arrives so that they refuse the help of the engineer who has come to rebuild the wall, but as Sally says impatiently when John points out that Andy Phelan's insults have 'ruined everything', 'With grown men that shouldn't matter',[12] again pointing to the immaturity or 'childishness' of their behaviour.

The island men wanted to keep out all outsiders, but as Frantz Fanon has pointed out:

> Far from keeping aloof from other nations, it is national liberation which leads the nation to play its part on the stage of history. It is at the heart of national consciousness that international consciousness lives and grows. And this two fold emerging is ultimately the source of all culture.[13]

The idea that it is more important to focus exclusively on one's own small problems than to concern oneself with global responsibility is another situation brought about by the collapse of colonialism and identified by Havel in post-communist Czechoslovakia. He says that vanity combined with provincialism causes the newly freed people to ridicule anyone who speaks of global responsibilities and encourages them to think only of themselves. When one of the men in *The Sea Wall* asks: 'And how do we know we wouldn't have a load of taxes put on us, to pay for that wall after?', he shows that a focus on economics has caused them to neglect the security of the island. They do not seem to realize that without security no economy can flourish. The islanders' wish for isolation, which is brought about by lack of confidence, has not only caused them to put the security of their island at risk, it has also prevented them from showing concern for future generations. When one of them says '"It will do our time." John gets indignant. "What about our time? ... Don't we matter at all?"'[14] Havel points out that although these things are seen as 'icing on the cake', when 'solidarity, concern for future generations, respect for the law and the culture of interpersonal relationships' are all trivialized there is nothing left 'to put the icing on'.[15] Dillon expresses this sentiment through Sally, when Sally explains what will happen if the sea wall is not rebuilt. 'Little by little, the lower part of the island will be washed away until the job of protecting Inisharcain from the sea will be so big that no one alive will be able to do it.'[16] Sally struggles to convince the people that they will only be secure when they see themselves as part of Europe and participate in the affairs of the greater world. She is saying that without this true liberation her island will disappear into oblivion.

Many feminist critics have pointed out the connection between nationalism and masculinity. Because colonial powers identify their subjects as feminine, passive, in need of guidance, the newly independent people aspire to the traditionally masculine role of power. Due to the insecurities left by colonial subjection, there is an effort to construct identification with the colonizer and his patriarchal values. This applies particularly to Irish nationalism where women were doubly marginalized by being reduced to cultural icons such as Mother Ireland or Cathleen Ni Houlihan.[17] This pattern of dominance and dependence is internalized in the minds of the people and is confronted by Dillon in her stories through her representation of very strong women. Sally is initially the only person in the community with any foresight and she doesn't give up until she has achieved her goal of having the wall mended properly. The contemptuous dismissal of Roddy Hernon when he says, 'Stand aside, Sally! This is no place for women',[18] is in such contrast to the action of the story that it merely serves to enhance her competence and good sense, especially as he himself is one of the ringleaders in turning away the engineer, and is portrayed as being aggressive and lacking in foresight or diplomacy. The image that Hernon has of himself is 'valued on the basis of its specular similarity to British cultural and institutional *models*'.[19] His failure to allow Sally to speak is both phallocentric and imperialist, and mimics colonial structures of power. When Sally, in a spirit of self assertion, finally calls on the good sense of the other women, saying: 'Women of Inisharcain! No one is asking you what you think',[20] the women are able to take control of the situation and they escort the engineer up to Sally's house. The men have no option but to follow.

The only weak woman in the story is Mrs Connor, who resorts to tears for even the most trivial of reasons. Instead of doing something practical to solve her problems she dissolves into tears and waits for someone else to solve them for her, thus portraying a typical image of the feminine. Sally, however, doesn't attribute Mrs Connor's 'moaning and lamenting' to the fact that she is a woman. It is just the way she is: 'A person's mind is like their body. If you're born with a strong one, you can do wonders and no thanks to you. It's as easy for you as it is for the weak people to do the little they're able for.'[21] As the story shows, weakness is not necessarily a female characteristic. In this way Dillon challenges the basic assumptions and myths that underlie the formulation of Irish national identity. Sally recognizes and points to the undervaluing of women in society, an undervaluing that comes from the notion that 'the feminine is simply the negative reflection of the masculine, whose "lack" confirms masculine wholeness'.[22] When John is writing the letter to the county council she tells him not to put her name at the bottom of the letter because 'a woman's name would be no good. It must be a man's name or they won't come.'[23]

The imitation of colonial structures of power comes across in other ways. In his essay, 'The Post-Colonial Personality', Vincent Kenny compares an authoritarian parent treating children as if they had no rights at all to an imperial power. He says: 'In this we see a repetition and a parallel process to the national experience where our autonomy, independence and confidence was systematically crushed by our treatment at the hands of other authority figures.'[24]

In Dillon's story, *The Cruise of the Santa Maria*, Colman Flaherty is an example of a parent as an authority figure who imposes the same type of constricting oppressions on his children that foreign oppressors imposed on the nation. Colman had quarrelled with his whole family because he belonged to a generation that did not expect children, even adult children, to question their parent's judgement. He had six children but he had driven them all apart from him because of his authoritarian manner. Jim says: 'I think I know why all those boys of his went to America ... Did you ever see such a cranky old rasper?'[25]

Colman would be quite astonished at the thought that anyone would be afraid of him. He does not see himself as crushing the autonomy and independence of his children. He simply believes that he knows best and he is behaving, John realizes, 'as he thought the father of a family should do, or perhaps an army general'.[26] He is in fact using the colonizer as a model.

Morgan MacDonagh, a character in the same story, also shows how oppression repeats itself. Dillon draws attention to this aspect of internalized subjection by having her young narrator, John, say of Morgan:

> it struck me then, as it often did later in my life, that it was a strange thing for a man who had suffered oppression himself to have treated someone else as badly. One would have thought he would have learned from his own sad life to be charitable and generous in his dealings. With him as with many another it seemed to have worked the other way: he had become sour and jealous of the good fortune of everyone else.[27]

Frantz Fanon in *The Wretched of the Earth* explains this by saying that colonization is a 'systematic negation of the other person'[28] and often brings about a mental pathology which is the direct product of oppression. Where identity is threatened it becomes crucial to assert it, so each person who is oppressed by someone more powerful than himself finds someone less powerful to whom he can become a tyrant in his turn. The psychology of the colonized causes Morgan to be a bully because he himself is being bullied by his mother. Also, Morgan wasn't just interested in marrying Sarah for love. He was 'after the island too – the bit of land she'd have here'. When Tomas asks Colman about his own land Colman says: 'There is land and money there but it's not mine.' He paid the money into the bank for his mother and he says 'Always she'd have it counted, she'd tell me. Only once, I kept a few pounds but she knew it when I got home.'[29] Both Colman and Morgan, each in their own way, display the mental pathology explained by Frantz Fanon and it takes the Spaniard, Tomas, to sort things out, because 'Tomas had a way of forcing Colman's interest on to new things, so that he almost seemed to forget to rage and shout'[30] and he dismisses Morgan's mother as a 'silly old thing'. Because he is an outsider and, more importantly, perhaps also because he comes from another colonial power and has not himself been subjected to oppression, Tomas has a clearer view and recognizes political and economic imperialism for what it is. He says 'the people should have put a stop to [these] games long ago'.[31] John is astonished at his air of authority: 'In all my life I had never heard such straight talk. We don't have the habit of it in Connemara – we take the easy, roundabout way whenever we can, perhaps from politeness, perhaps to avoid trouble.'[32]

Another example of the pervasiveness of colonialism is an obsession with land, and Dillon shows this process at work in *A Herd of Deer*. In this story we see how the plot arises from the prejudices of the people and their obsession with land. When Michael Joyce, the returned second-generation Irish-American, bought a house and some land in Connemara, he was realizing a dream:

> All the while I was growing up, my father was talking about Ireland and the beautiful country of Connemara. Long before I saw it I knew what the sunset was like there, and how the moon looks over a calm sea on a summer's night. I knew about the smell of a turf fire, and how the people sit in the evenings telling stories about the great heroes of long ago.[33]

But 'attachment to the imagined past, to the past which has been installed in memory by books, buildings, statues and pictures entails a leap over the immediate past'[34] and there were some things his father had not told him. He had not told him how the Connemara people would feel about what they perceived as a resident foreigner with 700 acres, while they struggled to make a living out of twenty or thirty acres – especially when he stocks it with 'a queer class of an animal'.[35] Both Michael Joyce and the Connemara people have been affected by tradition in different ways and Joyce's selective knowledge of the past does not help him to understand his immediate environment of the present. The old men want to 'fight for the right to use the sacred soil of Ireland to rear children, and decent animals like cows and pigs', and even though the younger men remind them that 'That fight is long over and won',[36] they themselves are not impressed by a deer farm either and would like to see the land divided out among the local people. All of them, except Michael Joyce, associate deer with the old landlord classes who had been known to clear out their tenants and stock the land with ornamental deer instead, and their prejudices show that the old insecurities are not far away.

In John B. Keane's play *The Field,* and the subsequent film of the same name, the theme was a man's obsession with land and the ruthless lengths to which it drove him. Just as *The Field* demonstrates 'how different the Irish American mind had evolved from the native Irish', and also 'how dangerous this obsession with land becomes, where even the native Irish are alienated from one another',[37] so *A Herd of Deer* explores the same obsessions, prejudices and outrage. As well as their resentment of the rich foreigner with his herd of deer, the locals are deeply resentful of the Scottish herdsman who doesn't allow anyone to trespass on the

land. They believe that their claim on the land supersedes even the owners' rights, and the idea that anyone could stop them from walking on
the 'sod' of their own country infuriates them. The narrator, Peter, has
had his own assumption of hospitality repulsed when he wanted to camp
on the land and he tells the owner: 'Let me tell you, Mr. Joyce, if you
never had a herd of deer there's no place in Ireland where the people
would stand for that way of doing things.'[38] In Ireland 'the land itself was
counted a holy thing, to be respected and prized'.[39] Just as Bull McCabe
in *The Field* does not respect the priest or the travellers because they are
not of the land, so the local people in *A Herd of Deer* have no respect for
Colman Donnelly because he 'hadn't the wits' to mind his land and sold
it to the foreigner. The idea of selling your land like any other com-
modity was totally alien to them and they regarded Donnelly with
derision. Ned Hernon says 'Colman is only half a man'.[40]

Because the narrator has a foot in both camps he can present both
sides of the argument. 'There is', Peter says, 'right on both sides as far
as I can see'.[41] His balanced viewpoint shows how misunderstanding
can turn into violence, and while this story doesn't result in murder as
The Field did, it does have one or two nasty moments, brought about
because the value of the land 'is set by history, politics, repression and
bloodshed'.[42]

Michael Joyce is finally accepted into the community mainly because
of his ancestry. Patsy says: 'But we never knew your father was a Joyce
from Casla. If we had known that in the beginning, things might have
been a bit different.'[43] This failure of inclusion is an aspect of the repression of others which, although understandable in their efforts to
repossess their own land, posits a notion of 'authentic' Irishness
which as we shall see further on in this chapter can result in racism or
neo-imperialism. In order to assert their own identity it becomes
necessary to suppress those who are seen as different. The search
for authenticity in order to assert a security of identity becomes what
'could be termed the "paranoid" moment of post-colonial discourse,
the dual passage between self-affirmation and self-defence'.[44] It also
follows colonial practices in that it attempts to define the boundaries
between us and them, a necessary pre-requisite of colonial authority.

As these stories show, true freedom is about more than a regaining
of territory and the after effects of colonialism are more pervasive than
its obvious geographical or political limits. It leaves a fear of officialdom, an unwillingness to take on responsibilities, an obsession with
land and it often imitates the parent-child metaphors that underpin
imperialism. As Vaclav Havel has pointed out, young people are more

likely to be free of these problems and so we can see them grow and develop a sense of autonomous identity. The analogy in these stories is with a young country which is also growing and neither the children nor the country can develop without pushing out their boundaries. John Stephens in *Language and Ideology in Children's Fiction* says that it can be a problem to represent growth in a character. The problem is 'to find strategies which will represent growth rather than just present it, which will demonstrate it, rather than merely assert it'.[45]

In Eilís Dillon's stories it is possible to trace the gradual maturing of the young protagonists. For example, in *The Sea Wall* the children move from a point where 'John's tongue refused to move', to where he is able to explain exactly what they wanted. We follow the growth and maturing process of the children from the first hesitant letter to the council to their eloquent plea at the council meeting, and we see that there is hope for the future when they take public affairs into their own hands. John, the more adventurous of the two, found that 'it was easy once he had made a beginning'.[46] He sees that Pat is a little slower to try new things, and resolves to 'get Sally after him' to persuade him to be more daring, because otherwise 'you never learn anything'.[47]

When the identity of a people has been threatened with extinction, that identity becomes more intense, more important. In an effort to rid themselves of their old colonial complex and ensure that their different identity was acknowledged, many more mistakes were made, chief among these being a withdrawal into themselves as a nation and a notion of 'authentic' Irishness that was exclusive rather than inclusive. Dillon's stories show that a love for national culture and a respect for the cultures of others is not incompatible. Her use of Hiberno-English coupled with her use of folklore and customs both contrasts Irish and European stories and also points out what they have in common.

In *The Aran Islands*, Synge quotes an old man who says: 'A translation is no translation unless it will give you the music of a poem along with the words.'[48] This mirrors Dillon's view that music and rhythm were very important in language. She disliked stage-Irish dialects, preferring, like Synge, to write in an 'English into which toxins of the Gaelic mode of speech and syntax had been injected'.[49] Her daughter, Eiléan Ní Chuilleanáin, remembers her mother trying out the sentences in Irish first before translating them into English.[50] Thus we have sentences such as 'I'm thinking he'll only laugh at me'[51] using the progressive tense formed with the present participle as we would in the Irish language, or sentences where the imperative is formed with 'let' as in 'Let you run up and tell him the good news'.[52] This language, as well as infusing her stories with a sense of place, also fore-grounds the presence of the oral tradition. The Irish story-telling tradition is closely adhered to with the phrases and images from spoken Irish and also with the first person narrator used in most of her stories.

There are many different aspects of culture – language, stories, songs, food and traditions. The young reader of Eilís Dillon's stories, as well as learning about the traditional belief in ghosts and other superstitions, also learns the idea of 'visiting houses', the habit of blessing a house when entered, and the layout of the houses. They also learn that the people's diet consisted mainly of potatoes and soda-bread, supplemented with a little bacon or salt fish. In this way, she makes a way of life that is in danger of being forgotten, 'once again a portion of the imagination of the country'[53] and gives the young reader a link with the past and a sense of continuity. It is clear that it is important to her that children should have a knowledge and respect for their own distinctive Irish dialect and culture. In *The Cruise of the Santa Maria,* Juan explained why he knew so much about Ireland, even though he had been born in Spain and had lived there all his life. His mother, he said, had told him stories and sang him songs.[54]

However, it is also important that children should have respect for the culture of other countries. In his introduction to *The Folklore of Ireland* Sean O'Sullivan says:

> Ireland's geographical position as an island on the extreme west-ern edge of Europe ensured that, while its people were close enough to borrow lore and ideas from their European neighbours, they were enabled at the same time to preserve a fairly accurate picture of what belonged to themselves traditionally.[55]

Pat, the narrator of *The Singing Cave,* confirms this when he talks about the air on the island of Barrinish as being 'full of strange wild scents and tastes that seemed to have been carried on it from faraway places and mixed delightfully with our own homely smells of salt and seaweed and turf-smoke and spring grass'.[56]

By making connections between different cultures as well as pointing out the differences, Dillon encourages her young readers to have a more open view of the world. In *The Singing Cave* Pat discovers an inner chamber in a cave which is known locally as 'the singing cave' because of the sound the wind makes as it moves through the inner chamber. Inside the chamber is the skeleton and tomb of a Viking warrior: 'He wore a bronze helmet, decorated with short, straight horns. His bony fingers lay listlessly on the hilt of a long sword. Thus he had sat I supposed, for a thousand years, exactly as his friends had left him.'[57]

The Breton fishermen in this same story find that the singing cave on Barrinish is just like their own 'grotte qui chante',[58] which, when they first opened it, also had a Viking inside. The Viking skeletons which have been found in all the caves mark the uncovering of a civilization in its broader European context and also serves to place Ireland in that European context. This is something that was very important to Synge too and in *The Aran Islands* when Pat Dirrane, the storyteller, tells him the story of The Faithful Wife, Synge relates it to similar versions in other countries and he says: 'It gave me a strange feeling of wonder to hear this illiterate native of a wet rock in the Atlantic telling a story that is so full of European associations.'[59]

In *The Cruise of the Santa Maria* John, the narrator, finds the courtesy of the Spanish men 'astonishing' and remarks that he 'had often observed the same in the men of Rossmore'.[60] He also compares the Spanish women, with baskets of washing on their heads, to the women who sell fish in Galway and who also 'carry their baskets on their heads'.[61] The differences are pointed out too. In *The Singing Cave* when Louan says 'we are a hospitable people just like the Irish'[62] and invites Pat and Tom to enjoy a meal of shellfish, it was little to their taste. Tom plans to get his own back when Louan next visits Barrinish. He tells him: 'We would like to return your hospitality by giving you a fine dinner of potatoes and sour milk.'[63] Louan bowed politely but the idea did not seem to make him happy. The repeated patterns which the boys find in the Spanish and Breton communities, along with the cultural differences, are a way of recognizing the world. They allow for 'the recognition of multiplicity, variety and irregularity in the recognition of self-similar patterns'.[64]

As her use of language and folklore shows, Dillon emphatically sees herself in a national tradition and she believes in the vital relation of our past to our present and future development. However, one of the most important things to be learned from folklore is a more open view of the world and the way in which it places Ireland in its European context, showing that whatever differences of tradition exist with other European nations there are also many similarities that can be identified. She shows the way forward to reconcile the concern for national culture with the openness of Europeanism. In an article called 'The Multiculturalist Misunderstanding', K. Anthony Appiah distinguishes between 'liberal' multiculturalism and 'illiberal' multiculturalism:

> a decent education will teach children about the various social identities around them. First, because each child has to negotiate

the creation of his or her own individual identity, using these collective identities as one (but only one) of the resources; second, so that all can be prepared to deal with one another respectfully in a common civic life ... But there is another side to multiculturalism that wants to force children to live within separate spheres defined by the common culture of their race, religion, or ethnicity.[65]

The first of these is of the kind that Dillon advocates in stories such as *The Cruise of the Santa Maria* or *The Singing Cave*. It attempts to reconcile for Irish children their European identity with an understanding and admiration for their own Irish identity. The second, or 'illiberal' multiculturalism, is the kind which 'sets out to force on each child its "proper" identity'[66] and which sees its idea of culture as above everyone else's. It also sees culture as being something apart from the actions of everyday life. This is again a symptom of post-colonialism that characterized the Ireland of the 1940s, 1950s and 1960s, but as Vaclav Havel has pointed out, you cannot view culture in this way. Culture is part of everyday actions and endeavours.

We have seen examples of political and economic imperialism in the stories of Colman and Morgan in *The Cruise of the Santa Maria*, but culture too shows the pervasiveness of imperial attitudes. Edward Said believes that 'there is in all nationally defined cultures ... an aspiration to sovereignty, to sway, and to dominance'[67] and the Ireland of Eilís Dillon's youth was no exception. She was born in 1920 and grew up in a time which Sean O'Faolain describes as: 'one of the most sad and stagnant phases of our long struggle to recognise that, in every age, the past is but the twilight of the dawn'.[68]

O'Faolain puts this down, at least partly, to the fact that the background of all previous nationalist politics had been a semi-educated peasantry, so that our nationalism, having no industrial class to inject a social content into it, developed as a 'mystique'. 'Politics', he says, 'as the technology or blueprint of a new way of life was beyond it'.[69]

Censorship, which began in 1929 under the first Free State and continued throughout de Valera's regime, was a tool for those who feared outside influences. It was what Eilís Dillon herself called 'the last sign of post revolutionary fervour which strove to make Ireland once more an island of saints and scholars'.[70] Julia Kristeva explains in *Nations Without Nationalism* why this might happen. She says that when we no longer know who we are, and are searching for identity, we 'take shelter ... under the most massive, regressive common denominators: national origins and the faith of our forbears'.[71] We are provided with an insight into the truth of this in the post civil war society in which

Eilís Dillon grew up. For example, in January 1995 the largest file among the newly released cabinet papers covered the activities of the 1926 'Committee on Evil Literature'. During this period over ten thousand authors were banned under the pretence that they were indecent, but Sean O'Faolain suggests, 'actually to silence every frank attempt to delineate the society in which he lived'.[72] These state papers also reveal that the commission on emigration discussed a proposal, as late as November 1948, that girls under the age of 21 be prohibited from leaving the state. The comment of the Archbishop of Dublin, Dr McQuaid, that every member of the committee who voted against the ban 'contributed to the continued flight of immature young persons into moral, national, and social perils',[73] articulates the endemic fear of outside influences. Maurice Goldring points out that:

> Thunderous excommunications, whether in republican ranks or cultural circles, share the same logic as Communist parties with the resulting danger of a totalitarian state. Democracy, on the other hand, must first learn to recognise that different ideas must be understood, tolerated and maybe even considered as not necessarily wrong.[74]

Dillon was born, she says, 'into a world of ghosts',[75] where the spirits of the 1916 rising still lingered, and it is with the ghosts of the past that the book I will discuss in this section concerns itself. Tracing the developments of her own writing in a paper given at a conference on children's literature, she says: 'as time went on I found that it was possible to make the background support of a story more sociological than adventurous'.[76] This is certainly true of *The Island of Ghosts*, published in 1990. The preoccupation in this story is with the questions, which Sean O'Faolain says are controversial in all post-revolutionary periods: 'Past or Future? Progress or Stasis?'[77] The alternative would be to adapt old traditions to new circumstances, but in Ireland, 'we lived', O'Faolain says, 'under the hypnosis of the past, our timidities about the future, our excessive reverence for old tradition, our endemic fear of new ways'.[78] *The Island of Ghosts* investigates the fact that this kind of withdrawal into oneself as a nation portends 'a decline of individualities, cultures, and history ... to the advantage of subjective, sexual, nationalist and religious protectionism',[79] and as such, it illustrates the close connections between culture and imperialism.

One way of overcoming imperialism is to try to discover an essential, pre-colonial self but as Edward Said points out, there are dangers of chauvinism and xenophobia in this. While it is true that nationalism and the assertion of a separate identity can advance the struggle against domination, it often becomes a chauvinist and authoritarian conception of nationalism. In *The Island of Ghosts*, one of the protagonists, Mr Webb, is introduced as an outsider: 'His name was George Webb, and try as they would no one has ever been able to put Irish on that. A more foreign name couldn't be imagined.'[80] As the story progresses, it is not difficult to equate him with that other 'unique dictator' with a foreign name, namely Éamon de Valera, the most significant figure in the political history of modern Ireland. The similarities are too numerous to be coincidental. De Valera has been described as being 'on the border line between genius and insanity',[81] a description which also fits Mr Webb very well. Brendan says: 'He's out of his mind'[82] and Mr Lennon says 'That man is a genius'.[83]

The amazing mathematical capacity of de Valera is common knowledge. Desmond Ryan says that: 'He was recognised as one of the greatest mathematicians in Ireland of his years and had he continued his mathematical career it is possible that the historians of the future would put him on a pedestal side by side with Hamilton Rowan.'[84] Sean O'Faolain in *The Irish* describes him as 'a combination of realism, sentimentality and ruthlessness' adding his belief that 'all idealists are ruthless'.[85] Mr Webb too is described as an idealist with a wonderful capacity for mathematics. 'Mathematics', he says, 'when you pursue the subject far enough, presents the ideal world, a world of order, a world under control'.[86] He is an engineer, and, he says, a good stonemason and plumber too. He is able to make his own electricity and his own irrigation system, and generally make the island, to which he has abducted the boys, almost completely independent and self-sufficient. In fact, his plans for their life on the island bears great similarity to de Valera's vision of an ideal Ireland with its idea of 'frugal comfort'; a vision which was put forward in the St Patrick's Day broadcast of 1943 entitled 'The Ireland That We Dreamed Of'. It seems that de Valera's ideal Ireland and Mr Webb's Hy Brazil are one and the same place. However, as Barbara, the co-narrator, says, and as de Valera's 'athletic youths' and 'comely maidens' were to find out, 'there's no such place as Hy Brazil'.[87] One of the problems is that, in their efforts to revive the indigenous tradition which they feel is being threatened:

> individuals transform the indigenous tradition into a doctrine or into an ideology ... The practiced beliefs of the traditional reactionaries are practically never identical with those traditions they seek to reinstitute; the latter are very selectively reconstructed. The revival of a tradition almost inevitably involves changing the tradition.[88]

We can see an example of this in Mr Webb's indifference to the bones he has found on the island, even though he admits like the others to having seen the ghost. Despite the traditional belief that until the bones had a 'decent burial' and the right prayers said the soul could not rest, he left the bones of the mother and her child under the turf rick. He had also used part of a cell left by St Brendan where he had founded a little monastery and the headstones from the graveyard to build extensions to his own house. Mr Webb had used tradition to suit himself. When the bones have finally been laid to rest by the islandmen, Dara reproaches Mr Webb: 'There's a tradition in front of your nose. You're always talking to us about traditions and traditional living. How can you have respect for one tradition and not for another?'[89]

'It is ... a mark of quality in a book that it differentiates its values rather than fusing them in composite and (perhaps fraudulently) homogeneous groups.'[90] Eilís Dillon has great respect for the intelligence of her young readers. 'They miss nothing', she says, 'and they savour every nuance and every detail that inspiration sends one'.[91] The debate is complex and acknowledges multiplicity and diversity. In spite of the fact that they have such different aspirations neither Dara nor Brendan's roles in life are presented as deserving higher value than the other. Both boys have courage and integrity; these qualities are not necessarily dependent on the choices they make. Both knew from the beginning what they wanted to do. Brendan is not interested in 'frugal comfort'. He has envisaged a few new practices along with the traditional way of doing things and is more interested in 'a big grassy farm somewhere in the midlands'.[92] He thinks that the Island of Ghosts 'was a good place in its day. But who would want to live with ghosts?'[93] He was going to be a farmer, he said, but not quite like his father before him: 'No. He lives in the Stone Age. I'm going to have modern methods.'[94] Later he says: 'I have nothing against stones but I mightn't want to spend the rest of my life with them.'[95] Edward Shils explains that:

> What has happened is that there are some persons in the receiving culture who have acquired elements of the alien tradition while retaining the indigenous tradition in all other respects ... When a relationship occurs over a great distance, through colonists, missionaries or conquerors, the active transmitting agent may remain unchanged; they might add words to their vocabulary and artefacts; a small number of the members of the society might learn the new language, gain new knowledge, but their use of their own language, their own traditions of arts, remain as they were and so do their religious beliefs.[96]

Brendan is following in the footsteps of his father in that he still wants to be a farmer but he has different ideas about how to go about it. Dara on the other hand says: 'I like our life here. I'm an islandman all my life',[97] and all the attractions of the old way of life are presented through his eyes. Even the ghostly woman has two points of view and seems to embody the ambivalence of acknowledging the past while at the same time realizing that inevitably there must be changes. When Dara asks Brendan what he thinks she would have to say to Bardal, Brendan replies: 'Nothing. I think she's angry with him because he brought us here, and still she's glad to have us, to have people come to live here again.'[98]

Mr Webb is not presented as a bad man, more a misplaced idealist. There is more than one road to take. It is a matter of choice and of having the freedom to make that choice, and this is the problem with Mr Webb. He doesn't trust the boys to be able to move forward and at the same time to stay in touch with their past.

The complexity of the argument is further evident from the fact that Dara, like Peter in *A Herd of Deer*, has a foot in both camps. Brendan was his 'greatest friend'[99] and he sympathized with his position, but he himself enjoys his life on the island, even though he is there against his will, and he has great admiration for Mr Webb who has taught them so much. He tried to explain to Brendan how he felt but Brendan has no sympathy at all with these feelings. He says: 'We might as well be in a concentration camp ... I don't know how you can find a good word to say for him'.[100] He suggests that Mr Webb is making use of them. 'He wanted to live here but he was afraid to come alone.'[101] It is true that Mr Webb felt let down by his previous society and hopes for redemption in the myth of Hy Brazil. He lost his wife in an accident when they were both engineers working on a plane, and now even the sight of a plane from the outside world flying over the island caused him to fly into a rage.

Edward Said explains that 'the power to narrate, or to block other narratives from forming and emerging is very important to culture and imperialism and constitutes one of the main connections between them'.[102] There are many examples in *The Island of Ghosts*, particularly in the exchanges between Mr Webb and the boys, which make it clear how closely the operation of power in society is associated with language. Mr Webb operates from a position of power which comes partly from his love of the traditions he wants to safeguard and fear that they will be lost, and partly from his assumption of adult superiority. In her discussion of power in conversational exchange Jenny Thomas shows how her findings on the language of power are generalizable across all 'unequal encounters'. She describes 'particular strategies employed by the "powerful" participant in an interaction ... which enables him/her to keep the upper hand'.[103] Many of these strategies can be identified in the encounters between Mr Webb and the boys. For example one of the ways of 'blocking the addressee's bolthole' is the use of 'upshots'. This means that 'the dominant speaker presents the hearer (H) with an "upshot" (a brief summary by the dominant speaker of a long contribution by the subordinate) ... in response to which H is required to make clear or simply to confirm the intended pragmatic force of his/her utterance'.[104] An example of this can be seen in the following exchange. After the boys explain that they must get home because their parents will be worried, Mr Webb says:

> 'They'll get over it, ... I noticed that they were letting you go off to Galway without a murmur out of them.'
>   'We would come back', I said. 'We were only going to school.'
>   'And after that?' As we made no answer he went on: 'You know very well that hardly anyone comes back, once they've been away to school.'[105]

The pragmatic tactics used by Mr Webb has completely silenced the two boys.

His position of power is demonstrated in other ways, such as the fact that they are inhabiting what he calls 'my kingdom'. In other words the interaction takes place on his home territory which adds to the power differential. He 'orders' them to do things instead of asking. In this way he succeeds 'in making explicit [his] own speech act force, thereby removing any polite ambivalence and giving the utterance a "sledge-hammer effect"'.[106] Again, he demonstrates his position of assumed power in his refusal to answer the boys when they try to tell him that they must get back home before the storm prevents them from leaving. Dara says: 'He paid no attention to me, just continued on his way so that we had to follow.'[107]

In *Language and Ideology in Children's Fiction*, John Stephens discusses novels where a main character's life is described as that of a slave. He says: 'This draws our attention to the subjection of the individual by social practices embodied in the power exercised by parents or by instructors.'[108] There are several references in *The Island of Ghosts* which draw attention to the master-slave relationship between Mr Webb and the boys. Dara says: 'He was our master, and though he gave his orders kindly enough it was clear that he expected us to jump to obey him.'[109] It is Brendan, however, who identifies their situation as slavery when he says: 'He has two slaves now, and that's what we'll be forever if we don't make a run for it.'[110] He also draws our attention to the censorship of the period when he says: 'He even carries that little radio of his in his pocket, so that we won't find out what's going on in the outside world.'[111]

Towards the end of the story, when their parents and neighbours come to rescue the boys, Mr Webb produces a revolver, saying 'if anyone tries to take away these young people, I'll shoot them all'.[112] This has echoes of de Valera's statement that 'the lesser evil is to see men die rather than that the safety of the whole community should be endangered'.[113] It is ironic that in an effort to gain control Mr Webb uses the now discredited ideology of 'pedagogic improvement' and reverts to the disturbingly familiar idea of 'subjugating and virtually enslaving the natives'.[114]

De Valera was aware that ideology is bound up with language. In the St Patrick's Day broadcast mentioned above, he says that the national language is more than a symbol; it is an essential part of our nationhood. Ignoring all that has happened in between, he says: 'The Irish language spoken in Ireland today is the direct descendant, without break, of the language our ancestors spoke in those far-off days.'[115] Mr Webb too is aware of the connection between ideology and language and he is very good at word games. He has a scrabble board and offers to show Dara how to play, though Dara admits that Mr Webb was nearly always able to beat him at the game. Brendan, however, absolutely refuses to play, in fact he would scarcely speak to him. Jenny Thomas stresses that strategies consciously employed by the dominant participant, or 'metapragmatic acts' (MPAs), are not effective in and of themselves. Their effectiveness, she says, 'lies in a combination of the MPA + the power relationship obtaining between speaker and addressee'. Thomas suggests that these strategies are only effective in situations where both participants are, whether consciously or not, compliant with the 'status quo'. She goes on to say that 'in interactions in which one participant refuses to accept the dominant ideology ... tactics such as those I have described will not work'.[116] While Dara is basically compliant because even though he is there against his will he finds the life there very pleasant, Brendan, on the other hand, recognizes that he is always the subordinate participant in an unequal encounter and so he will always be powerless. He attempts to subvert the power relationship by physically overpowering Mr Webb but when his plan fails he falls back on the only other course open to him.

He completely withdraws from the encounter, refusing to play language games and almost refusing to even speak to him. The ideological gap between them makes communication impossible without some kind of compromise and Mr Webb does not compromise: 'His dream, Hy Brazil, filled his mind completely, leaving no room for anything else.'[117]

Cait is the only one who can sometimes beat him at his own game. She also knows the importance of language as we realise when she suggests changing the name of the island. When Dara asks her if she would live there with him when they are old enough to get married she says: 'Of course I would, but we'll have to give it another name.'[118] This gives a sense of the power of language to change the way in which we interpret the world and also demonstrates how colonialism 'conceptually depopulated countries' by 'looking through the native and denying his/her existence'.[119] The name of the island is changed from 'Island of Ghosts', a name which leaves Brendan outside of history, back to its original name, which was 'Brendan's Island', ironically called after St Brendan the Navigator. Brian Friel's *Translations* showed the importance for the colonizer of Anglicizing place names, while 'one of the first tasks of resistance was to reclaim, rename, and reinhabit the land'.[120] In the same way, Brendan had been dispossessed by the ghosts but by changing the name he is reinstated, showing that there is more than one kind of nationalism and that there are multiple perspectives to be reconciled. As Roy Foster comments in his Foreword to Hubert Butler's *Children of Drancy*, 'Solipsistic "ideal" communities are not the way to a better world'.[121]

While emphatically seeing herself in a national tradition, as is evident by both the politics and poetics of her storytelling, Eilís Dillon believed that the culture of a nation is an ever developing process, a living thing that grows and changes rather than the resumption of a fixed past identity. When he was outlining the points he considered necessary for transforming the Czech state, Havel left culture to the end because he considered it to be the most important. He said, 'it is not true that culture is a superstructure that sometimes lives a parasitic existence on a flourishing economic base'. It can be measured, he said, 'by what skinheads shout in the bar U Zabransk Yeh, by how many Roma have been lynched or murdered, by how terribly some of us behave to our fellow human beings simply because they have a different colour of skin.'[122] This is how we should think about culture and identity. As Havel goes on to say, the people who rant on about national identity and try to engender fear of its loss obviously understand identity as something we are given; something over which we have no control and this is not so. 'Identity', he says, 'is above all an accomplishment, a particular work, a particular act. Identity is not something separate from responsibility, but on the contrary, is its very expression.' In spite of Havel's pleas the Czechs are now erecting walls and barbed wire fences and throwing curfews around gypsy camps; not unlike limited internment.[123] On this basis and in the present racial climate, we need to think about 'how we give substance to our identity'.

As her use of folklore shows, Dillon does believe in the vital relation of our past to our present and future development. However, while her stories celebrate Irishness, they have a more comprehensive idea of what Irishness is, and it is not the narrow nationalism put forward by Mr Webb. Said's *Culture and Imperialism* shows that 'neither culture nor imperialism is inert, and so the connections between them as historical experiences are dynamic and complex ... cultural forms are hybrid, mixed, impure, and the time has come in cultural analysis to reconnect their analysis with their actuality'.[124] President Mary Robinson expressed similar sentiments in her address to the Oireachtas in 1995, when she said:

> This island has been inhabited for more than five thousand years. It has been shaped by pre-Celtic wanderers, by Celts, Vikings, Normans, Huguenots, Scottish and English settlers ... Whatever the rights and wrongs of history ... how could we remove any one of these things from what we call our Irishness.[125]

This inclusiveness is confirmed by the conclusion of *The Island of Ghosts*, where both boys fulfil their ambitions in their own way: Dara and Cait on Hy Brazil, and Brendan and Barbara on a grassy farm in Tipperary. Brendan, however, has been damaged by his experience in that he can on longer bear to even speak of either Mr Webb or Hy Brazil, proving that Mr Webb's efforts have produced more harm than good. This has its parallel in the backlash of shame in Irish culture experienced in the 1950s and 1960s, when the young turned towards England or America.

Dillon does not promote the ideology of either of the boys, but she helps her readers to understand them. In this way she can help them to grow beyond the divisive political attitudes of their parents. This is especially important in today's world, in a time of renewed nationalism, where Julia Kristeva points out that, 'the cult of origins easily backslides to a persecuting hatred' and 'we could witness a loss of concern for personal freedom, which was one of the essential assets in the "Declaration of The Rights of Man and Citizen'".[126] K. Anthony Appiah points to the fact that 'the trouble with appeal to cultural difference is that it obscures rather than illuminates the situation'.[127] It is not the different culture that the racist disdains but the people.

A writer with this richness of material does not need exceptional ingenuity in order to discover ways of entertaining children. According to Walter Benjamin, 'children are particularly fond of haunting any site where things are being visibly worked on'.[128] Dillon does not assume that children's books should lack complexity. In fact she says, 'it has always been comforting to be sure of such an intelligent audience',[129] and this is reflected in the level at which issues are discussed. The children who read these stories are not just being entertained; they are also seeing how colonial practices can be reproduced in their own community and, as a corollary to this, they are learning to outgrow it. It is this engagement with the politics of Irish life that connects Dillon to other political and literary writing in Ireland and sets her children's stories firmly within the main body of Anglo-Irish literature.

NOTES

1. Letter of Gustave Flaubert to Louis Bouilhet (19 December 1850). Quoted in Richard Terdiman, *Present Past: Modernity and the Memory Crisis* (New York: Cornell University Press, 1993).
2. Seamus Deane, *Strange Country: Modernity and Nationhood in Irish Writing since 1790* (Oxford: Clarendon Press, 1997), p.1.
3. Chris Tiffin and Alan Lawson (eds), *De-scribing Empire* (London: Routledge, 1994), p.4.
4. Ibid., p.9.
5. Vaclav Havel, 'The State of the Republic', Paul Wilson (trans.), *The New York Book Review of Books*, XLV, 4 (5 March 1998), pp.42–6.
6. Ibid., p.42.
7. Eilís Dillon, *The Sea Wall* (Dublin: Poolbeg, 1994), p.39.
8. Frantz Fanon, *The Wretched of the Earth* (Harmonsworth: Penguin, 1990 [1961]), p.237.
9. Dillon, *The Sea Wall*, p.34.
10. Ibid., p.52.
11. Ibid., p.20.
12. Ibid., p.24.
13. Fanon, *The Wretched of the Earth*, p.199.
14. Dillon, *The Sea Wall*, p.16.
15. Havel, 'The State of the Republic'.
16. Dillon, *The Sea Wall*, p.48.
17. See Eavan Boland's essay *A Kind of Scar: The Woman Poet in a National Tradition* (Dublin: Attic Press, 1989).
18. Dillon, *The Sea Wall*, p.23.
19. Chris Prentice, 'Problems of Response to Empire', in Tiffin and Lawson (eds), *De-scribing Empire*, p.47.
20. Dillon, *The Sea Wall*, p.115.
21. Ibid., p.70.
22. Prentice, 'Problems of Response to Empire', p.47.
23. Dillon, *The Sea Wall*, p.10.
24. Vincent Kenny, 'The Post Colonial Personality', *Crane Bag*, 9 (1985), pp.77–8.
25. Eilís Dillon, *The Cruise of the Santa Maria* (Dublin: O'Brien Press, 1991), p.76.
26. Ibid., p.76.

27. Ibid., p.155.
28. Fanon, *The Wretched of the Earth*, p.200.
29. Dillon, *The Cruise of the Santa Maria*, p.161.
30. Ibid., p.175.
31. Ibid., p.177.
32. Ibid., p.159.
33. Eilís Dillon, *A Herd of Deer* (London: Faber & Faber, 1969), p.15.
34. Edward Shils, *Tradition* (London: Faber & Faber, 1981), p.53.
35. Dillon, *A Herd of Deer*, p.35.
36. Ibid., p.59.
37. Jacqueline Moore, 'Gender, Representation and Ireland' (Unpublished Essay, 1994).
38. Dillon, *A Herd of Deer*, p.87.
39. Ibid., p.87.
40. Ibid., p.58.
41. Ibid., p.87.
42. Moore, 'Gender, Representation and Ireland'.
43. Dillon, *A Herd of Deer*, p.185.
44. Prentice, 'Problems of Response to Empire', p.48.
45. John Stephens, *Language and Ideology in Children's Fiction* (New York: Longman, 1992), p.281.
46. Dillon, *The Sea Wall*, p.106.
47. Ibid., p.110.
48. J.M. Synge, *Plays Poems and Prose*, ed. Alison Smith (London: J.M. Dent & Sons Ltd., 1992), p.345.
49. Declan Kiberd, *Synge and the Irish Language* (London: Macmillan Press Ltd., 1979), p.199.
50. Conversation with Eileán Ní Chuilleanáin, 1 December 1994.
51. Eilís Dillon, *The Island of Ghosts* (London: Faber & Faber, 1990), p.7.
52. Ibid., p.21.
53. Quoted by Robert O'Driscoll, 'Return to the Heartstone: Ideals of the Celtic Literary Revival', in *Place, Personality and the Irish Writer*, ed. Andrew Carpenter (Bucks: Colin Smyth Ltd, 1977), p.43.
54. Dillon, *The Cruise of the Santa Maria*, p.135.
55. Sean O'Sullivan, *The Folklore of Ireland* (London: B.T. Balsford Ltd, 1974), p.12.
56. Eilís Dillon, *The Singing Cave* (Dublin: Poolbeg, 1992), p.12.
57. Ibid., p.25.
58. Ibid., p.81.
59. Synge, *Plays, Poems and Prose*, p.270.
60. Dillon, *The Cruise of the Santa Maria*, pp.112–13.
61. Ibid., p.113.
62. Dillon, *The Singing Cave,* p.174.
63. Ibid., p.175.
64. Lissa Paul, 'Imitations of Imitations', in Peter Hunt (ed.), *Literature for Children* (London: Routledge, 1992), p.76.
65. K. Anthony Appiah, 'The Multicultural Misunderstanding', *The New York Review of Books*, XLIV, 15 (9 October 1997), p.34.
66. Ibid.
67. Edward Said, *Culture and Imperialism* (London: Vintage, 1994) p.15.
68. Sean O'Faolain. *The Irish* (London: Penguin Books, 1969), p.159.
69. Ibid., p.148.
70. Eilís Dillon, *Inside Ireland* (London: Hodder & Stoughton, 1982), p.155.
71. Julia Kristeva, *Nations Without Nationalism* (New York: Colombia University Press, 1993), p.2.
72. O'Faolain, *The Irish*, p.161.
73. 'State Papers Reveal Preoccupation with Evils of "Injurious" Literature', *The Irish Times*, 2 January 1995.
74. Maurice Goldring, Foreword, in *Pleasant the Scholar's Life: Irish Intellectuals and the Construction of the Nation State* (London: Serif, 1993), p.10.
75. Dillon, *Inside Ireland*, p.73.
76. Eilís Dillon, 'Literature in a Rural Background'. Paper given at Loughborough Conference on Children's Literature, Trinity College Dublin, 1981.

77. O'Faolain, *The Irish*, p.146.
78. Ibid., p.162.
79. Kristeva, *Nations without Nationalism*, p.2.
80. Dillon, *The Island of Ghosts*, p.2.
81. Quoted in J.P. O'Carroll and J.A. Murphy (eds), *de Valera and His Times* (Cork: Cork University Press, 1986), p.184.
82. Dillon, *The Island of Ghosts*, p.44.
83. Ibid., p.134.
84. Desmond Ryan, *Unique Dictator* (London: Arthur Baker Ltd, 1936), p.24.
85. O'Faolain, *The Irish*, p.163.
86. Dillon, *The Island of Ghosts*, p.9.
87. Ibid., p.25.
88. Shils, *Tradition*, p.246.
89. Dillon, *The Island of Ghosts*, p.132.
90. Peter Hunt, *Literature for Children*, p.38.
91. Dillon, 'Literature in a Rural Background'.
92. Dillon, *The Island of Ghosts*, p.14.
93. Ibid., p.34.
94. Ibid., p.14.
95. Ibid., p.15.
96. Shils, *Tradition*, p.276.
97. Dillon, *The Island of Ghosts*, p.133.
98. Ibid., p.107.
99. Ibid., p.3.
100. Ibid., p.105.
101. Ibid., p.106.
102. Said, *Culture and Imperialism*, p.xiii.
103. Jenny A. Thomas, 'The Language of Power. Towards a Dynamic Pragmatics', *Journal of Pragmatics* 9 (1985), p.767.
104. Ibid., p.773.
105. Dillon, *The Island of Ghosts*, p.48.
106. Thomas, 'The Language of Power', p.769.
107. Dillon, *The Island of Ghosts*, p.44.
108. Stephens, *Language and Ideology in Children's Fiction*, p.255.
109. Dillon, *The Island of Ghosts*, p.50.
110. Ibid., p.60.
111. Ibid., p.105.
112. Ibid., p.130.
113. Quoted in O'Carroll and Murphy (eds), *de Valera and His Times*, p.169.
114. Said, *Culture and Imperialism*, p.307.
115. Maurice Moynihan (ed.), *Speeches and Statements by Eamon de Valera 1917–1972* (Dublin: Gill & Macmillan, 1980), p.419.
116. Thomas, 'The Language of Power', p.776.
117. Dillon, *The Island of Ghosts*, p.66.
118. Ibid., p.113.
119. Tiffin and Lawson (eds), Introduction, *De-scribing Empire*, p.5.
120. Said, *Culture and Imperialism*, p.273.
121. Roy Foster, Foreword, in Hubert Butler, *The Children of Drancy* (Mullingar: Lilliput Press, 1988), p.viii.
122. Havel, 'The State of the Republic', p.45.
123. Hugo Hamilton, 'Hostages to Fortune', *The Irish Times*, Weekend Supplement, 8 August 1998.
124. Said, *Culture and Imperialism*, p.15.
125. 'Cherishing the Irish Diaspora', *The Irish Times*, 3 February 1995.
126. Kristeva, *Nations Without Nationalism*, p.2.
127. Appiah, 'The Multicultural Misunderstanding', p.36.
128. Marcus Bullock and Michael Jennings (eds), *Walter Benjamin, Selected Writings*, Vol.1. 1913–1926 (Cambridge, MA: Harvard University Press, 1996), pp.449–50.
129. Dillon, 'Literature in a Rural Background'.

3

The Importance of History to Cultural Identity: Marita Conlon-McKenna

Prisoners on parole from history,
Striving to come alive as I think I am

Cromwell[1]

In the present intellectual debate over the function of history, children's writers too have a part to play. In this area, Marita Conlon-McKenna has not only made a substantial contribution to her young reader's knowledge of modern Irish history, but she also contributes to the debate on revisionism. The topics covered in her trilogy include the Great Famine, emigration and the Land-War. These topics, as well as being of historical interest, are also of great contemporary significance in that our reading of them can affect how we see ourselves in the present.

Hayden White, the critical theorist, has said that if one wants to liberate oneself from narrative closures of the past then everything depends on how one studies it and to what end.[2] He believes that we should study and use history in such a way as to make a responsible transition from the present to the future; find a way of thinking about the past that makes us responsible for our present condition because our present condition is always, at least in part, a product of human choices and can be changed by further choices. 'We choose our past in the same way that we choose our future',[3] therefore, we can make our lives different for ourselves and for our children by realizing the uncontrollable nature of history and by using the remaining traces of the past in a positive way to encourage a different future.

White's idea is that all history is interpretative and never literally true. In his essay, 'The Historical Text as Literary Artifact', he says that his insistence on the fictive element in all historical narratives annoys historians, because they believe that they are dealing with real events while the fiction writer deals only with imagined events. Simultaneously, it disturbs literary theorists who believe that literature's interest in the 'possible' is radically opposed to historical fact.[4] However, exactly the same detailed events can be construed in different ways so that whether historians admit it or not, there is an ideological component in every account of the past while fictional stories are usually made out of 'chronicals'. This idea of historical works as a translation of fact into fiction may not be popular with historians, but different interpretations of the same set of historical phenomena do not mean that we cannot distinguish between good and bad historical accounts. We can always 'fall back on such criteria as responsibility to the rules of evidence, the relative fullness of narrative detail, logical consistency, and the like to determine the issue'.[5] In her paper 'The Art of Realism', Jill Paton Walsh remarks that: 'A work of fantasy compels a reader into a metaphorical frame of mind. A work of realism, on the other hand, permits very literal-minded readings, even downright stupid ones.'[6] Walsh was comparing fantasy and realism in children's fiction, but the remark would also hold true for a comparison between historical fact and certain kinds of historical fiction.

In writing this chapter I have drawn on Hayden White's idea that a theory of language and narrative provides the basis for a more subtle presentation of history. His idea, which is developed in *Tropics of Discourse,* is that narrative strategies can illustrate and give meaning in different ways. For example, he says in *Metahistory*: 'If in the course of narrating his story, the historian provides it with a plot structure of a Tragedy, he has "explained" it in one way; if he has structured it as a Comedy, he has "explained" it in another way.'[7] This is the key to interpretation and can help us understand how a writer can participate in the liberation of the present from 'the burden of history' by writing about the past in such a way as to provide perspectives on the present that can be used in a positive way. This does not mean altering events. It means that history can be used in a positive way by the arranging of the events in a different order; by telling one kind of story rather than another.

In *A Kind of Scar* Eavan Boland talks of a woman she met in Achill when she was a student. She says:

> She was the first person to talk to me about the famine. The first person, in fact, to speak to me with any force about the terrible parish of survival and death which the event has been in those regions. She kept repeating to me that they were great people, the people in the famine. Great people. I had never heard that before.[8]

Marita Conlon-McKenna's stories have a way of marking off the events contained in them from other events which we would expect to read in any factual historical chronicle of the times she is concerned with in her trilogy. By relating history on a human level, she directs the reader's attention to a secondary area, different in kind from the events that make up the primary area but giving an equally valuable perspective. For example, in *Under the Hawthorn Tree*, the first book of the trilogy, the facts of history which have caused controversy, such as the corn leaving the country during the famine, are mentioned, but they are unimportant in this instance because they are not understood by the child protagonists in the story and therefore do not directly affect their actions. Levi-Strauss in *The Savage Mind* explains that in so far as it aspires to meaning, history must be selective. 'A truly total history', he says 'would cancel itself out'. He explains this in terms of the French Revolution: 'When one proposes to write a history of the French Revolution one knows (or ought to know) that it cannot, simultaneously and under the same heading, be that of the Jacobin and that of the aristocrat.'[9] Because their respective stories (even though each is 'anti-symmetric' to the other) can be equally true, one must choose between them because to recognize them equally renders them both meaningless. This means that historical accounts are determined as much by what we leave out as by what we put in. In Conlon-McKenna's historical account, what matters most are the human qualities; the stories of grief, and most of all, of courage and survival, and the scenes chosen in *Under the Hawthorn Tree* allow for the creation of a new set of signs. The soup queues and coffin ships of those desperate times have not been forgotten. Indeed, the descriptions of the scenes they meet on their journey, such as the man on horseback pulling a slide on which were piled skeleton-like bodies, are particularly harrowing. However, the intention is not to tell the *whole* truth about the Famine but *one* truth about it, and whether one meets life with a belief in the possibility of surviving and overcoming or sees one's self as a permanent victim is the more important issue now, and this is reflected in the novel's perspective.

In their book *Kafka: Towards a Minor Literature*, Deleuze and Guattari define minor literature as the writings of minorities within major languages which they modify in making their own. They say that 'minor no longer designates specific literatures but the revolutionary conditions for every literature within the heart of what is called great (or established) literature'.[10] The formula is to find one's 'own point of underdevelopment'; in other words to write making a virtue of impoverishment. In the words of Reda Bensmaia, minor literature then becomes 'a continent where reading and writing open up new perspectives, break ground for new avenues of thought, and above all, wipe out the tracks of an old topography of mind and thought'.[11] This also works very well for writers of children's books, especially when dealing with such a volatile subject as Irish history to which most adults come with preconceived ideas. If we have been previously imprisoned by the old interpretations and meanings that we as adults have learned, then 'minor' language in the form of children's literature can be the perfect instrument to break the circle, especially if we are assuming that children are less likely to be approaching the past with a fixed set of ideas. If you are writing for children you can make a virtue of impoverishment by stressing the positive aspects of our history rather than the negative aspects. Thus, the writer is able to create a space which is not only free from preconceived ideas, but one which creates a new subject position for the reader. In this case, Conlon-McKenna can make a virtue of impoverishment by directing her readers to a new perspective.

What I have been arguing so far is that Marita Conlon-McKenna, through the different trope of writing for children, can give a different view of the past; one that encourages Irish children to change from being the victims of Irish history to being the authors of it. According to John Stephens, 'discourse comprises the complex process of encoding [a] story which involves choices of vocabulary, of syntax, of order of presentation, of how the narrating voice is to be orientated towards what is narrated and towards the implied audience'.[12] I want now to look at how these components function within the text of *Under the Hawthorn Tree*, because an analysis of this kind will help us understand the factors which work to bring about a secondary reading which concentrates on the human elements rather than the facts of history. The story of this book is a retelling of the famine. It is a factual account, and this is reinforced by the epilogue 'A Simple History of The Great Famine. 1845–1850', but it is refocused as experienced by three children.

Even in its inception there is a difference in the way this history is presented and the way the discourse of history is usually rendered. The event which sparked off the first book came from a human story which the author heard on the radio rather than a previously analysed version of the famine. This immediately moves the history to a different level of significance. In an interview with Robert Dunbar, Conlon-McKenna says: 'It all started when I heard a story on the radio about an unmarked children's grave which had been found under a hawthorn tree.

"There must", I thought to myself, "be a story there!"[13] And indeed the first story begins with the sickness and eventual death of Baby Bridget who was buried under the hawthorn tree in the back field. The priest was ill and the coffin maker had already died. There were no funerals so it was decided to 'bury her decently in her own place'.[14] Later, in the same interview Conlon-McKenna says:

> The Famine is clearly a turning point in our history: it had its depressing and horrific aspects. But the children who lived through it had a marvellous capacity to bounce back ... What I tried to capture was the emotional aspect of survival. And that's where I found the notion of the journey, which is at the centre of the book, very useful: the young reader experiences a sense of progress and comes to understand something of the nature of responsibility ... the progress of the children is paramount.[15]

As a nation we have come a long way since the 1840s and this co-incides with the narrative structure of *Under the Hawthorn Tree*. The children's difficult journey and eventual safe arrival function as a metaphor for the national journey. The notion that the young reader 'comes to understand something of the nature of responsibility' also ties in with Hayden White's idea that our present position is at least partly something that we ourselves are responsible for; a product of the choices we have made along the way. Eily was not responsible for the Great Famine or the fact that she was left at 13 with a younger brother and sister to look after, but she *was* responsible for the de-cision to make the journey to Castletaggart and for the decisions and choices she made along the way. She must decide how they should make their escape from the group going to the workhouse; what to do when Michael gets blood poisoning; how to cope when Peggy gets ill with fever. In later years Peggy remembers and reminds Eily that, 'at barely thirteen you saved Michael and me from the workhouse and brought us all the way from Duneen to Castletaggart. You pushed us and made us walk and got food for us and forced us to survive the famine.'[16] To think about history in this way ensures not only that a young reader should experience a sense of progress, but also that they realize that we must take responsibility for our own future.

The controlling metaphors in this book, as in all three of the books in the trilogy, are those of courage, resourcefulness, loyalty and sur-vival. All important human qualities which are transhistorical and which contrast with the negative emotions of anger and resentment attached to many versions of our history. These controlling metaphors are made manifest by a combination of the angle of narration and the use of language. John Stephens explains:

> If, with reference to the existents represented in a text – its objects, events, people, landscape, etc., we ask the question, 'Who Sees?', we are trying to determine the perceptual point of view, the vantage point from which something is represented as being visualized. Such visualization can be an activity of the narrator of the text, or of a character situated within the text. Another way to put this is to say that phenomena are *focalized* by some perceiving agent, whom we can call the focalizer.[17]

Although sometimes, as in first person narratives, the two functions are fulfilled by the same agent, the narrator may be defined as the voice that speaks, while the focalizer is the agent through whose perspective the narrative is filtered and is very important to any consideration of subjectivity or ideology. Identification with focalizers is one of the chief methods by which a text manages to reconstitute its readers as subjects within the text. Very often in *Under the Hawthorn Tree* direct speech is employed to allow the characters to speak for themselves. In these instances, focalization becomes internal in that it is limited to the perspective of the speaker and therefore, limited to the present tense of the represented narrative world. This allows Conlon-McKenna to depict an allegedly unmediated version of events as they happen.

Eily is the main focalizer of *Under The Hawthorn Tree* and she is a survivor. This is important because being placed as she is in the events as they happen, she has not yet formed any opinions of these events; her history has not yet been formed into a narrative. Mark Twain in *Huckleberry Finn* used a similar strategy in that he used a child's mind to explore the racist society of the American post-Civil War society at a time when racism and slavery were facts of life. Much of the genius of *Huckleberry Finn* comes from the fact that, like Eily, Huck is placed in history as it happens. Twain shows Huck's mixed feelings about slave ownership arising from the fact that even though in his heart he feels it to be wrong, the codes of his society are based on it. This enables us to see ourselves live through the times in question and see that 'for any one of these individuals, each moment of time is inexhaustibly rich in physical and psychical incidents which all play their part in his totalization'.[18] Milan Kundera says that when we think back we focus on action, meaning, content, but, '*in real life:* dialogue is surrounded by dailiness which interrupts it, slows it down, affects its development, changes its course, makes it unsystematic and illogical'.[19] The use of

Eily as a focalizer in *Under the Hawthorn Tree* ensures that, at least for the duration of the story, the reader's own knowledge is effaced and he/she internalizes the perceptions and attitudes of Eily, whose main concern is that of survival. Unlike those of us who have been trained to see the famine in the way we have been taught, children identify personally with Eily and participate in her hardships and especially in her final triumph. She shows them their progressive development – how far they have come.

Indeed, Eily herself knew how to use history to her advantage. Her mother had been used to telling the children stories about her childhood in the town of Castletaggart:

> 'Tell us about when you were a girl – go on, please', they all begged.
>
> 'Are ye not all fed up with my old stories', she chided.
>
> 'Never', assured Michael.
>
> 'Well then', she began. 'Mary Ellen, that was my mother and your grandmother, what Eily's called after, lived with her two sisters Nano and Lena ...'.[20]

It is this link with the past that gives the children hope for the future. Instead of looking back longingly and comparing her mother's childhood with her own unhappy situation, Eily, spurred on by her younger brother and sister, uses her mother's stories in a positive way to give them an alternative to the workhouse: 'No workhouse for them! They'd find their way to the aunts. In the town of Castletaggart there would be someone who knew them, who belonged to them.'[21] The stories her mother had told her about her past were what gave Eily the inspiration for dealing with their present problems. By using history in this way she shows us how we too should benefit from the past.

The secondary reading of *Under the Hawthorn Tree* is also reinforced by what Stephens calls 'linguistic discourse', that is 'stretches of language perceived to be meaningful, unified and purposive'.[22] Five years *after* Conlon-McKenna's book was published, Cathal Póirtéir, in a book called *Famine Echoes*, published to coincide with the RTE radio series of the same name, says:

> To have no voices of many of those most badly affected by the hunger, diseases and deaths caused by the Famine is a notable gap indeed in our record of those terrible events. The perspective of those who saw their districts depopulated by death, eviction and emigration is not one which is to the fore in official documentation of the period.[23]

Póirtéir criticizes both revisionist and nationalist orientated historians for ignoring folklore and oral history material. He points out that a close examination of the oral sources might disappoint the nationalist propagandists because placing blame rarely plays a part in the many accounts that were passed on orally. The emphasis in the oral accounts is almost entirely on the local situation and local personalities. Conlon-McKenna's approach is a mixture of intuition, solid research and stories heard from her mother.[24] When Eily's mother returns from the village her account of what is happening goes beyond 'official documentation'. It reinforces Conlon-McKenna's idea of relating history on a human level in that the usual researching and analysing of statistics is replaced by a listing of local families and individuals in an undramatic and ordinary way:

> into the ground every single one of them, all those five sons and Mary O'Brien, the kindest woman that ever lived. The Connors and Kinsellas have both left. Nell Kinsella had enough put by, and they plan to buy tickets and sail to America. No one knows where the Connors are. Francie O'Hagan has closed up her draper's shop ... Poor Father Doyle is very bad and hasn't stirred at all in weeks – his housekeeper Annie died a few days back. The few men that are left were sitting by the fire in Mercy Farrel's, and not even one was having a sup of porter.[25]

The list goes on, not statistics but flesh and blood people recalled as they were, so that there is a strong sense of the way things are changing which is particularly moving.

This foregrounding of the human element is continued in the way that the theories usually applied to the Famine are dealt with. The account of the incident at the harbour where the grain is being shipped to England is one example. When the crowd gather around and attempt to prevent the grain from being loaded on to the boats, the children do not know what is happening. "'Eily what will we do?" questioned Michael. "I don't like this place, its too dangerous. Let's leave it."'[26] The stigma of 'souperism' and proselytizing is also mentioned, but again it is not understood by the children.

> That night they slept in Kineen, as it was rumoured that the soup kitchen would reopen at midday again the next day. During the night an old man shook them and told them to be on their way, as the heathens would try to convert them in the morning and if they took another mug of soup they may as well take the Queen's shilling. The children were puzzled, but simply ignored him.[27]

An adult reading this book would realize that what for them were the important events are unimportant to the children because, while it may have helped to bring about their situation, it can have no bearing on how they are going to get out of it. Despite the horrors they faced Eily knows that 'they must have hope'. She has courage and is determined that 'They would survive'. This courage and determination to survive are also expressed by Kitty O'Hara, a young girl who is now alone because everyone belonging to her had died. She tells Eily: 'I'm glad to be going to the workhouse. At least there'll be a meal and a roof over our heads. They're all gone, every single one. I'm the only one left and *I'm going to live*.' (my italics)[28] The determination, courage and hope presented here reaffirm the philosophy of the text.

How a narrative is resolved is important. Although *Under the Hawthorn Tree* has a satisfying ending in that the children have reached their goal, it has no easy answers. Mother and father do not come back. Eily, Michael and Peggy, with a little help from the great aunts they have heard about in their mother's stories, have to make their own way from now on. We cannot wipe out what has happened but we must move on:

> Lena had stood up and was holding her arms open to them. Eily relaxed at last knowing that they would be safe in their new home with Nano and Lena. But, at the same moment, she knew their hearts would always belong to the little thatched cottage with the flat stones outside, and the small overgrown garden, and the fields around it with the breeze blowing softly through the hawthorn tree.[29]

There is closure in the sense that they have arrived safely at their destination, but there is some degree of openness in that their future remains indeterminate. We too have arrived safely at this point in time but our future, like that of the children, depends to a large degree on the further choices we make. The formal closure in the epilogue connects the story to real history, underlining the truth of the assumption made throughout the book, that what we must take forward with us are the qualities of courage, resourcefulness, loyalty and survival and the memory of the 'great people' of the famine times. For those who may think that it is a betrayal to foreground these qualities over the necessity of attributing blame, Eily has the answer. When Michael asks, 'What if mother and father come back and everything is gone – what will they think?' Eily replies: 'They'll know we had to survive. It's better than us all staying, with no food and the disease all around us.'[30]

To find the positive aspects of this time in our history may be difficult, but it is infinitely better than staying in the past with the disease
of anger and resentment all around us. The current thinking in our
society would seem to agree with this. In fact, the famine commemoration of 1997 had the title 'Triumph Over Disaster'. However,
Marita Conlon-McKenna's book was first published in 1990, before
the 150th anniversary and when the Famine was not such a fashionable
subject as it has since become. We should also note that M.A.G.
O'Tuathaigh has remarked, four years after the publication of this
book, that, 'it is disappointing how few practicing historians seem
prepared to contemplate or, more accurately, to address the implic-
ations for their work of the writings of White and other critical
theorists'.[31] In this case, not only can children's literature be seen to
be reflecting the concerns of our time, it is leading the way.

Given the facts of Irish history which feature a massive exodus, particularly after the Famine, it is not surprising that the second book in
this trilogy, set seven years later, deals with emigration, and in common
with other aspects of Irish history the experience of the diaspora has
also undergone a revaluation. Alan O'Day, in an essay that traces the
development of the literature concerning the Irish abroad during the
nineteenth century, points out that, 'Motivation for striking out on the
emigrant trail varied. Nationalist tradition insisted that the prime cause
was the British misgovernment of Ireland ... Modern authorities have
been more impressed by the allure of better prospects overseas.'[32] In
this story it is Peggy, the youngest of the three children from *Under the
Hawthorn Tree* and now 13, who emigrates alone, and it is her fortunes
that we follow. Although there was a high proportion of young, single,
female migrants, until recently the experience of these women emigrants has often been ignored. Patrick O'Sullivan begins his introduction to *Irish Women and Irish Migration*, published in 1995, by stating:

> Every chapter in this, the women's history and women's studies
> volume of *The Irish World Wide*, begins by remarking on the
> paucity of research into the experiences of migrant Irish women
> and the paucity of comment on women in earlier studies of the
> patterns of Irish migration ... This ignoring of women is extra-
> ordinary. Donald Harman Akenson has said, 'One half of the
> great Irish diaspora was female. Between the Act of Union of
> 1800 and independence of southern Ireland in 1922, about four
> million Irish females left the homeland.'[33]

Some of the questions now being asked include: Who were these women? Why did they leave? What impression did their new home make on them? How well did they settle there? These are the issues that are addressed in *Wildflower Girl*, where Peggy's experience gives an insight into the lives of many Irish women immigrants to America in the years after the Famine. Conlon-McKenna does not short-change her young readers. Her research was just as meticulous as if she were writing a recognized historical account. She travelled to Boston to find out from talking to people and visiting Irish centres and museums how these people lived and what their new lives were like. The pattern set up in the first book, where there is a definite shift from pathos to action, is continued here as we see Peggy face another challenging journey, this time across the Atlantic to America.

Ireland after the Famine had little to offer any of its children but least of all women. Many of these women left because there was no place for them in the social order that existed in Ireland, while in America opportunities beckoned. As we have seen from the account of Peggy's earlier journey, these women were survivors. They were not passive and accepting but active, courageous and enterprising, ready to seize their chances when they came. When Eily tries to put Peggy off going by telling her 'You're too young. You'd never survive in a strange country on your own', Peggy, using 'every ounce of O'Driscoll stubbornness to get her way', reminds her of her own achievement in getting them through the Famine, and when asked if she isn't frightened of going alone, Peggy replies: 'No, no. I remember things that were worse, a lot worse.'[34] The ordeals they had come through during the Famine had fitted them well for their undertaking. It is often remarked upon how well the Irish have done in America, and indeed how successful the Irish diaspora throughout the world has been both socially and economically. They have been a significant force in the countries to which they emigrated, playing a prominent role in politics and commerce, but the qualities of courage, resourcefulness, loyalty and survival learned and reinforced during the Famine years have stood them well and we should not be surprised at their successes. These qualities are the legacy which the 'great people' of the Famine have passed to us. They tell us something about these women who left and the reasons for their success. They also serve as a concrete example to Conlon-McKenna's young readers of the positive aspects of our history.

One of the reasons given by Hasia R. Diner for the high number of young single women emigrants was the structure of the modern Irish family: 'Other than the very poor, the Irish who emigrated as single men and women did so because of their unfavourable place in the fam-

ily land arrangements of the Irish countryside.'[35] The policy of clear-
ance and consolidation which had begun to take shape immediately
after the Famine led to the growing security and acquisitiveness of
those farmers who had survived. The memory of the result of the pre-
Famine fragmentation of holdings ensured that there must be no divi-
sion of the land. F.S.L. Lyons explains the consequences of this in
Ireland Since The Famine.

> Instead, one son ... must be elected to succeed, and one daughter
> (perhaps) equipped with the dowry that would enable her to
> make a suitable dynastic alliance with a neighbour whose affairs
> were in a satisfactory condition. Upon the rest of the family this
> unifying, centralising tendency had of course the effect of pre-
> senting them with two bleak alternatives – either to emigrate or
> to remain at home as relatives assisting on the farm, with little
> hope of ever breaking out of the pattern of perpetual bachelor-
> dom or spinsterhood that had been devised for them.[36]

This shows how for many young people in a family, particularly
women, there was no possibility of having a place of their own and the
alternatives were unappealing. Each emigrant must have had her own
story on why she was leaving Ireland. There were of course many reasons why people left, but there is a difference between the massive dis-
locations endured at the height of the Famine and the more optimistic
journeys taken later on. It has been established that after the Famine
emigrants tended to flee less from hunger and disease and more from
a desire for new opportunities. Many of them left on a positive and
cheerful note, full of anticipation and ambition although saddened by
the knowledge that they would probably never see their homes and
families again.

There is an acknowledgement of other stories: Kitty's family had
left Ireland in 1847 when the great famine was at its worst and most
of her family had died on the journey; Nell Molloy who travelled with
Peggy was going to join her husband who had gone to America two
years before and worked hard to earn enough to bring his family out;
Mags Halligan, who had emigrated twenty-five years before, is testament to the fact that emigration had always been part of Irish life.
However, in *Wildflower Girl* we are given Peggy's story, and the notion
of the reluctant and pathetic emigrant is quickly dispelled by the image
of Peggy 'bursting with excitement' at the sight of the sheet of paper
which was their passport to America. During the Famine and also in its
aftermath several agencies assisted Irish men and women to emigrate.

Some landlords too helped their tenants to leave, and a letter of application for a ship's voucher, such as the one that Peggy had, was for many people their opportunity for a fresh start in the New World. Peggy had originally hoped that they would emigrate as a family, but when Eily points out their responsibility to Nano, who has cared for them since they arrived starving at the door and is now too old to make the journey, she realizes that this is impossible. Later, when Eily decides to marry John Power and Michael gets a longed-for job as a stable boy at the Big House Peggy surveys her prospects for the future: 'A settle bed up at Power's farm, miles from the town and friends! No chance of a job, only helping Eily with the house!'[37] This was in fact the prospect that faced many young single women and accounted for the fact that while most of the immediate Famine exodus was made up of those who because of hunger and disease had no choice, now they made the journey in search of greater opportunities and a status that they could never have at home during the times they lived in. It was a chance of adventure and opportunity against the knowledge that they had nothing to lose.

In spite of her older sister's opposition to the idea of her going, Peggy persists. She answers Eily's objections by saying, 'But I want to go. It's not just what you want, this is something *I* want!'[38] Her stubbornness and determination to get her own way do not mean that Peggy thinks only of herself. Certainly she wants more from life than she could look forward to at home, but she also looks forward to getting a job and being able to send money home to ease things for those she has left behind. Hasia Diner points out that for many Irish emigrants 'the move to America did not represent a search for a new identity, nor did it constitute a break with the past'.[39] In fact, she remarks on the 'cultural persistence over time' of Irish emigrants compared to their Italian or Jewish counterparts. She says the Irish family 'bent and stretched ... itself', managing to integrate their own traditional values with new situations.[40]

The symbols of the ties with her own traditions and values can be seen in the gifts Peggy received before she left. On the eve of her departure the house is filled with friends and neighbours who have come to say their goodbyes. This kind of farewell party was known as an American wake because everyone knew it was unlikely that they would ever see the traveller again in this lifetime. Peggy takes the opportunity to look at all the friends around her: 'Hard lives and bad times and yet they could still smile. I'll never meet the likes again, she said to herself, sealing their faces and stories into her memory.'[41] When all the well-wishers have left, Peggy accompanies her old aunt upstairs for the last time. Nano goes to the old oak chest of drawers and hands Peggy the family Bible. When she opens it and sees the names and birthdates inside that constitute a family tree, 'Peggy realised that it was more than just a Bible she was being handed. It was her history – the keeping of a tradition.'[42] Michael's gift symbolizes the closeness of the three children. He has made her a horsehair bracelet by plaiting together the black, chestnut brown and golden hair from 'the three best horses in the stable' to bring her luck and speed and strength he said. 'Peggy looked at it and loved it straight away, knowing what it meant.'[43] The last gift comes from Eily, the mother figure. Apart from putting together enough food to do for all the weeks at sea, Eily's gift is her best shawl. 'Peggy clutched it close to her ... It would enfold her just like Eily had always wrapped her and kept her safe'.[44] While these things had little material value, they would be an invaluable link between the Old world and the New. They would give Peggy a past that could be touched and measured; give her the power to have her own identity, history and tradition. For her part, one of the first things that Peggy does when she has some money is to send back a photograph of herself. Having rejected the idea of wearing one of the costumes offered by the photographer because 'it wasn't her', she decides to be photographed in her uniform. The photograph shows that while many things may change some part of her will stay the same; 'an image that will withstand anything that might happen'.[45] Eily, Michael and Nano looking at this picture of Peggy in her uniform can 'trace a story backwards for years and forwards for at least a few hours'.[46] This reinforces the sense of identity, history and tradition because 'fragile images [family photographs] often carried next to the heart, or placed by the side of the bed, are used to refer to that which historical time has no right to destroy'.[47]

What Peggy must do next, and what Edward Said has said is needed now if we are to be free from 'monopolizing attitudes' towards history and be able to integrate, is to 'go on and situate these in a geography of other identities, peoples, cultures'.[48] Said says that survival is about the connections between things rather than the separation. When she arrived in Boston after her nightmare journey Peggy quickly found that 'Empire Hill, Boston, America – it didn't matter where in the world you were, a bed was a bed and sleep was sleep'.[49] Again when she found herself looking out 'over field after field of grass and corn' she realized that 'it's just like home'.[50] She wandered around gathering the wild flowers just as she had done in the fields around Castletaggart on the morning she had left home. Flowers that, like these Famine children, might be flattened by the elements and by man 'but they would still spring back again and dance and bow in the summer breeze and sun'.[51] This ability to have our own identity and yet to see how it overlaps with others, is what Said calls 'the intellectual and cultural challenge of moment' and Peggy has faced the challenge and overcome it and now she can move on.

In *Culture and Imperialism* Edward Said quotes Hugo of St Victor, a twelfth-century monk from Saxony: 'The person who finds his home-land sweet is still a tender beginner; he to whom every soil is as his native one is already strong; but he is perfect to whom the entire world is as a foreign place.'[52] He notes that Hugo makes it clear that the 'strong' or 'perfect' person achieves independence and detachment by *working through* attachments, not by rejecting them. When Peggy's first job ends in disaster her first thought is of home and how much she misses her family and friends, but Mags Halligan tells her that her tears will save her:

> Just know this – there isn't a girl in this house that won't shed tears like you've done. It may not be at this time, it may be in six months' time or a year's time or the day she will wed or have her first child. Sometime in her future. But you – you're lucky it has happened so early on. You'll get over it. You're a born survivor.[53]

And she is. In the last paragraph of the book Peggy realizes that 'sitting here in the kitchen at Rushton, celebrating her first American Thanksgiving, she felt at home'.[54] She is no longer a 'tender beginner'. While it is true that many Irish emigrants achieved great success, this is not to imply that they did not suffer many hardships. They worked for small wages in mills and factories as well as in private homes. Sarah, the girl whom Peggy had befriended on the boat journey from Ireland, works in a shirt factory. When Peggy goes to visit Sarah on her first day off, she finds her 'pale, with deep purple shadows under her eyes, her hands were zigzagged with cuts and looked sore and stiff. The nails were broken and chipped, and blackened and darkened from the but-ton work'.[55] Peggy, like the majority of Irish women chose kitchen work. Because domestic workers generally lived with their employer and also had no expenses of food, lodgings or transport, it fitted in with the needs of these women, offering a chance to earn and save. It was also the kind of work that no one else wanted so there were ample opportunities to find employment. Hasia Diner tells us that American women considered domestic work beneath them. Women of other immigrant groups also chose lower paid jobs rather than go into domestic service, consequently domestic work became synonymous with Irish female emigrants.[56] Peggy found that life as a kitchen maid was exhausting work. Her day began at dawn and continued until late at night by which time her 'bones and muscles ached'. There was also negative stereotyping attached. The stereotypical 'Bridget' or 'Norah' was often not very clean, not very bright, and not to be depended on. Roxanne, the daughter of the house where Peggy was employed, shows the generalized image when she says of Peggy: 'Why couldn't that stupid maid, Bridget or whatever she's called, keep her filthy hands to herself.'[57]

Jean Kennedy Smith, a US ambassador to Ireland and whose grandfather Fitzgerald was the mayor of Boston – the first Irish Catholic mayor in America – has talked about the prejudice against Irish Catholics. Even though she came from a very privileged family she remembers that her father moved to New York 'because there was such a prejudice in Boston against Catholics, against Irish Catholics. It was still a time when some signs said "No Irish need apply".'[58] In the contemporary period Irish emigrants have a high profile, partly due to President Robinson's insistence on the inclusion of the Irish Diaspora as part of our identity. On the other hand, Ireland itself is providing an asylum for migrants from other parts of the world and the response is not always what might be expected from a country that has exported so many people and has been the victim of much racist sentiment abroad. While the question of immigration into Ireland has come later and would not have been to the forefront of her mind when writing this novel, we know that Conlon-McKenna is interested in the question of racism. Another of her books, *The Blue Horse*, which has as its theme anti-traveller sentiment, shows this. After reading about some of the negative stereotypes which Irish emigrants encountered in the last century, and the problems and dangers that they faced both in their journey and after their arrival, Irish children might be more aware about the position and response of Irish people to the refugees, both political and economical, who are beginning to enter this country. They are, after all, a sign of our present growing prosperity.

As Eavan Boland has often reminded us, both in her pamphlet *A Kind of Scar* and also in her poetry, too often Irish history has ignored the experience of women and this is also true of emigration history. With the second story in her trilogy, *Wildflower Girl*, Conlon-McKenna addresses this omission and with her account of Peggy's experience she reclaims for her readers the life stories of those who stood 'Their hardships parcelled in them. Patience. Fortitude. Long-suffering in the bruise-coloured dusk of the New World. And all the old songs. And nothing to lose.'[59]

The final book of this trilogy, *Fields of Home*, continues the stories of Eily, Michael and Peggy and introduces the next generation. Eily is now married with two small children and the family faces eviction from their cottage, while Michael loses his job as a groom at the Big House when his landlord is burnt out. Both of these strands deal with another important area of Irish history, that of agrarian unrest, where again there have been many changes in the historiography during the past two or three decades.

Meanwhile, Peggy's story is continued in five chapters that are inserted here and there throughout the book, and, as G.V. Whelan rightly says, the excitement is somewhat dissipated by the chopping and changing of plots.[60]

When we pick up Peggy's story, Roxanne, the daughter of the house, is about to be married. On the morning of the wedding, when the kitchen staff stand in line to offer their congratulations, Peggy stands in line with the rest. Normally she would have had little to say to Roxanne who had often made her life miserable and whom she had earlier described to Kitty as a 'shrew', but now she is suddenly surprised to find that:

> They were no longer enemies.
>   'I wish you happiness and many, many good things in the future, Miss Roxanne, I really do!' said Peggy warmly.[61]

And she really means it. Whelan, in her review of the book, sees this as 'passive and uninteresting'. She argues that, 'All the fire has gone out of her struggle with the spoiled daughter of the house, which so held one's interest in *Wildflower Girl*. Now Roxanne's racialism ... is washed away by the wearing of a pretty wedding dress.'[62] I think it has more to do with character maturation. In a trilogy that has been so concerned with showing growth and complexity of character, it seems unlikely that it would move towards closure of Peggy's story without a summation of this theme. John Stephens says that, in an effort to represent growth,

> the conventional strategy is to situate the character within a complex of social practices so as to construct a number of self-other interactions. The crucial ideological implication is then whether the self demands that the other replicate the self's desires ... whether the other overwhelms the self (a common possibility at the outset of an interaction), or whether the self can negotiate with the other so as to encourage personal growth.[63]

Conlon-McKenna shows Peggy move from the second of these possibilities to the third. In *Wildflower Girl* there are a number of interactions between Peggy and Roxanne: when Peggy is restitching Roxanne's dress and accidentally gets blood on it through pricking her finger; Roxanne's knowledge of Peggy's fear of dogs and her subsequent jeering; her false accusation of Peggy when Bonaparte, the dog, dirtied her dress; and finally her attempt to have Peggy dismissed for theft when her ring goes missing. While Roxanne definitely has the upper hand in the first two incidents, in the second two Peggy is eventually able to prove her wrong, thus illustrating a gradual movement towards personal growth. During the last of these incidents and before she has proved her innocence, Peggy is lying in bed watching a tiny spider working on a web. 'The draught kept blowing through the wood and knocking her off her perch. Undefeated, she'd jiggle back up her swinging life-line and begin again.'[64] The spider symbolizes Peggy's courage and determination to survive; it shows how she has gradually and painstakingly earned her place until, now, she has overcome opposition and made a place for herself in the new world. I would see Roxanne's smile and accompanying gesture of shaking Peggy's hand as an acknowledgement and acceptance of this.

It is also a sign that Roxanne too has grown substantially from the 'right little minx' we met in the last book to a young woman who has an increasing awareness of how she relates to others. Now she has the grace to blush when it is Peggy's turn to wish her happiness, probably remembering previous encounters. When Peggy lifts her eyes to meet Roxanne's, she sees 'happiness and hope and nervousness and sadness all jumbled together'.[65] Each girl has had her own struggles with self-discovery and has moved to a position of personal growth. In Roxanne's case, personal growth means that she has moved away from her own self-absorption.

There are other signs that the immigrants have settled down and grown in confidence. Kitty, the kitchen maid who had befriended Peggy when she had first come to work at Rushton House, has also risen in the world. She is to go with Roxanne as her personal maid and 'advise her on household management and the like'. Years before, when she had heard the story of Kitty's hard life, Peggy had decided that she would do her best to make up to her for all the things she had missed out on in life. She had taught Kitty to read and write and scolded her for her lack of ambition, asking 'Do you want to stay a stupid skivvy for the rest of your days?' Now Kitty has changed from the weak-spirited girl who thought that 'It doesn't matter that much what

I can or can't do', to a self-sufficient young woman able to make decisions for herself and confident that, as a sort of chief housekeeper, she 'should be able to manage'. This is also a good example of the successful informal female networks that gave support and sustenance to those who were less strong. Hasia Diner tells us that 'from all accounts – personal, journalistic, literary – Irish women did in fact rely on their extensive female social networks, and their friendships with each other played important social roles in Irish communities'.[66] These informal support systems which contributed to the advancement of many Irish women 'reflected fundamental Irish values'[67] being based on the 'traditional patterns of female support that had sustained women in the old setting during periods of crisis – illness and death, widowhood and old age, childbirth and domestic strife'.[68] By the late 1850s or early 1860s, around the time when this story is set, 'the Irish had already so engulfed urban America as to be the single largest immigrant group in Boston, New York and Philadelphia and the second largest in Baltimore and Cincinnati'.[69] This urban concentration – due partly to the urban friendship networks – was seen as the cause of the continuing poverty of many of them. Thomas D'Arcy McGee who had escaped to America in the aftermath of the 1848 rising and who was closely associated with journalism in North America, was an active proponent of settling the Irish in the West. He forecast in 1852 that: 'Whatever we can do for ourselves as a people, in North America, must be done before the close of this century, or the epitaph of our race will be written in the West *"too late"*.'[70] He knew that the Irish were a rural people, and places like Iowa, Nebraska, Oregon, Wisconsin and Kansas had readily available tracts of cheap land.

When Sarah first tells her of her decision to go west with her two brothers in search of a place of their own, she invites Peggy to come along with them but, although she has come a long way, Peggy still has something to learn about independence and detachment. She decides to stay: 'She had a good job and was earning good money. Every month the bank collector called to the back-kitchen door and she would give him another small deposit from her wages ... This was her independence.'[71] Or so she thought, until she tried to imagine life in Boston without Sarah, John and especially James. This is what brings her to the point where she can transcend the limits of possessions and place. When, on the eve of his departure, James declares his love, Peggy is again ready to risk everything. Her decision to go west with James in a wagon train could be seen as proof that she has reached the final stages of Hugo of St Victor's 'strong' or 'perfect' person: 'The tender soul has fixed his love on one spot in the world; the strong person has extended his love to all places; the perfect man has extinguished his.'[72] Now, as she sits beside her new husband on the canvas-covered wagon that was to be her first home, she reflects that 'her whole life, well, all the important pieces of it, seemed to involve a journey of some sort or other'.[73] The first two books of this trilogy saw Peggy make long and dangerous journeys and arrive successfully at her destination. The final paragraph of her story, in what is described on the cover as 'the final book in the famine trilogy', shows her starting off on a new and different kind of journey, and once again the journey functions as a metaphor for the national journey:

> Ahead of them lay miles and miles of unexplored territory. It was a long road and a hard journey ahead but that didn't bother Peggy a bit, now that she had James beside her. She was on a wagon train, going near half-way across America, just imagine! But this was one journey she really wanted to make.[74]

Always, Peggy has been inclined towards innovation and an ability to move on when necessary, while at the same time managing to remain in contact with her own traditions and values. This is what true independence is about, although there remains for me an uneasiness that there is no mention of the Indian displacement or the imperialist settlements that will give them that independence.

Interpretations of the Land War have also changed somewhat over the past couple of decades. Here too there has been a rethinking of prevailing ideas. Paul Bew, in *The Making of Modern Irish History*, says that 'The landlords are now the subject of a treatment which is considerably less unsympathetic.' Bew goes on to quote Cormac Ó Gráda who says: 'Few historians now believe that Irish landlords were typically the predatory or vindictive ogres of nineteenth-century farmer propaganda (though some were) or that the Land War of the 1880s was the inevitable outcome of landlords' injustice.'[75] This revisionism is also evident in Conlon-McKenna's account of the collapse of The Big House and in her representation of the rising Catholic middle class. Although she certainly does not deny that there is a genuine cause of tenant grievance, which is shown in the eviction scenes and the storming of Eily's home by the landlord's agent, there is also sympathy for the trauma suffered by the occupants of Castletaggart House. Some years ago (July/August 1997), there was a debate in *The Irish Times* about whether the Cork writer, Elizabeth Bowen, was Irish or English. Certainly Elizabeth Bowen saw herself as an Irish writer. This question of how we define our Irishness and also 'the notion of the essential unity of the challenging collectivity of the peasantry'[76] is central to the account given of the demise of the Big House in *Fields of Home.*

In the six years since he has come to work at the Big House at the top of the rhododendron-lined avenue, Michael has learnt a lot about the Big House and its ways. While Lord Henry, the owner, is described as a kind and fair man, Michael has seen that 'every fish that swam in the river and lake, every pheasant and woodcock that inhabited the undergrowth, every apple or cabbage that grew from the rich brown soil was part of the vast Buckland estate'. He has also seen that the forty tenant farmers who worked the estate lands were given only 'a patch of ground where they could only grow barely enough to feed their own families'.[77] While sometimes Lord Henry would join them and make polite conversation when they were queuing to pay their rent, his estate manager, George Darkley, was barely civil to them. Michael could sense a growing unease and a desire for change among these tenant farmers and he describes the 'wooden' look on their faces, 'their eyes set, their hearts hardened'.

On the other hand, Castletaggart House and its occupants raise questions about civic and ethnic concepts of national identity which are still relevant. The fire is described as chasing its way 'across the heavy, century-old damask curtains'. Lord Henry says, 'These old houses are like tinderboxes'. Our attention is drawn many times to the age and beauty of this house and the length of time the Bucklands have been here. But, 'The large hall where kind old Lady Buckland had been waked, where the Castletaggart hunt had met, where visitors had called to pay their respects, was now a huge, open, gaping, pain-filled mouth as the old house lay dying.'[78] Since he had come to know Miss Felicia, the young daughter of the house, Michael liked her. She reminded him very much of his own younger sister Peggy: 'Full of spirit'. When, on the night her home was burnt to the ground, there were mutterings of 'Burn them out!' and 'Go back to England!' it was she who faced the crowd and pointed out that:

> 'I was born in that front room there.' She pointed towards the house. 'I am as Irish as any of the rest of you. But you don't care about that. If we go away who will you blame then? I'll tell you what'll happen,' she laughed hysterically. 'You'll all fight among yourselves, that's what my father says. You'll fight and kill each other one by one, that's what you'll do. Each and every one of you can go to hell. See if we care!'[79]

Her sentiments are echoed by Toss, who had spent fifteen years at Castletaggart House as head groom, when the next day he anticipated the gombeen men of Yeats' 'September 1913': 'What do ye think will happen the land now when the landlords go? It'll be the townies and middle-men that will decide and fight over it. Half the people you see around you will be off the land in a week or two.'[80]

In fact, the fire hadn't even been started by a tenant farmer with a genuine grievance but by a jockey who had been threatened with dismissal for his treatment of the horses, which Toss had described as 'Careless! Stupid! Cruel!' Peadar Mahoney had been seen standing with a group of tenant farmers when the fire was raging but he was not one of them; he was seeking revenge rather than justice.

In Eily's story we see that Toss' fears about middle-men are well founded. We also see another side to the landlord question. Louis MacNeice maintained that the Big Houses, with a few exceptions, contained no culture worth speaking of – 'nothing but an obsolete bravado, an insidious bonhomie and a way with horses'.[81] This describes very well Denis Ormonde, who is the new landlord to Eily and her neighbours, and whom Michael says is, 'the kind of man who liked to have a bit of a bet ... he's hoping to build up his stables. He doesn't care about farming, he reckons racing's the thing.'[82] While there was a degree of sympathy for landlords such as Lord Henry, Ormonde will neither receive nor deserve sympathy when his turn comes. He is the epitome of those landlords who, like Maria Edgeworth's dissolute Irish family, the Rackrents, bring about their own downfall through a mixture of carelessness, dissipation and disinterestedness.

When Eily goes to visit her friend and neighbour, Frances Hennessy, Frances is worried about this new landlord and his agent William Hussey – 'that gombeen man'.[83] She tells Eily 'he wants us to work like slaves so that we can pay him a higher rent ... Hussey is going to try and make us surrender our holdings and evict us!' The eviction of the Widow Quinn shows that her worries are warranted. This eviction is a brutal scene with three men on horseback, two policemen and a bailiff, all there to enforce an eviction order on one elderly woman from the only home she has ever known because 'Mister Hussey plans to plough up this whole piece of land'.[84] The description of the distressed old lady gathering together the few belongings that remained of her family life, while the bailiff orders the constable to 'smash that door down', ensures that the trauma is not overlooked.

Finally, it is the turn of Eily and John to have their rent doubled and the reason for the evictions becomes clear. John learns at a meeting of tenants that Ormonde plans to merge many of the small holdings and farms, getting rid of what he considered the poor and useless tenants before selling the land to pay his large betting debts. Hussey was to get one of these newer enlarged farms which explains his interest in getting rid of as many small tenants as possible. He had his eye on John and Eily's place and was making it impossible for them to meet his exorbitant demands. It is ironic that it was the generosity of Lord Henry in giving Michael the two race horses that allowed Eily and John to finally become the owners of the land. This underlines the complexity of the relationship between landlords and their workers.

It also revises the belief that the peasants were totally devoid of economic skills. Seamus Deane has pointed out that in Maria Edgeworth, 'Irish peasant society is presented as little more than a feudal residue ... utterly devoid of the economic skills that would make it a serious political presence'.[85] Michael's deal with Ormonde, in which he sells him a horse and promises to 'give him a bit of advice on getting that shambles of a stable he has into some kind of shape' in return for Eily and John's small holding, gives the lie to this notion. Ormonde's previously mentioned gambling debts and 'shambles of a stable' show him to be financially incompetent, whereas the acceptance of the horses in lieu of wages, and the deal done with Ormonde, shows Michael's economic competence.

Toss also shows economic rationality. In his case, he overturns the Yeatsian idea of the heroic national character which contrasted the image of the imaginative and poetic Irish peasantry with that of the commercial 'gombeen man'. In Toss we have an image of the modern Irish character who can combine poetry and traditional virtues with economic sense without betraying either. He is a transitional figure in whom we can see the beginning of the modernization of Irish society. The poetic side of Toss is seen in the 'gift of whispering' to horses. Just before he moves to England with the Buckland family he passes this gift on to Michael. He invites Michael to stand close to him and listen to him whisper to the racehorse Glengarry:

> Michael, you know I have no children, no sons. Today I want to give you a gift ... This was passed from my father to me. He got it from his father before him ... Toss whispered of wind in the trees and green grass growing, of soft rain that fell, and the night sky that drew in and stars that watched from above. He spoke of times past, times present and times to come. He spoke of the races she'd run, the foals she'd had and would have, and the races they too would run.[86]

Michael knows that he has been given 'a rare thing'. At Toss's bidding he tries it out on the young foal, Morning Boy. 'Morning Boy, born as the moon dipped and the sun rose warm from earth'. This beautiful and poetic writing shows one side of Toss. The negotiation with Lord Henry that acquired these two horses for Michael shows another. He explained to Lord Henry that the injured racehorse and the frightened colt would not survive the journey to England. When Michael is offered and accepts the injured racehorse in payment for money owed, Toss speaks out: '"Begging your pardon, your Lordship", interrupted Toss, "them two are a pair and Michael here would be the only one with a chance of making something of either of them. Let him have the two."'[87]

If we see in Edgeworth a separation between sensibility and economics, such as that shown between Thady and his son Jason, here they are reconciled. In *Fields of Home*, Toss makes the transition into modernity by exhibiting both traditional traits and by transcending the limits previously attributed to national character by a writer like Edgeworth and also by the later Literary Revival which was also dominated by this contrast between imagination and commerce. In his opening address to the Merriman Summer School (August 1997) Professor Declan Kiberd pointed to the talent Irish people had revealed for enterprise in the previous three or four years. Conlon-McKenna shows that it has always been there. Toss has not only bridged the gap between imagination and commerce, he has taught the younger man, Michael, how to do the same. This has proved – by the deal Michael has done with Ormonde – to be the first step to recovery of the land.

Seamus Deane points to a difference in the Irish battle for the land and the battle for the soil in the nineteenth century, 'even though the two merge and interfuse at various points'. He says: 'Soil is what land becomes when it is ideally constructed as a natal source, that element out of which the Irish originate and to which their past generations have returned ... soil is eternally possessed by a community; land is temporarily owned by an individual.'[88] This sentiment is echoed by Agnes Quinn, the widow who had been evicted from her home, when she says, 'They can tumble my cottage, tear it down stone by stone, but they can't take away the fact that me and mine lived and died here ... The O'Briens will always be a part of this place. No one can change that!'[89]

At the end of this trilogy about the Famine and the post-Famine transition, when the land finally becomes their own, Eily calls her daughter Mary Brigid to her and places a sod of earth in her hands: 'Eily placed the sod in Mary Brigid's open hands. The earth felt hard and heavy and damp. It smelt of peat and new grass and all the things that had grown in it for hundreds and hundreds of years.'[90] I am immediately transported back to where the first story began and to the memory of Baby Brigid buried under the hawthorn tree. This is not just a sod of earth. It is made up as much from memories as it is from layers of soil. It is as though all the dead have been 'turned to earth, incorporated in it, dispersed into the landscape'.[91]

This idea of landscape carrying the weight of history is not new. Simon Schama in *Landscape and Memory* quotes the opening pages of Conrad's *Heart of Darkness*, with its 'vision of English history bobbing on the roadstead tides' as an example. The notion of the Thames as a line of time as well as space gives us a clearer understanding of the Irish relationship with land and gives us an idea of what Eily felt when she placed the sod in her daughter's hands and bid her to: 'Remember this day and this night! This is the day that these fields and this land and this hard-worked soil finally became ours!'[92] Her words are loaded with memories of the generations behind and hope for those yet to come.

Usually, we think of fire as the element of annihilation but 'both mythographers and natural historians know better: that from the pyre rises the phoenix, that through a mantle of ash can emerge a shoot of restored life'.[93] At one of the hardest times on their journey in *Under the Hawthorn Tree*, the children come across a part of the landscape where everything is charred and blackened. There has been a fire and a spell of very dry weather has caused it to spread over the area. 'Nothing stirred in this bleakness, not a bird or an insect or a bee or an animal. It was too quiet. Fields of what had been gorse and heather and pasture had been laid bare.'[94] The desolation is such that Peggy thinks she is in hell, but we know that the grass will grow back and the animals will return. Again, after the burning of Castletaggart House in *Fields of Home*, Toss is pessimistic: 'Just like the famine that spread among us, this fire – this fire, I'm telling you, will spread across the land. Things will never be the same.'[95] And of course they won't. Schama, however, reminds us that:

> Once rooted, the irresistible cycle of vegetation, where death merely composted the process of rebirth, seemed to promise true national immortality ... even fires that could strike the wooded hillsides ... while superficially devastating, actually promoted the natural cycle of renewal. Beneath the ashy crust, we knew, there would always be blessed vitality.[96]

Schama's *Landscape and Memory*, he says, shows a way of looking at landscape that, instead of being another account of what we have lost, can also be a way of re-discovering what we already have or indeed an exploration of what we may yet find. This alternative way of looking has been at the heart of Conlon-McKenna's attempt to offer her readers a more positive view of history, which, while it does not contest the reality of what has happened, reveals the richness and complexity of our heritage and shows how much we stand to lose if all we see is tragedy. While this trilogy commemorates the darkest of times in our past, and takes us through what Eavan Boland describes as the 'wrath and grief of Irish history', it is not a lament. The story is fundamentally one of survival, symbolized by the children's transcendence of the problems of history, their victory over it, and finally their liberation from it.

While these stories are historical, and true to the historical facts, they are also about ourselves as we are now. One can understand the reservations of Richard Roche who, referring to the State commemoration of the 150th anniversary of the Famine, writes in *The Irish Times* about 'the glaring impropriety of "celebrating" such tragedies'.[97]Concern has often been expressed about an 'Anglo-centric, revisionist dominance of Irish historical scholarship'; traditional historians fear that 'the baby has been thrown out with the bathwater'.[98] However, these stories manage to revise our national history without discounting the suffering and courage of those who made us what we are. Too often our memory of the past has occupied our social and psychological thinking in a negative way. It has placed constraints upon the present by painting a picture of ourselves as victims and thereby prohibiting our ability to see ourselves as the complex beings we really are rather than the passive objects of history. Conlon-McKenna has managed to assimilate the past into the present in a way that enables Irish children to liberate themselves from previous patterns and face a future freed from that past. At the end of his essay 'Historicism, History and The Imagination' Hayden White says, 'Robert Frost once said that when a poet grows old he *dies* into philosophy. When a great work of historiography or philosophy of history has become outdated it is *reborn* into art.'[99] With Marita Conlon-McKenna's historical trilogy a whole section of our history has been 'reborn' for a new generation.

NOTES

1. Brendan Kennelly, 'A Soft Amen', in *Cromwell* (Dublin: Beaver Row Press, 1983), p.146.
2. Hayden White, 'The Burden of History', in *Tropics of Discourse. Essays in Cultural Criticism* (Baltimore, MD: The John Hopkins University Press, 1990 [1978]).
3. Ibid., p.39.
4. Hayden White, 'The Historical Text as Literary Artifact', in *Tropics of Discourse* p.98.
5. Ibid., p.97.

6. Jill Paton Walsh, 'The Art of Realism', in Betsy Hearne and Marilyn Kaye (eds), *Celebrating Children's Books* (New York: Lothrop, Lee & Shepard, 1981), p.38.
7. Hayden White, *Metahistory: The Historical Imagination in Nineteenth-Century Europe* (Baltimore, MD: The John Hopkins University Press, 1993 [1973]), p.7.
8. Eavan Boland, *A Kind of Scar: The Woman Poet in a National Tradition* (Dublin: Attic Press, 1989), p.5.
9. Claude Levi Strauss, *The Savage Mind* (London: Weidenfeld and Nicolson, 1962), p.258.
10. Gilles Deleuze and Felix Guattari, *Kafka: Towards a Minor Literature* (Minneapolis, MN: University of Minnesota Press, 1986), p.18.
11. Reda Bensmaia, Foreword, in Deleuze and Guattari, *Kafka: Towards a Minor Literature*, p.xiv.
12. John Stephens, *Language and Ideology in Children's Fiction* (New York: Longman Publishing, 1992), p.17.
13. Marita Conlon-McKenna talks to Robert Dunbar, *Children's Books in Ireland*, (3 December 1990).
14. Marita Conlon-McKenna, *Under the Hawthorn Tree* (Dublin: The O'Brien Press, 1990), p.24.
15. Marita Conlon-McKenna talks to Robert Dunbar, *Children's Books in Ireland*.
16. Marita Conlon-McKenna, *Wildflower Girl* (Dublin: The O'Brien Press, 1992), p.26.
17. Stephens, *Language and Ideology in Children's Fiction*, p.27.
18. Levi Strauss, *The Savage Mind*, p.257.
19. Milan Kundera, 'A la recherché du Present Perdu', in *Testaments Betrayed* (London: Faber & Faber, 1996 [1995]), p.136.
20. Conlon-McKenna, *Under the Hawthorn Tree*, pp.16–17.
21. Ibid., p.51.
22. Guy Cook, *Discourse* (Oxford: Oxford University Press, 1989), p.156. Quoted in Stephens, *Language and Ideology in Children's Fiction*, p.11.
23. Cathal Póirtéir, *Famine Echoes* (Dublin: Gill & Macmillan, 1995), p.3.
24. Although she spent a lot of time in the National Library checking sketches and official reports of the time, Conlon McKenna also drew on the many stories passed on by her mother and by elderly friends and relatives in West Cork. She also included folklore. For example, a child would be buried under the hawthorn tree because folklore tells us that the hawthorn tree is a fairy tree and as such no one would dare to cut it down. The child would be protected by the fairies. Although her research is always rigorous, she likes to weave it with elements of intuition and folklore. Conversation with Marita Conlon-McKenna, 31 March 2008.
25. Conlon-McKenna, *Under the Hawthorn Tree*, p.37.
26. Ibid., p.104.
27. Ibid., p.82.
28. Ibid., p.56.
29. Ibid., p.150.
30. Ibid., p.53.
31. M.A.G. O'Tuathaigh, 'Irish Historical "Revisionism": State of the Art or Ideological Project?', in Ciaran Brady (ed.), *Interpreting Irish History: The Debate on Revisionism* (Dublin: Irish Academic Press, 1994), p.325.
32. Alan O'Day, 'Revising the Diaspora', in D. George Boyce and Alan O'Day (eds), *The Making of Modern Irish History* (London: Routledge, 1996), p.190.
33. Patrick O'Sullivan (ed.), *Irish Women and Irish Migration*, in *The Irish World Wide. History, Heritage, Identity*, Vol.4 (London: Leicester University Press, 1995), p.1.
34. Conlon-McKenna, *Wildflower Girl*, pp.26–9.
35. Hasia R. Diner, *Erin's Daughters in America* (Baltimore, MD: The John Hopkins University Press, 1986 [1983]), p.33.
36. F.S.L. Lyons, *Ireland Since the Famine* (London: Fontana, 1989 [1971]), p.52.
37. Conlon-McKenna, *Wildflower Girl*, p.24.
38. Ibid., p.26.
39. Diner, *Erin's Daughters in America*, p.xiv.
40. Ibid., p.45.
41. Conlon-McKenna, *Wildflower Girl*, p.31.
42. Ibid., p.33.
43. Ibid., p.36.
44. John Berger and Jean Mohr, *Another Way of Telling* (New York: Pantheon, 1982), p.36.

45. Ibid., p.109.
46. Ibid., p.119.
47. Ibid., p.108.
48. Edward Said, *Culture and Imperialism* (London: Vintage, 1994), p.401.
49. Conlon-McKenna, *Wildflower Girl*, p.77.
50. Ibid., p.121.
51. Ibid., p.122.
52. Said, *Culture and Imperialism*, p.407.
53. Conlon-McKenna, *Wildflower Girl*, p.94.
54. Ibid., p.172.
55. Ibid., p.132.
56. Diner, *Erin's Daughters in America*, p.83.
57. Conlon-McKenna, *Wildflower Girl*, p.118.
58. 'Jean Kennedy Smith talks to Eileen Battersby', *The Irish Times*, 3 July 1997.
59. Eavan Boland, 'The Emigrant Irish', in *The Journey and other Poems* (Manchester: Carcanet, 1987), p.54.
60. G.V. Whelan, 'Book of the Day', *The Irish Times*, 5 June 1996.
61 Marita Conlon-McKenna, *Fields of Home* (Dublin: The O'Brien Press, 1996), p.50.
62. Whelan, 'Book of the Day', *The Irish Times*, 5 June 1996.
63. Stephens, *Language and Ideology in Children's Fiction*, p.282.
64. Conlon McKenna, *Wildflower Girl*, p.141.
65. Conlon-McKenna, *Fields of Home*, p.50.
66. Diner, *Erin's Daughters in America*, p.126.
67. Ibid., p.138.
68. Ibid., p.120.
69. Ibid., p.40.
70. Quoted in ibid., p.40.
71. Conlon-McKenna, *Fields of Home*, pp.90–1.
72. Quoted in Said, *Culture and Imperialism*, p.407.
73. Conlon-McKenna, *Fields of Home*, p.186.
74. Ibid., p.187.
75. Cormac Ó Gráda, 'Too Slow to Evict', *Times Literary Supplement*, 22 July 1994, quoted by Paul Bew in *The Making of Modern Irish History* (London: Routledge, 1996), p.94.
76. Bew, *The Making of Modern Irish History*, p.94.
77. Conlon-McKenna, *Fields of Home*, pp.30–1.
78. Ibid., p.113.
79. Ibid., pp.115–16.
80. Ibid., p.119.
81. Louis MacNeice, *The Poetry of W.B. Yeats* (London: Faber & Faber, 1967), p.97.
82. Conlon-McKenna, *Fields of Home*, pp.181–2.
83. Ibid., p.130.
84. Ibid., p.56.
85. Seamus Deane, *Strange Country: Modernity and Nationhood in Irish Writing since 1790* (Oxford: Clarendon Press, 1997), p.39.
86. Conlon-McKenna, *Fields of Home*, p.140.
87. Ibid., p.123.
88. Deane, *Strange Country*, p.71.
89. Conlon-McKenna, *Fields of Home*, p.63.
90. Ibid., p.189.
91. J. Hillis Miller, 'Topography and Tropography in Thomas Hardy's "In Front of the Landscape"', in *Tropes, Parables, Performances: Essays on Twentieth-Century Literature* (London: Harvester Wheatsheaf, 1990), p.210.
92. Conlon-McKenna, *Fields of Home*, p.189.
93. Simon Schama, *Landscape and Memory* (London: Harper Collins, 1995), p.19.
94. Conlon-McKenna, *Under the Hawthorn Tree*, p.108.
95. Conlon-McKenna, *Fields of Home*, p.119.
96. Schama, *Landscape and Memory*, p.6.
97. Richard Roche, 'When Famine Stalked the West', *The Irish Times*, 5 July 1997.
98. Damien Kiberd, 'Making History of Our History', *The Sunday Business Post*, 14 April 1996.
99. Hayden White, 'Historism, History and the Imagination', in *Tropics of Discourse*, p.118.

4

Modern Ireland: Cormac MacRaois

And may we have neither the mania of the One
Nor the delirium of the Many –
But both the Union and the Diversity–

'Dialectician's Prayer'[1]

If Marita Conlon-McKenna has attempted to break away from
national myths, Cormac MacRaois has opted to return to old stories
in his attempt to show us what we are. While the previous two chapters
have dealt with post-colonialism and revisionism as they apply to Irish
situations and concerns, it has also been evident that these are concerns which have more than simply Irish meaning and application. The
same is true of Cormac MacRaois' Giltspur trilogy in which he blends
adventure with ancient Irish myth in order to underline the problems of twentieth-century society. In getting to the heart of the problem
in Ireland, he also gets to the heart of the estrangement of the modern
world.

In an article in *The Lion and The Unicorn*, MacRaois has defined
Irish mythology as stories our ancestors told one another and which
arose out of their understanding of themselves and of the society in
which they lived. These stories had, he says, 'serious political, historical, and religious (pre-Christian) significance for the tellers and their
audience'.[2] MacRaois takes these old myths into the present by setting
the normal family life of two Irish children of our time against the
backdrop of our old stories, and once again they have serious 'political, historical and religious significance'.

According to John Stephens, 'because intertextuality is a strategy
whereby a text relates to existing discourses and achieves intelligibility,
it often plays a major part in attempts to produce determinable meanings and to acculturate the audience'.[3] For example, the use of myth
carries a clear pre-textual connection in that it belongs to the realm of

the magical or mysterious, is pre-scientific and pre-rationality. It also serves as a reminder that we cannot sever our links with the past. In this case, intertextuality is exploited when contemporary social discourse is questioned by weighing it against a discourse constructed from tales from Irish mythology in such a way as to comment on the present and its values. Set in North Wicklow at the foot of the Sugar Loaf Mountain, the situations depicted give MacRaois' vision of an Irish cultural crisis. They also may be said to stand for the cultural crisis that has reached its height generally in this postmodern era with its culture of individualism and moral nihilism.

In *Postmodernism, or The Cultural Logic of Late Capitalism*, Fredric Jameson identifies several features, which he says characterize postmodernism. These are depthlessness, the disappearance of the subject, loss of expression and loss of history. All of these features can be found in this trilogy in the Morrigan or her Shadow Slaves. In the old Irish mythological cycle the Morrigan is a shape changer who foretells and attends on battle slaughter and who drains away the courage of warriors. This chapter investigates the fact that, in MacRaois' trilogy, she seems to be a personification of the culture of postmodernism, while her Shadow Slaves are described by Glasan as, 'wretched beings unable to resist her will, taking whatever shape she wants them to'.[4] The threat for the young protagonists of these stories is that of becoming a slave to the postmodern monster. In opposing and resisting the Morrigan and her creatures, the children are questioning the kind of society which they will inherit.

In his essay, 'Welcome to the Teen World',[5] Bryan Appleyard expresses a belief that the young are working hard to rediscover the 'complex and frequently hidden net of custom and value that unites, stabilises and sustains societies'. Tired of being told that they have no past and no future, they are trying to restore the sense of family, authority and morality which we have disposed of on their behalf. In this trilogy, children are obviously of great importance as mediators in producing change. They are often referred to as Manannán's 'chosen ones'. Glasan tells them: 'The power that called me back to Ireland obviously did not intend me to meet Manannán myself ... It was for this moment you were chosen.'[6] In the midst of the final battle Imbas also tells them that he would 'spare [them] all the dangers of this conflict but I have a deep certainty in my heart that you have a vital part to play in this struggle, a part beyond the understanding of anyone here'.[7] Like the old mythological heroes they are mediators between earth and heaven. If we agree with Appleyard that the high school is 'the happening place' and that the 'socialising process comes from below, not from above', then it follows that literature for children is a good place to begin the questioning of social practice.

John Stephens points out that 'the questioning of one social practice can only be carried out from within the value systems of another'. This alternative ideological practice is, he says, 'even more inescapable when the protagonists of a narrative are children, for whom the struggle against adult power will not eventuate in structural change'.[8] Any major change is likely to be a change from one socialized subjectivity to another. MacRaois' apparent ideological purpose is to replace what he sees as a society with no fixed points of reference with a return of the Sacred. To this end, Glasan and the people of Tir Danann are represented as being beautiful, intelligent, caring, skilled in warfare, poetry and music, but unimpressed by technology. When the children and Donnan, one of the citizens of Danann, are comparing life in Tir Danann to life in modern Ireland we can see one example of how meaning is produced at the point of interaction. Ronan expresses surprise that after all these years the people of Tir Danann have not yet invented many machines. They still use horses and chariots and defend themselves with swords. Donnan however tells the children:

> If you had known two thousand years of peace, I doubt if your people would have wasted their time and wealth on the terrible weapons of destruction that the great nations of the earth now hold ... We long ago discovered that to develop the power of our minds – what your people would call magic – was a much more useful and far deeper kind of progress than just improving machines.[9]

One of the important functions of this exchange is to deconstruct the notion of technology as progress and to compare the value systems of the two societies.

The first and most obvious feature of postmodernism Jameson describes as a kind of 'flatness or depthlessness, a new kind of superficiality in the most literal sense'.[10] There are several literal instances of this superficiality in MacRaois' trilogy. For example, in the first book of the series when the children and Glasan are fleeing from their attackers, they find their way ahead engulfed in fire so that they were trapped. Glasan, however, hesitates only for a second before urging the children on.

"Go on!" He urged. "This is a trick. It is not real fire. Go on!"

> Niamh and Daire looked at the red flames leaping higher than their heads, the black smoke drifting and the sparks flying. It was impossible not to believe the fire was real.[11]

At Glasan's urging the children walk through the flames and smoke and discover that it was indeed an illusion. When they have all passed through, Glasan moistens the tip of a hazel wand in his mouth and draws it through the flames. Scarnan's creatures following behind are driven back by the heat. Niamh is puzzled and asks why they also did not walk through the flames. Glasan tells her that this is because his flames are real and not mechanically reproduced copies. The authentic is more difficult. He says: 'Imaginary fire is an easy trick. Real fire takes longer to learn.'[12]

In the same way, when they appeared to be surrounded by a writhing mass of serpents, these were found to be depthless images. When Daire swings his sword at one of them the blade passes clean through but the creature is unharmed and Glasan tells him, 'They're only air.'

The final example of this confusion between the real and the unreal comes when the wolves are transformed into their own images:

> another pair of wolves, exactly like the first pair. More and more appeared until there were nine pairs of wolves, each of them exactly the image of Greyfang and Deathtooth.
> 'Are these also images of fear?' cried Niamh.
> 'Two of them are real', said Glasan.
> 'Which two?' said Daire, as the wolves began to close in.
> 'I cannot tell', replied Glasan.[13]

This 'flatness' or 'depthlessness' is found not just in objects or animals, but also in the human subject. It has its physical manifestation in the Shadow Slaves who are to be found, with all the life drained from them, chanting and grovelling at the feet of the Morrigan. There is a deathly quality about these pathetic creatures that has nothing to do with death and everything to do with the disposition of the subject. They have literally faded to shadows – 'a ghostly army of the lost'[14] – and are therefore a fitting example of the disappearance of the individual subject. They serve perfectly to illustrate Jameson's idea of beings that are 'no longer that of the old monadic subject, but rather that of some degraded collective objective spirit'[15] whose loss of depth gives rise to the mechanical reproduction mentioned in the last paragraph.

These literal and physical examples of depthlessness are underscored by a corresponding depthlessness in expression and feelings or emotions. Jameson's comparison of Van Gogh's painting, *Peasant Shoes*, with Andy Warhol's *Diamond Dust Shoes*, illustrates how ex-pression and emotion can be lost. In the Van Gogh painting the peasant shoes are the symbol for some greater reality. To Jameson they represent agricultural misery and rural poverty. He says that, if the painting is to have any meaning, we must be able to ground it in some situation which is now in the past. The fact that we can mentally restore the initial situation from which the work has emerged and to which it responds, prevents the painting from becoming a mere 'inert object'. He compares this to Warhol's *Diamond Dust Shoes*, which he describes as 'a random collection of dead objects' which 'leave us no way to complete the hermeneutical gesture, and [to] restore to these oddments that whole larger lived context'.[16] Without its context, the painting calls forth no emotion. This holds as much for human subjects as it does for objects. If we remove ourselves from 'the larger lived context' then the resulting loss of subjectivity brings a loss of feeling or emotion. This can be seen in the Morrigan's inability to *feel*, which is what causes Niamh to pity her:

> Niamh looked sadly at the Morrigan. 'All you can see is evil', she whispered. 'We see it too, but we also *feel*. We feel pity and love. You have lost that. You are more lost than all your unfortunate victims. I pity you more than all the rest.'[17]

As Jameson points out, there can be no feeling if there is no longer a self present to do the feeling.

According to Jameson, the disappearance of the individual subject 'engender[s] the well-nigh universal practice today of what may be called pastiche' whereby 'the producers of culture have nowhere to turn but to the past: the imitation of dead styles, speech through all the masks and voices stored up in the imaginary museum of a now global culture'.[18] Jameson goes on to say that this leads to what Henri Lefebvre has called the increasing primacy of the 'neo'. This attempt to appropriate a missing past has, he says, a huge effect on historical time because the past has simply become 'a vast collection of images'. This culminates in a situation where 'the past as "referent" finds itself gradually bracketed, and then effaced altogether, leaving us with nothing but texts'.[19] In other words, 'real' history is replaced by 'aesthetic styles'; a situation which results in a lack of narrative continuation and prevents us from organizing past and future into any kind of coherent experience. Jameson says that if we are unable to unify the past, present

and future of our own biographical experience, then we become schizophrenic. In MacRaois' trilogy this schizophrenic tendency manifests
itself in the fact that the Morrigan, in keeping with the pluralism and
perspectivism of postmodernism, must keep changing her appearance.
When Ronan asks which out all the disguises is the *real* Morrigan,
Glasan tells the children:

> She is the witch of a thousand shapes ... That is her strength and
> her weakness. The Morrigan is the restlessness of greed, the
> unease of envy, the tearing apart of frustration. Her deepest
> unhappiness is that she has lost her real self. This is what drives
> her to so much dreadfulness. She no longer knows who she is, so
> she cannot settle to be one of her many selves. She must keep end-
> lessly changing without rest.[20]

In *Fantasy: The Literature of Subversion*, Rosemary Jackson says
'whereas "faery" stories and quasi religion tales function through nostalgia for the sacred, the modern fantastic refuses a backward looking
glance'.[21] MacRaois' stories shift back towards the former in that they
do indeed function through nostalgia for the sacred, but this time the
emphasis is on tradition and continuity rather than nature, as it tends
to be in traditional fairy stories. It has been said, that 'in a society
where myth and/or magic are prominent ... praxis is embedded in an
undifferentiated unity between humanity and nature'.[22] However,
Daniel Bell, in his 1977 essay 'The Return of The Sacred?', asks
whether there is a future for religion in modern culture. He believes
that there is and he predicts that:

> If there are to be new religions – and I think they will arise – they
> will, contrary to previous experience, return to the past, to seek
> for tradition and to search for those threads which can give a per-
> son a set of ties that place him in the continuity of the dead and
> the living and those still to be born. Unlike romanticism, it will
> not be a turn to nature, and unlike modernity it will not be the
> involuted self; it will be the resurrection of Memory.[23]

The trend forecast by Bell seems to be borne out in this trilogy. One of
the effects of using the mythic mode is to remind us that we cannot
sever our links with the past as postmodernism tries to do. In the first
pages of *The Battle Below Giltspur*, the first book of the series, when
the scarecrow, Glasan, comes to life on the feast of Bealtaine, 'he was
trying to remember something, something long ago and far away'.[24]
For Glasan, 'praxis' comes with memory rather than unity with nature.

His early attempts at magic hang upon relearning or remembering. He tells the children 'The power was stronger in the old days ... but a little of it is returning to my hands'.[25] He also tells them that 'passing from one world to the other is not easy. It is like wakening from a long deep sleep, so that it takes a long time to remember who you were and what you were able to do.'[26] His power thus comes from something that is innate since it is something that can be *re*learned or *re*membered.

At this first meeting with the children when Niamh and Daire ask his name, he tells them: 'My name is Glasan. But that doesn't really tell you who I am.'[27] Selfhood is more complex than that. When they in turn tell him their names he replies: 'What fine names! Daire, the oak wood, strong, tall and trusted. Niamh the beautiful, fair of face and fair of heart.'[28] If naming is the first step in recognizing the selfhood of the other, by giving the original meaning of their name Glasan immediately makes a connection between tradition and selfhood. As Bell has put it, 'The thread of culture – and religion – is memory'[29] and the emptiness of contemporary culture leaves a space for those who wish to defend the bonds of tradition and find that pre-existing meaning by stripping away the covering layers.

In this same essay, Bell gives his idea of the forms any new religions might take. One of these he calls 'redemptive' and this he describes as deriving from two sources. The first comes from the retreat from the excesses of modernity, whereby:

> one can face death, perhaps, not by seeking to be self-infinitizing, but by looking back ... In this sense, religion is the awareness of a space of transcendence, the passage out of the past from which one has come, and to which one is bound, to a new conception of the self as moral agent, freely accepting one's past ... and stepping back into tradition in order to maintain the continuity of moral meanings.[30]

In this case the continuity of moral meanings is maintained through Glasan, who has, he says, been here many times before. He has been 'a druid, a poet, a soldier, a fool, a priest, an eagle, a swan – and now a scarecrow'.[31] The thread of culture stretches back through Glasan a long, long way; 'longer ago than your history books can tell you', and he tells the children that he will be 'always parting [from them] and always meeting again'.[32] It seems that he will be always there to remind us when we are in danger of losing some things we may have been unaware of or may have forgotten about, and ensuring that we retain a sense of history that includes both the past and the future. Glasan's task is to re establish continuity and he tells Niamh that he has 'never been defeated before'.[33] In the midst of the battle when Niamh is in trouble, she blows the horn given to her by Manannán: 'it echoed from the mountains to the sea and back through all the years to when Fionn guarded the lands of Ireland'.[34] An answering call comes from a 'tall fair-headed warrior' with a horn exactly like Niamh's and it brings to her aid the Fianna, charging down the mountainside and scattering the evil Scarnan's army before them.

The narrative strategy of time travel stresses this interconnection between past and present. Whereas the trilogy begins with Glasan bringing the past into the present, in the second book the children travel from their present into the past, while the third book situates them between past and future. In this book, through the powers of the Morrigan, the children are afforded a glimpse of their future. This reinforces the notion of the simultaneity of past and present and their connection to the future.

The method of time travel also reinforces the closeness of that other world. Twice, in the first and third books, Glasan crosses over on what were important feasts in the old days of Ireland; Bealtaine, 'a sort of magical night celebrating the summer'[35] and Samhain, the start of the Celtic year. In the second book Niamh and Daire and their cousin Ronan are magically transported to the land of the people of Danann when they stand on a cairn where it is reputed a Chieftain lies buried. Glasan explains to the children that 'just as there are places in this world closer to the Otherworld, so also there are times of the year when the barrier between the worlds grows thinner'.[36]

The notion of the simultaneity of past and present is strengthened by the co-existence of time. When the children journey to Tir Danann it takes up none of the present time. When Niamh expresses concern that her parents will be worried about them, Foras tells her: 'The time you spend in this world is not taken from the time you spend in your own. If you were to return to Ireland now, you would be back at exactly the same moment that you left the hillside beside Giltspur. So no one will be looking for you and no one will be worried.'[37] MacRaois thus introduces what M.A.L. Locherbie-Cameron calls 'the notion of simultaneous though differing perceptions'.[38]

Foras also tells the children: 'Our worlds are not unconnected. If the powers of evil triumph here, it will not be long before they reach out to your world as well.'[39] Niamh realizes that this has already begun to happen. She has already seen in Greystones the same 'plague of seaweed' that is preventing the people of Danann from reaching Inis Og. This enchantment, brought about by the Formorians for the destruction of Tir Danann, is also threatening her own time and place. This reinforces the notion of simultaneity and challenges the narrowness of our concept of linear time.

Again, returning to the passage mentioned above where the children and Donnan are talking about life in Tir Danann compared to life in modern Ireland, Daire expresses regret that his world hasn't developed in the same way as that of Tir Danann. Donnan says: 'We weren't always so wise. When we lived in Ireland we were as warlike and selfish as everyone else. We have changed since then ... We have thousands of years in which to learn wisdom.'[40] As well as causing the children to question the value of the progress of modern life, this exchange also widens the boundaries of the notion of linear progression in that it places the importance of imaginative growth above the progression of time. It also has the strange effect of making the people of the past those with post-knowledge and consequently further questions our narrow conception of linearity, a concept that Jean Baudrillard says 'must have seemed entirely fictitious, wholly absurd and abstract to cultures which had no sense of a deferred day of reckoning, a successive concatenation of events and a final goal'.[41] Our present conception of linearity is, he says, a scenario that only established itself with great difficulty. This timelessness, a characteristic feature of myths, is a movement away from the idea of the abstracted fate of the individual in postmodern times as nothing more than 'solitary individuals successively advancing through time until they arrive at death'.[42] Instead, as Bell says, the use of myth 'evokes the totality of things. Its purpose is not to discover sequences but to uncover solidarity'.[43]

The second source of Bell's idea of 'redemptive' religion may be, he says, in the growth of 'mediating institutions' such as family and community which will resurrect the function of caring for each other – one of the oldest sources of human attachment and a form of love that Bell says 'has been crushed between rationalized *eros* and profaned *agape* and superseded by the welfare state'.[44] The children in MacRaois' stories, Niamh and Daire, together with their parents, are a traditional middle-class farming family. When Glasan stood outside the lighted window he saw

> a comfortable well-lit kitchen. The family was seated at the table. Mrs. Durkan was pouring tea and the warm steam rose up towards the light. There was a plate of brown bread in the centre of the table, and butter and jam and currant scones ... He wished

he was inside, sitting at the table, talking and laughing with everyone else.[45]

This is just the sort of stable family unit that had traditionally been seen as the cornerstone of Irish society and it becomes clear in these stories that their mediation is necessary if we are to successfully fill the moral vacuum at the centre of our society.

The importance of the family unit is made clear by the fact that, in her final attempt at domination, the Morrigan begins by attacking the trust between Niamh and Daire and their parents. If she can destroy this she will have made her task a lot easier. The children are at their lowest point when the Morrigan has managed to fill their home with worry and unhappiness; they are in trouble for lying and their parents are shouting at each other. 'Daire had never seen a row between his parents before. It left him feeling lonely and lost.'[46] This is the point at which Niamh comes closest to being lost. The Morrigan says: 'She was at the tips of my fingers. One second more and she was down, down at my feet to grovel and beg for mercy to me.'[47] However, when Glasan asks Niamh whether she thinks that at the next try the Morrigan might succeed in dragging her across to her world, Niamh's 'eyes wandered down to where the Durkan farmhouse stood solidly among the familiar fields' and she replied firmly 'She will not succeed'.[48] By emphasizing the importance of a loving and stable family unit and its importance as mediator in the scheme of the story, MacRaois emphasizes the need to reinstate family life as a 'reaction against central government, large scale bureaucracy and the mega-structures of organisation'.[49]

It seems appropriate to question at this point whether this is merely another example of pastiche since MacRaois' notion of the family would seem to have little in common with the experience of many of today's children and may itself be no more than a mere 'aesthetic retrieval'.[50] Although, in the last paragraph of *Postmodernism, or The Cultural Logic of Late Capitalism* Jameson is at pains to point out that his is 'not a call for a return to some older kind of machinery',[51] still, it must be noted that Bell, Jameson and of course MacRaois himself, are all returning to the past; either a return to the sacred or a return to Marxism. Paradoxically, this neo-conservatism or neo-Marxism, as well as being a reaction to the excesses of postmodernism, could also be viewed as an example of pastiche and therefore in itself a prominent feature of postmodernism.

In contrast to the stable, loving family of the Durkans, Carl Craven's father is a bully and his mother a 'terrified rabbit'. 'As a small child Carl used to lie in bed clutching his teddy and crying quietly to himself in the dark. If his father heard him he would shout angrily at him for being silly, but he would never allow him to put on the light.'[52] Carl's dysfunctional family life is reflected in his behaviour to others. He himself is a bully who takes pleasure in tormenting his victims. He also shouts his mother down in any argument and bullies her into giving him his own way. Carl Craven's unloving family produces a troublesome, unhappy child who is unable to integrate socially. The thing that changed his attitude was the discovery that Glasan actually liked him. Once he realized that someone cared about him, 'he experienced an overwhelming urge to be liked for his strength instead of feared and hated'.[53] It caused him to come to the rescue of Niamh, Daire and Ronan when they were set upon by three youths in Bray, showing how the function of caring can bring about the complete transformation of an individual and make him a valued member of the community.

The importance of the community as a mediating institution is also stressed. Before he can take over, the evil Scarnan must first entice the community to destroy themselves by driving them mad 'with greed and hate and fear'.[54] His intention is to 'set them at each other's throats and laugh as they destroy each other' and he begins to accomplish this by causing friends and neighbours to argue and fight with each other. In the second book of the series there is a stress on how much more difficult it is to destroy a community in unison rather than one acting as individuals. As Foras explains the tangle of ancient Irish history and why he needs the children's help, he tells them that the only way his people have been able to protect themselves so far, since they have been denied the water of youth, is by the power of the assembled Council. When they work together 'the combined power of the Council reaches out to everyone in the city, awakening each person's strength to resist the enemy'.[55] The children see the truth of this when the enemy is trying to search Niamh's mind in order to discover her secret. She can feel fear weakening her self-control until Daire and Ronan join forces to help her. 'She could hear their voices clearly saying "Resist! Resist!" With a surge of relief she realised that their minds had united with hers to help her.'[56] The enemy was powerless against their united effort. Later, when they are once again under threat, Glasan shows them how they can 'perform magic' by combining the energy of their minds along with his. When they need to swim a long way underneath the surface of the water he advises them to: 'Think *seal* ... Think this thought clearly: once you touch the water you will become a seal.'[57]

In *Errata: An Examined Life*, George Steiner reminds us – if we need reminding – that our age is the blackest in human history. While he concedes that it may seem worse than other ages simply because we are informed through the news media of horrors which we would not have been able to know about in earlier epochs, this, he says, cuts both ways. 'Our very awareness of what man is inflicting on man should trigger outrage and intervention ... Almost invariably, however, the frequency, the packaged unreality of media representation leaves us either numbed or rapidly forgetful.'[58] It is, he believes, 'difficult to deny that the twentieth century has lowered the threshold of humanity'[59] because the bestial released in the killer makes something less than human both of his victims and of himself. In spite of this, Steiner also finds it undeniable that some human beings 'are capable of altruism, of active compassion, of self-sacrifice to the point of death ... At any given time, the sum of everyday humaneness, of applied love, can be considerable, and more often than not anonymous.'[60] Even if most of the time we are good and act altruistically out of self interest, it remains true that most people still believe that moral behaviour is an end in itself and many *are* capable of the kind of altruism Steiner talks about. While this love of humanity still exists it saves us from our natural savagery. Perhaps this is what redeems humanity. Certainly, in MacRaois' trilogy, this is what finally defeats the Morrigan.

The greatest conceptual difficulty that the Morrigan faced was the phenomenon of altruism. Being inherently selfish she did not understand it and could not fight against it. On the other hand, every time the children are in danger of being drawn into her net, it is their concern for others that saves them. The first time Glasan sends them to Manannán for help they find themselves in a wonderful orchard. Although they have been warned by Glasan that if they eat anything there they will never be able to return, they are sorely tempted: 'Niamh felt a great wave of longing rising inside her. She so much wanted to stay among the blossoming trees in this happy green place above the calm sparkling sea. She had only to reach up and pluck the fruit. One sweet bite would be enough. It would be so easy.'[61] It is the thought of Glasan waiting alone on the rocks below Bray Head and relying on them to bring help that prevents her from succumbing. When they resist the temptation Manannán says: 'You have shown yourselves willing to give up your own happiness for the sake of others. You have passed the test.'[62] Again, when Foras asks the children to stay in Tir Danann and help his people, in spite of the dangers Niamh replies: 'even if the evil power of Formor couldn't reach us at home, I still think we can't just go off and leave a whole country full of people to be killed or turned into slaves'.[63] Niamh even feels pity for the

Morrigan, which causes Glasan to say: 'In this you are far greater than she. Knowing your true self, you can feel pity for her. She is without pity.'[64]

Altruism, however, is a contingent state and cannot be taken for granted. Under the spell of the Morrigan, Niamh at one point became vain and uncaring to the extent that she helped to tie her brother to the stone altar and almost murdered him at the Morrigan's command. When she is explaining what happened to the High Council, Niamh tells them: 'The lady found the evil hidden in me and used it against me. I never realised before that I could become such an evil person.'[65] Imbas explains to Niamh that the Morrigan uses many disguises. In the guise of a beautiful lady who wants to help the children, she placed a medallion called the Balor Eye around Niamh's neck. This draws together every evil urge in the person who wears it. John Stephens says: 'To construct a new subjectivity the self needs to comprehend, confront, and struggle with the other.'[66] In Niamh's case she must struggle, not only with the Morrigan, but also with her own vanities. The High Council is impressed with her understanding of what has happened to her and also with her powers of resistance. Imbas tells her that by understanding how the Morrigan can use the power of evil, which is already in each of us, she has understood the Morrigan's power exactly. He tells her: 'You overcame not only the Morrigan but yourself. This is the true magic – the power within you to resist evil and do good.'[67] He goes on to say that Niamh's strength in resisting her will have weakened the Morrigan's power. Once she has had the courage to face evil and see it for what it is, it is powerless against her. Had the Morrigan succeeded in overcoming Niamh, Imbas tells her that she would have sucked the life from both her and Daire. The Morrigan's perpetuation depends on absorbing the lives of the children.

When her final attempt to break Niamh's resistance fails, the Morrigan tells her that she has believed too many high-minded stories and that it is time her eyes were opened and she saw the *real* world. Commanding the children to 'Look at the mirror of Life!' she unfolded a vision before them of political atrocities – genocide, dictatorships, world wars.

> From the shimmering horizon, a long line of ragged people was struggling towards the children. Their haunted eyes stared from skull-like heads and in their wasted arms they held out the bodies of their starving children, pleading for help, help that would never come. On and on they came, hundreds, thousands, millions wailing in their misery.[68]

Following on this vision she shows them where 'well-fed men secretly planned their wars for money, power, or to satisfy their own hunger for revenge'.[69] Centuries of human misery passed before their eyes in the Morrigan's effort to bring the children to despair, but the end comes when Niamh tells her: 'All you can see is evil ... We see it too but we also *feel*. We feel pity and love. You have lost that. You are more lost than all your unfortunate victims. I pity you more than all the rest.'[70] This is the end for the Morrigan. The power that had tried to dominate the children has failed because she has no power that can overcome Niamh's persistent belief in the worth of the human race.

One of the reasons why the Morrigan's vision of human misery did not fill Niamh with despair was because Niamh already knew that the world was a 'terrible place'. Joshua Foa Dienstag in an article, 'The Pessimistic Spirit', writes about pessimism as distinct from scepticism and nihilism. Dienstag says: 'there is a sense in which a dose of pessimism, rightly administered, could serve as a vaccine against the paralyzing effects of disorder and disenchantment, our true post-modern afflictions. Pessimism can enable us, that is, to understand better our world and to act within its limits.'[71] The Morrigan's vain striving for unadulterated happiness leads to a sense of injustice and self-pity. This in turn leads to despair, which causes her to see the world as irredeemable and not worth the effort. In the end, we too can feel pity for the Morrigan. She is tired, frustrated and hopeless. A striving for happiness that replaces a traditional sense of kinship with a theory of individualism has parallels in Edmund Burke's ideas on the French revolution. Burke argued that the Enlightenment's replacing of tradition and religion with reason was the source of many social problems in the eighteenth century. According to Burke, the French revolutionaries' 'barbarous philosophy had destroyed all the foundations of traditional civilization and had gone so far as to produce an alteration in human nature itself ... It had converted a society into a plebeian mob; most of all, *it had raised theory to an unprecedented position of power in European politics and social thought*'.[72] (my italics)

On the other hand, Niamh's 'pessimistic' realization that happiness for society as a whole is unlikely, allows her to have a positive plan for doing the best she can, even if the world will remain a disordered and disenchanted place. When the Morrigan tries to force her to see that 'there is no hope', Niamh tells her:

> I'd rather live a short life of cheerful courage than live forever like you, feeding on hatred and misery. That's all you can see but there's a lot more to us than that. Those poor starving babies were

wrapped in the arms of mothers who loved them ... We *know* the world is a terrible place. We're making the best we can of it. Considering all the wretchedness we've had to endure, I think the human race is marvellous to have survived at all.[73]

Niamh has refused to succumb to the paralysis of despair. At the core of her ethics is a fundamental recognition of the vulnerability of human life, so, without wilfully negating reality, she insists that we must continue to try to remain responsible. In the conclusion to *The Wake of Imagination*, Richard Kearney writes about ethics as something which 'presupposes the existence of a *narrative identity*: a self, which remembers its commitments to the other (both in its personal and collective history) and recalls that these commitments have *not yet been fulfilled*'.[74] This 'narrative self' has the ability to understand itself both as an individual and as one person among others who share a common humanity. It can only be someone who knows that they are part of a narrative which is never complete and with a commitment that is never exhausted; a 'tale of creation and obligation that never comes to an end'.[75] As Julia Kristeva says: 'This concept ... links the destinies of *life, narrative,* and *politics*: narrative conditions the duration and the immortality of the work of art; but it also accompanies, as historical narrative, the life of the *polis,* making it a political life, in the best sense of the word'.[76] I said earlier in this chapter that one of the effects of using the mythic mode was to remind us that we cannot sever our links with the past. By placing us in a larger narrative, the use of myth also extends our notion of personal identity to include that of a communal identity. This means that our responsibility to others stretches beyond personal history to include a collective history. The story must be endless, as MacRaois' is, because 'to abandon this story would be to condemn ourselves to the circles of empty imitation which predominates today, to renounce all hope of imagining alternative forms of cultural and political practice'.[77]

This is why Niamh feels pity for the Morrigan. She has no belief in progress and she has no link with the past. Isolated from both past and future she reduces herself exclusively to the present or 'to the illusion of a permanent undying "presence"'.[78] She has no 'narrative self'.

Seamus Deane in *Celtic Revivals* says that Yeats believed that the way to retain our Irish culture was to stay aware of metaphysical questions because in this way we not only kept our own identity, but also our links with ancient European culture. Deane points out that, with Yeats, 'to be traditionalist in the modern world was to be revolutionary'. He goes on to say that this is 'a conviction which has a true revolutionary impact when we look at the disappearance from the western mind of the sense of eternity and of the consciousness of death'.[79] Deane suggests that Yeats believed that it is the fear of death which makes people 'unredeemable from the things of earth ... His abhorrence of the neutralization of death in the middle-class consciousness led him towards disciplines and interests in which the notion of death was pre-eminent and the contemplation of it a crucial activity.'[80] This notion remains intact in the sense of crisis in MacRaois' trilogy. It is her inability to come to terms with life and death that causes the Morrigan to be the way she is. On the other hand, the sense of wholeness that Niamh has as a result of her relationship with the past, present and future allows her, in spite of the difficulties of life, to be optimistic about its value.

Following on the vision of all the misery of life, the Morrigan shows the children a vision of themselves growing old and dying. She tells them: 'It's all like this ... Everything comes to me in the end. There's nothing else but withering, destruction, death. Everything falls apart. There is *no hope*.'[81] The difference between Niamh and the Morrigan is their understanding of death. Bell quotes Hobbes: 'The source of conscience, said Hobbes, is the fear of death; the source of law, the fear of violent death.' Bell then goes on to say that, 'within a religious culture, death could still be viewed – though feared – as the prelude to *something* beyond. But what if there was nothing beyond?'[82] For the Morrigan there is nothing beyond, there is only the void and life has become hell for her. The realization that she has come to this point draws from her 'a cry of such despair, such pain as had never been heard before. It was a cry for all that was young and innocent, long ago, for all the goodness that could have been. It was a cry of rage against everyone, but mostly against herself.'[83] Her efforts to escape this predicament cause her to make a Faustian pact with Crom and his Twelve Lords of Night.

On the other hand, Niamh's optimism enables her to transform the Morrigan's vision into something of transcendent significance and give a metaphysical dignity to Being. She replies:

> So the three of us will grow up and grow old and eventually die ... That's no dreadfully shocking news. We know that already. Everybody knows it ... We haven't discovered yet how to make everyone good, but most of us are trying to be generous and kind, even if we often fail ... Most people are really good and incredibly brave and I'm proud of them![84]

Niamh knows and accepts that human existence is about being-in-the-world. When she sees her friends Glasan and Foras standing together in Manannán's orchard and realises that they have come to the end of *their* journey, she begins to wish that she too could stay here in this peaceful place, but Manannán tells her: 'Your time will come, but not yet. You are all young and have many years of growing to do. There is much to be achieved in your own world, many challenges to be met, many victories to be won before your last battle is fought.'[85]

What matters in a myth is whether it enables us to live; to keep going. MacRaois' Giltspur Trilogy has sometimes been dismissed as a repeat of the old battle between good and evil. The most obvious and frequent comment is that the stories are echoes of C.S. Lewis' Narnia series. Certainly there are obvious and intentional similarities. Both use fantasy as a means of communicating their protest against the values of their time: Lewis' battle takes place between the forces of Christianity and the forces of evil, MacRaois' between humanity and a sense of kinship as against a postmodern loss of subjectivity and meaning. Both were convinced that, although each individual was unique, they were also part of a larger unity. Both have Christ figures: Lewis in the guise of Aslan and MacRaois in the guise of Manannán. However, there is, I think, one very important difference. I would agree with David Holbrook, who finds *The Last Battle* to be 'full of hate'. He says: 'In C.S. Lewis there is a particular emphasis on a *continual* aggressive stance: indeed, in a sense, nothing happens in the Narnia books except the build-up and confrontation with paranoically conceived menaces, from an aggressive posture of hate, leading towards conflict.'[86] Holbrook finds the Narnia books to be primarily aggressive, confrontational and paranoid and marked by cruelty and hate towards opponents. On the other hand, MacRaois' protagonist, Niamh, feels pity for the Morrigan on more than one occasion. When Glasan was explaining that 'The Morrigan is the restlessness of greed, the unease of envy, the tearing apart of frustration' and that she has lost her 'real self', Niamh 'felt a pang of pity for the dreaded witch'.[87] Again, when she is trying to force them to see the world through her eyes, Niamh feels sadness for the Morigan. After the final battle in the series, Manannán tells the victors to help their enemies: 'Now, my friends ... We have much healing to do on this shore. Today my power is doubled in your hands. Let us attend the wounded. Do not neglect your injured enemies, for this is a day to heal all wounds.'[88] To the men of Tir Bolg he says: 'Your ancient resentment against the People of Danann must now end. Be free of the burden of your anger. Leave it buried here among the dead. Return in peace to brighten the homeland that you have made grim and gloomy by your long discontent.'[89]

Holbrook makes the observation that: 'Nowhere in the Narnia books are there causes to be served, in terms of the mysteries of this world, the possibilities of man or the satisfactions of interpersonal encounter between human beings: love.'[90] Lewis' Narnia tales place no value or satisfaction on living in this 'shadowland'. For Edmund, Eustace and Jill, 'all their life in this world and all their adventures in Narnia had only been the cover and the title page'.[91] This is not the case with Niamh and Daire. MacRaois' trilogy is very much concerned with the possibilities of man and the satisfactions of interpersonal encounter. In *The Voyage of the Dawn Treader*, the fifth volume in the Narnia series, Eustace's conversion is brought about by Aslan's magic. In *Lightening Over Giltspur*, Carl Craven's conversion came about when 'with a jolt of astonishment he realised that the Scarecrow actually *liked* him'.[92] The difference is best exemplified by an incident that occurs in both *The Last Battle* and *The Battle Below Giltspur*. When the protagonists of *The Last Battle* come into Aslan's orchard they eat the golden fruit:

> Everyone raised his hand to pick the fruit he best liked the look of, and then everyone paused for a second. This fruit was so beautiful that each felt 'It can't be meant for me … surely we're not allowed to pluck it.'
>
> 'It's all right', said Peter, 'I know what we're all thinking. But I'm sure, quite sure, we needn't. I've a feeling we've got to the country where everything is allowed.'[93]

The ensuing description of the freshness, juiciness and sweetness of the wonderful fruit, after which 'all the nicest things in this world would taste like medicine', prompts Holbrook to question whether the ultimate reward will be 'a Super-hedonism, of Absolutely Guiltless Self-interest'.[94] In contrast, when Niamh and Daire first come into Manannán's orchard they resist the temptation to eat the fruit because they know that if they eat the golden apples they can never return and they know that, back in their own world, Glasan is depending on them:

> Niamh felt a great wave of longing rising inside her. She so much wanted to stay among the blossoming trees in this happy green place above the calm sparkling sea. She had only to reach up and pluck the fruit. One sweet bite would be enough. It would be so easy. This chance would never come again. She would spend her

whole life ever afterwards wishing she had taken it. She was about to reach up when Daire said, 'Glasan!' He was talking to himself as if he was trying to remember. Glasan! Suddenly Niamh could see him standing alone on the rocks below Bray Head, with Rusk at his feet and Scarnan's horrible creatures climbing over the wall from the cliff path.

'No!' she cried loudly.

The children looked at each other. It was as if they had awakened from a dream. The tree still twinkled softly above them, but they no longer wanted to steal the fruit.[95]

Unlike the protagonists in *The Last Battle*, Niamh and Daire resist the golden fruit and make the existential choice. They choose love for humanity over the desire to eat the fruit and remain forever in Manannán's country. It seems that if C.S. Lewis' message is that the world is full of malignancy, MacRaois' message is that, yes, there is malignancy but there is also love. On their next visit they are able to eat the fruit and still return to their own world because they have 'earned the right'.[96] This is MacRaois' attempt to provide his young readers with a reason to keep going; some kind of moral framework, which will enable them to live in the world and within this postmodern moment. Over the course of the three books he asks important metaphysical questions about the nature of Being. In fact, he could be said to follow Yeats in that they both looked to myth as a source for a 'return to spiritual ideals lost in an overdeveloped modern Europe'.[97]

It seems indubitable that the Giltspur sequence, with its analogies of Paradise and Hell, is overtly ideological in its presentation of Christian doctrine as a way to understand and accept being-in-the-world. Although it should also be said that the use of myth, which is pre-conceptual, allows the Christian image to be substituted by any other symbolic image. It can of course be argued that this is not really facing death; it is just another form of avoidance. However, whether or not one sees this transcendence in the concept of Being as an illusion, it certainly seems true to say that the decline in religious belief, and the rise in the fear of nothingness beyond life on earth, brings its own problems. Probably because the existential questions that confront all human groups have not gone away. Daniel Bell suggests that religion is not an ideology, though he admits that it has in its institutional forms functioned in this way. 'It is', he says, 'a constitutive aspect of human experience because it is a response to the existential predicaments which are the *ricorsi* of human culture.'[98] It is something that is not manufactured or designed but which grows out of shared responses and shared experiences. In any case, it seems true to say that 'once humankind no longer has an end beyond itself, nothing stops it in the relentless exploitation of the world and itself'.[99]

Francis Fukuyama, the American social analyst, claims that the period from roughly the mid-1960s to the early 1990s has been marked by seriously deteriorating social conditions in most of the industrialized world, including Ireland.[100] But, we are now, he says, on the verge of a new era in which ordinary people will strive to live morally and insist that their bureaucrats and politicians do the same. The recent proliferation of tribunals in Irish society would lead us to suppose that this might very well be true. Jean Baudrillard has another way of looking at it. He says:

> A mania for trials has taken hold of us in recent times, together with a mania for responsibility, precisely at the point when this latter is becoming increasingly hard to pin down. We are looking to remake a clean history, to whitewash all the abominations: the obscure (resentful) feeling behind the proliferation of scandals is that history itself is a scandal.[101]

Baudrillard believes that, in the vain hope of escaping our present destruction, we are condemned to live everything through again in order to correct it all. He says that 'in the guise of revision and re-habilitation, we are cancelling out one by one all the events which have preceded us by obliging them to repent'.[102] We are, he says, 'cleaning and polishing' in an effort to wipe out all negative events from our memories until there will soon be nothing left of our history: 'all that has happened this century in terms of progress, liberation, revolution and violence is about to be revised for the better'.[103]

The disappearance of the subject as it is outlined in Jameson's essay and manifested in MacRaois' stories has not always been seen in a negative light. In *Modern Times Modern Places*, Peter Conrad reminds us of a time when Fernand Leger announced triumphantly that: 'Man becomes a mechanism like everything else; instead of being the end, as he formerly was, he is now the means.' Conrad makes the observation that: 'In 1923 this counted as an achievement – an advance beyond humanism and smug anthropomorphic sentiment. It is a measure of the moral history of our century that Leger's proclamation now sounds more like a threat than a promise.'[104] This is probably because we have come to see what it means to have nothing to hold on to; no past, no guidelines, and, most of all, no future. The way forward, as MacRaois sees it, is to stage a counter movement against the worst excesses of postmodernism and restore some of the social bonds of Irish traditions and values to a society that is in danger of losing its way because it no longer has any fixed points of identity and reference. He pits the social solidarity of family life, religion and community against the postmodern fragmentation of subjective rights, demand for instant gratification and nihilistic despair, not in an effort to turn back the clock, but rather as a way of pressing forward into the future. In the end, Niamh's resistance proves that all is not yet lost. As Glasan puts it, there is 'A Death's Chill, but not yet a Death'.[105] Niamh is the proof that the individual has not yet been exterminated despite the best attempts of a society created by science, industry and commerce.

NOTES

1. Kenneth Burke, 'Dialectician's Prayer', in *Collected Poems 1915–1967* (California: University of California Press, 1968), p.41.
2. Cormac MacRaois, 'Old Tales for New people: Irish Mythology Retold for Children', *The Lion and the Unicorn*, 21, 3 (1997), p.331.
3. John Stephens, *Language and Ideology in Children's Literature* (New York: Longman Publishing, 1992), p.86.
4. Cormac MacRaois, *Lightning Over Giltspur* (Dublin: Wolfhound Press, 1991), p.65.
5. Bryan Appleyard, 'Welcome to Teen World', *The Sunday Times*, Culture Section, 18 April 1999.
6. Cormac MacRaois, *The Battle Below Giltspur* (Dublin: Wolfhound Press, 1988), pp.103–4.
7. MacRaois, *Lightning Over Giltspur*, p.113.
8. Stephens, *Language and Ideology in Children's Fiction*, p.255.
9. Cormac MacRaois, *Dance of the Midnight Fire* (Dublin: Wolfhound Press, 1989), p.106.
10. Fredric Jameson, 'Postmodernism or the Cultural Logic of Late Capitalism', *New Left Review*, 145 (1984), p.60.
11. MacRaois, *The Battle Below Giltspur*, p.101.
12. Ibid., p.103.
13. Ibid., p.118.
14. Ibid., p.133.
15. Jameson, 'Postmodernism or the Cultural Logic of late Capitalism', p.126.
16. Ibid., p.60.
17. MacRaois, *Lightning Over Giltspur*, p.126.
18. Jameson, 'Postmodernism or the Cultural Logic of late Capitalism', pp.64–5.
19. Ibid., p.66.
20. MacRaois, *Lightning Over Giltspur*, pp.65–6.
21. Rosemary Jackson, *Fantasy: The Literature of Subversion* (London: Methuen, 1981), p.158.
22. David Held, *Introduction to Critical theory: Horkeimer to Habermas* (Berkeley, CA: University of California Press, 1980), p.155.
23. Daniel Bell, 'The Return of the Sacred?', in *The Winding Passage. Essays and Sociological Journeys 1960–1980* (Cambridge: ABT Books, 1980), p.349.
24. MacRaois, *The Battle Below Giltspur*, p.14.
25. Ibid., p.28.
26. Ibid., p.53.
27. Ibid., p.22.
28. Ibid., p.23.
29. Bell, 'The Return of the Sacred?', p.325.
30. Ibid., p.349.
31. MacRaois, *The Battle Below Giltspur*, p.53.
32. MacRaois, *Dance of the Midnight Fire*, p.157.

33. MacRaois *The Battle below Giltspur*, p.90.
34. Ibid., p.124.
35. Ibid., p.13.
36. MacRaois, *Lightning Over Giltspur*, p.65.
37. MacRaois, *Dance of the Midnight Fire*, p.26.
38. M.A.L. Locherbie-Cameron, 'Journeys through the Amulet: Time Travel in Children's Fiction', *Signal* 79 (January 1996), p.49.
39. MacRaois, *Dance of the Midnight Fire*, p.26.
40. Ibid., p.107.
41. Jean Baudrillard, *The Illusion of the End*, trans. Chris Turner (Cambridge: Polity Press, 1994), p.7.
42. Peter Conrad, *Modern Times Modern Places: Life and Art in the 20th Century* (London: Thames and Hudson, 1998), p.698.
43. Bell, 'The Return of The Sacred?', p.351.
44. Ibid., p.350.
45. MacRaois, *The Battle Below Giltspur*, p.14.
46. MacRaois, *Lightning Over Giltspur*, p.25.
47. Ibid., p.70.
48. Ibid., p.67.
49. Bell, 'The Return of The Sacred?', p.351.
50. Jameson, 'Postmodernism or the Cultural Logic of late Capitalism', p.63.
51. Ibid., p.91.
52. MacRaois, *Lightning Over Giltspur*, p.30.
53. Ibid., p.86.
54. MacRaois, *The Battle Below Giltspur*, p.86.
55. MacRaois, *Dance of the Midnight Fire*, p.90.
56. Ibid., p.114.
57. Ibid., p.138.
58. George Steiner, *Errata: An Examined Life* (London: Weidenfeld & Nicolson, 1997), p.107.
59. Ibid., p.108.
60. Ibid., p.109.
61. MacRaois, *The Battle Below Giltspur*, p.107.
62. Ibid., p.110.
63. MacRaois, *Dance of the Midnight Fire*, p.28.
64. MacRaois, *Lightning Over Giltspur*, p.66.
65. MacRaois, *Dance of the Midnight Fire*, p.94.
66. Stephens, *Language and Ideology in Children's Fiction*, p.257.
67. MacRaois, *Dance of the Midnight Fire*, p.95.
68. MacRaois, *Lightning Over Giltspur*, p.123.
69. Ibid., p.124.
70. Ibid., p.126.
71. Joshua Foa Dienstag, 'The Pessimistic Spirit', *Philosophy and Social Criticism*, 25, 1 (1999), p.72.
72. Seamus Deane, *Strange Country: Modernity and Nationhood in Irish Writing since 1790* (Oxford: Clarendon Press, 1997), p.7.
73. MacRaois, *Lightning Over Giltspur*, p.126.
74. Richard Kearney, *The Wake of Imagination* (London: Century Hutchinson Ltd, 1988), p.395.
75. Ibid., p.395.
76. Julia Kristeva, *Hannah Arendt: Life Is a Narrative*, trans. Frank Collins (Toronto, Buffalo, London: University of Toronto Press, 2001), p.8.
77. Kearney, *The Wake of Imagination*, p.396.
78. Richard Kearney, *Poetics of Modernity* (New Jersey: Humanities Press, 1995), p.40.
79. Seamus Deane, *Celtic Revivals* (North Carolina: Wake Forest University Press, 1985), p.49.
80. Ibid., p.41.
81. MacRaois, *Lightning Over Giltspur*, p.125.
82. Bell, 'The Return of The Sacred?', p.336.
83. MacRaois, *Lightning Over Giltspur*, p.126.
84. Ibid.
85. Ibid., p.136.
86. David Holbrook, 'The Problem of C.S. Lewis', *Children's Literature in Education*, 10 (March

1973), p.5.
87. Cormac MacRaois, *Lightning Over Giltspur,* p.65–6.
88. Ibid., p.131.
89. Ibid., p.132.
90. Holbrook, 'The Problem of C.S. Lewis', p.23.
91. Lewis, *The Last Battle* (London: Collins, 1998 [1956]), p.192.
92. MacRaois, *Lightning Over Giltspur,* p.86.
93. Lewis, *The Last Battle,* p.145.
94. Holbrook, 'The Problem of C.S. Lewis', p.22.
95. MacRaois, *The Battle Below Giltspur,* p.108.
96. MacRaois, *Lightning Over Giltspur,* p.135.
97. Edward Said, *Culture and Imperialism* (London: Vintage, 1994), p.274.
98. Bell, 'The Return of the Sacred?', p.347.
99. John O'Neill, *The Poverty of Post Modernism* (London: Routledge, 1995), p.86.
100. Francis Fukuyama, *The Great Disruption* (New York: Touchstone, 2000).
101. Baudrillard, *The Illusion of the End,* p.11.
102. Ibid., p.12.
103. Ibid., p.13.
104. Conrad, *Modern Times Modern Places,* p.402.
105. MacRaois, *Lightning Over Giltspur,* p.57.

5

Self-Differentiation and Self-Development: Mark O'Sullivan

Everything passes,
Everything changes,
Just do what you think you should do.
And someday maybe,
Who knows, baby,
I'll come and be cryin' to you.
　　　To Ramona (Words and Music by Bob Dylan, 1964)

The question of human subjectivity has long been one of great interest for both philosophy and psychoanalysis. Ever since Descartes' 'I think therefore I am', subjectivity has been interpreted in a variety of ways. These range from the essentialist, ahistorical 'I', whose truths are time-less and universal regardless of the situation in which they are located, to the postmodern idea, which, as we saw in the previous chapter, is that of a shallow subject that is shaped entirely by cultural practice and interpretation. Although academic interest has tended to swing from one extreme to the other, Frank Farrell in *Subjectivity, Realism and Postmodernism* says that there is little difference between these two polar opposites in terms of autonomy. It is, he says, as difficult to find a space for human activity in the idea of absolute freedom as it is in the power of the Divine will. They are both forms of absolute power. For most people, outside of theorists, the death of the subject, like the death of the author, is incomprehensible. So too is the idea of a subject already composed and unchangeable and whose truths are timeless and universal. Most believe that an individual subject, and indeed a work of fiction, has a central core of meaning that falls somewhere between the omnipotence of the author and the death of the author.

John Stephens says that 'the relationship between a subject's activities as a reader and a work of fiction which is the object of the reading both replicates other forms of subject/sociality interactions and constructs a specular, or mirroring, form of those interactions'.[1] In this chapter I want to look at the development of subjectivity and the way in which it can be mirrored in fiction. I will consider two novels by Mark O'Sullivan, *Silent Stones* and *Angels Without Wings*, both of which are testament to the fact that children's literature can play a valuable part in contributing to the discussion on the constitution of the subject, its development, and the role played by others in that development. The first of these stories is set in Ireland in 1999, the second in Berlin in 1934. In each case the reader can follow the subject choices available to the characters and the way in which they are defined by their given circumstances, by other characters, but also, and most importantly, by their own efforts. Of the two novels to be discussed here, one, *Silent Stones*, has two main focalizing characters, which not only illustrates each character finding their own subject position, but also the interaction or intersubjectivity between the two. The other, *Angels Without Wings*, literally sees the death of the author give existence to the characters, but first there is dialogue and understanding between them and still there is some level of determinable meaning. The essential core of the characters does not change. Even when they are able to control their own actions they each do so within the parameters of their given personalities.

Silent Stones is the story of two teenagers from different backgrounds trying to find their own place in the world. Robby, the son of an Irish Republican Army terrorist who was killed before he was born, has rejected the revolution of his father's generation. As he sees it, it has brought only cruelty and disaster. Mayfly is the child of New-Age traveller parents who have come to the ancient circle of stones at Cloghercree in the hope that the stones will work a miracle and cure her terminally ill mother. Her mother is dying from cancer and Mayfly blames her father who was part of the Cultural Revolution of the 1960s, because she believes that in the name of freedom, he has been self-indulgent and irresponsible. Both Robby and Mayfly feel trapped by what they consider to be the rhetoric of failed revolutions. This in turn fuels a form of reaction that renders them unable to take any positive action that will allow them to move forward and find their own subject position.

In an article in *The New York Review of Books*, Mark Lilla writes about the concept of reaction and the way in which it can bring 'serious political reflection down to absolute zero'.[2] He explains that this is because 'the reactionaries, no less than the revolutionary party, [have] placed themselves in the judgement seat of history and [have] abandoned the field of common political deliberation'. Reactionary rhetoric, he says, is simply an inversion of revolutionary rhetoric and has no real aims of its own. It is also, of course, a very common stance among those in their early teens where it can almost be seen as a liminal phase that allows the subject to rethink itself before proceeding to the next phase. Both Robby and Mayfly have to learn how to think and live in their own age and to define themselves by their own aims rather than in relation to the aims of their parents. Through the course of the book we see these two characters move away from the reactionary stance they have occupied and begin to find their own subject positions. The construction of subjectivity and its complexity is shown within the text by means of its structure, by giving access to the minds of characters through their inner thoughts, hopes and dreams, and finally in its concern with truth and perception.

Silent Stones is structured as a series of relationships between, on the one hand, Robby, his dead father, his mother, his step-father, his uncle and his environment and on the other hand, Mayfly, her father, her dying mother and the villagers with their stereotypical perception of new-age travellers. There is also a relationship between the two main characters themselves. By alternating the two main focalizers, Robby and Mayfly, and by interspersions which show the interaction between these characters, the structure links to the main theme of the book – that each of us is an amalgam of our background, inherited traits and our experiences, but we are also separate beings. As John Stephens puts it: 'The point is that past and present do interrelate, but with a process of interplay which includes both sameness and difference.'[3]

This is something that Robby has not yet grasped – the fact that he can have his father's traits and yet make different choices more appropriate to his own time. His biggest fear is that he is someone whose subjectivity has already been composed and decided. He thinks sometimes about the 'cold, clear determination'[4] that must be needed to deliberately lie in wait in order to kill another human being. Robby feared that coldness 'and he feared it all the more because he sometimes felt it in himself'. His fear that he may be destined to follow in his father's footsteps, despite his aversion to violence, is aggravated by the constant comparisons to his father. Tommy, the tramp, even calls him Sean. Robby's recurring nightmare, which had begun since he had come to live with his uncle Eamon two years before, was one of himself in a paralysed coma lying in a hospital bed in a white room and unable to communicate with those around him. The paralysis is a symbol of the frustration he feels in trying to define himself as what he is *not* rather than what he is – the constant need to stress that he is Robby, not Sean. As the events of the story begin to close in around him it seems to him that it is becoming increasingly difficult to divorce himself from the past, and the nightmare becomes worse than ever until eventually he feels that nobody is listening to him. He feels himself to be 'alone in the white room of his paralysis'.[5]

Because he has imagined his father in only one way, 'the gun-toting freedom fighter',[6] Robby feels he must cut himself off completely in his attempt to distance himself from the violence:

> He didn't visit his father's grave any longer; he hadn't for almost a year. The precise date of that last visit was etched in his memory. Thursday, 16 August, a grey morning at the tail end of a relentlessly grey summer. Three days later, a car bomb in Omagh had taken the lives of twenty-nine people – thirty-one, Robby always insisted, remembering the unborn twins who had died in their mother's womb. Men, women and children had been slaughtered and maimed, and to Robby it was as if his own long-dead father had driven the car into the heart of that town.[7]

This is the side of Sean Wade that Robby, encouraged by his uncle Eamon, has chosen to concentrate on. Other aspects of Sean have been overlooked: the young rocker who had idolised Phil Lynott; the talented hurler who had played with the County minor team; the aspiring engineer. Apart from the carefree teenager of Grace's memories and the memories of Sergeant Healy who trained the hurling team, the talk has always been about the myth rather than reality.

As the story progresses Robby finds that, in spite of his total rejection of the cause for which his father gave his life, they share many character traits both good and bad. Robby too is interested in music – a different kind of music. He is also a good hurler. At school when he was being bullied he had learned 'to see off his tormentors with a brutal ferocity that surprised even himself'.[8] This same defiance causes him to insist on bringing a wounded tramp to hospital even when the IRA fugitive, McCabe, is holding the barrel of a gun to his temple. Finally, his anger when he finds that McCabe has beaten his dog to death, brings him to the point where he faces McCabe with a gun and pulls the trigger:

> The trigger snapped under Robby's finger. There was no shot, just a loud metallic click that froze all three of them to the spot. Robby didn't know which was worse: the terror of McCabe's

reaction or the knowledge that he had been capable of pulling the trigger without thinking.[9]

Sean Wade too had been angry when he pulled the trigger on the young soldier in Fermanagh. Eamon says towards the end of the book: 'We did what we thought was right. You have to understand, Robby, it was the time of the hunger strikes. We were all fired up, watching the telly – those poor lads dying, one by one, and Maggie Thatcher letting them die like the hard, cold bitch she was.'[10] Even then Sean Wade hadn't done it easily, as we discover when McCabe says: 'Sean was a hero, a martyr, hah? I'll tell you what he was. What took him so long to fire the first shot, Eamon? He froze, didn't he? Froze so long he made a bloody target of himself. Sean was a gutless piece of shite who got himself shot because he lost his nerve.'[11]

It seems that Robby and Sean are not so different and this is what terrifies Robby. What he is unable to understand is the fact that his father's choices were made in different times and circumstances and do not necessarily have to be replicated by Robby himself. Sean was a mixture of things but because his life was cut short he was only remembered for one. As Grace says: 'Sean was just a boy who never, never, never had the chance to grow up!'[12] Who knows what he might have done with his life if he had had the opportunity to develop his talents when he had gone beyond the revolutionary mood of his time.

The mood of the time is another facet of what constitutes a subject. The present mood, of which Robby's feelings are an example, would seem to indicate that we have passed the point where the glory of the Nation is of more importance than human life. The epitaph on Sean Wade's tombstone – 'For Ireland and Ireland only' – is no longer acceptable. Vaclav Havel put it clearly in his address to the Canadian Senate when he said:

> Clearly, blind love for one's own country – a love that defers to nothing beyond itself, that excuses anything one's own state does only because it is one's own country ... has necessarily become a dangerous anachronism, a source of conflict and, in extreme cases, of immense human suffering.[13]

Eamon Wade has become an anachronism, unwilling or unable to see that the revolution is over and there is no support for a return to violence. Hence the IRA fugitive McCabe's difficulty with finding a safe house and the 'dwindling crowds at the annual Republican gathering'.[14] The idea that the Nation is more important than its people and the violence that this idea has spawned is no longer acceptable, but this evolution in thinking has not happened to Eamon because he has been completely subjected by the idea of revolution and he cannot accept that it has ended. The stagnation shown by his continuing blind belief that his country is more important than its inhabitants is reflected in several ways: the violence of his language, the traps he sets in his fields, but most of all in his lack of personal growth.

Eamon speaks the opening words of the novel. 'We'll have to shoot him'[15] he says, referring to Robby's dog, Rusty, who has been poisoned. Although he is so sure that he is right, as is shown by his dogmatic assertion that 'I know when a dog is finished. I've been around them all my life. And that one is finished',[16] he is proved wrong in retrospect when Mayfly's natural methods of healing are successful in curing Rusty. The violent McCabe later bludgeons Rusty to death. The badger traps too that Eamon sets are barbaric. It seems that the only solutions he knows are violent ones. The lack of subject growth and its consequences are represented in the first few pages of the novel by the modifiers used to describe Eamon. On the first page he is described as stiff and as having an 'unhealthily high colour'. He casts a 'lowering shadow over Robby and the dying dog'. What Robby sees when he looks back from the doorway at his uncle is a description of someone who remains trapped in the solipsism of a revolution that has ended, and who has failed to make the transition to the next step:

> At fifty-eight, Eamon had made an old man of himself. His hair, never washed or brushed, was a mouldering off-white, like an ancient tuft of sheep's wool caught on a barbed-wire fence. The sour cast of his features was unrelenting. Listless, lost in constant recollection, he was isolated by a bitterness that pervaded his every word and gesture.[17]

It is also a portrait of what Robby could become if he does not abandon his own reactionary stance, which is an inversion of his uncle's, in favour of more open habits of mind. In the space of a few lines the words 'mouldering', 'ancient', 'sour', 'unrelenting', 'listless', 'constant recollection', 'isolated' and 'bitterness' point relentlessly to a character whose intransigent attitudes have resulted in a complete lack of personal growth. The fact that only Eamon himself can change things is symbolized by the badger trap that Robby finds in the ditch and of which we are told that 'Eamon had made the trap years ago and ... All his traps ... had spring-locks only he could release'.[18]

Eamon's belief that Robby can become a replica of his father, an object rather than another subject, is indicated by the manner of naming him. Robby's mother, Grace, had wanted to put the Wade name on his birth certificate but she and Sean hadn't married and she hadn't the money to apply to the court. Eamon too had wanted the Wade name for Robby and he had paid all the legal costs but his ambitions for Robby were based on domination and subjection. He seemed to believe that if Robby took his father's name he would be the same; think the same way, do the same things. When it becomes obvious to Eamon that he cannot invent a single way of being for Robby and impose it upon him he becomes angry and tells Robby: 'You're not worthy of him. You're not worthy of this house, this land. You're not fit to be called a Wade.'[19] Robby, in his turn, feels that Eamon had bought him a name 'and now he wanted it back'.[20]

In contrast to Eamon, Sean Wade's widow, Grace, and her new husband, Liam O'Neill, have grown beyond the megalomania and solipsism of their youth and developed other sides of their identity. The description of O'Neill as 'track-suited and fit – and still lining out on the local hurling team – [bristling] with health and energy'[21] is in stark contrast to the mouldering image of Eamon and is a symbol of his successful efforts to reinvent himself. Although O'Neill had been part of the ambush where Sean Wade lost his life, he had long ago realized that the mood was different now and that human beings were more important than the state. He emphasizes that the struggle has, on both sides, been based on subjection and domination and he refuses to allow Eamon his mythic version of history. When Eamon talks about defending the Nationalist people of Northern Ireland, O'Neill says: 'Yeah, it started out like that, Eamon, but it got so it wasn't about people any more. It was about territory and driving the Protestants out. It was about revenge.'[22] Again, when Eamon says accusingly: 'You took the easy way out. You walked away from your comrades', O'Neill replies 'The hard way is to put down the gun and start talking, even when you're dealing with men who've walked all over you. The hard way is to believe they can change, if you can.'[23] In keeping with these more enlightened and democratic views of a new generation, O'Neill has learned to distinguish between national interests and human rights.

He has also developed other areas of his life. Vaclav Havel suggests that the emotional role, which the nation state has hitherto played in our lives, should be redistributed among the other areas that shape our identity. Areas such as family, community, profession, local region, 'all the way to our continent and ultimately our earth, the planet we inhabit'. These are, he says, 'the different environments in which our identities are formed and in which we live our lives'.[24] Unlike Eamon,

O'Neill doesn't need republicanism to give him an identity any more. Instead he has concentrated on making a new life for himself and his wife and building up his garage business, where the local lads find him to be 'sound – for a head honcho, like'.[25] His new start is also symbolized by the imminent birth of his first child.

Unlike Eamon's attempts to cast Robby in the mould of his father, O'Neill had always encouraged him to believe that he himself held the key to how others perceive him. At first, when Robby as a young boy had come from school complaining about being bullied, O'Neill had sympathized and assured Robby that his day would come. On his twelfth birthday, when he came home complaining yet again, instead of the sympathy he expected, what he got was O'Neill's palm across the face. In answer to Robby's plaintive 'You hit me', O'Neill replied 'You let me hit you'.[26] Although Robby did not feel grateful at the time, O'Neill was teaching him how to be in control of himself.

The self-other interaction that proves most enabling for Robby is that which takes place between himself and Mayfly, possibly because she judges him by his own actions and does not have any preconceived notions about him. Another reason may be that although the distance between their different ways of life is so great that it allows them to see each other as distinct identities, they also have things in common. Robby 'envied the freedom and easy-going lives of the few hippies and backpackers who came to Cloghercree'.[27] Mayfly in her turn longs to put down roots and have the benefit of a good education. They seem to want opposite things but really they both have the same problem; the conflict between their own generation and the previous one. When Mayfly decides to camp out in the derelict cottage that was Robby's childhood home she says: 'It's not the first time I've had to squat where I don't belong.' Robby's reply, 'I know the feeling', was 'like a song whose words Mayfly had been waiting to hear for a very long time'.[28] His affection for the music of Jeff Buckley and Bob Dylan sheds an interesting light on their dilemma. The songs he sings with Bubble, such as 'The Times They Are A-Changing' and 'To Ramona', suggests something about the way in which each generation must be in conflict with the one before.

If Robby feels that his freedom is curtailed because of the expectations of those around him and the limits of his existence, Mayfly is rebelling against the lack of limits in her family's lifestyle; a demonstration of the familiar adage that 'the opposite of freedom is too much freedom'. When her father, Bubble, tells her that when the time comes she can make her own way if she wants, she replies: 'Like I've got choices. Like you left me any choices.'[29] Nirvana, the pink and yellow converted delivery van that they live in, is to her parents 'Good old Nirvana' and it is 'gonna keep on going forever'. To Mayfly it is a 'scrap-heap' and 'hot as the pit of hell'. Moving from one encampment or commune to the next means that she does not have the opportunity to settle in school and make friends. 'As for going to university – that would cost more money than they'd ever see.'[30] As a result, Mayfly, like Robby, feels trapped by, what are to her, the empty slogans of failed revolutionaries, or what she calls 'dumb hippie clichés',[31] and she can see no way out.

The conflict between generations is not always caused by disagreement; sometimes it is caused by misunderstanding or thoughtlessness on both sides. Although she is aware of other people's intolerance and misconceptions, Mayfly too is guilty of misunderstanding her parents' way of life. She stages her own revolt when she comes in for unwarranted suspicion from a security guard at the shopping centre, where she had gone to buy the bamboo shoots necessary to make up the medicine for Rusty:

> When Mayfly emerged from the shop, the man followed her. The reflection of his arrogant little strut slid greasily along the shop fronts. With every step, Mayfly's concern for Rusty lost its immediacy. In its place a foolish indignation reared up and took possession of her.[32]

In spite of her own reservations about the social non-conformity of New Agers, 'foolish indignation' takes possession of her at the injustice of the security guard's racist notions regarding her. She doesn't see any parallels between her own assumptions about Bubble and his generation and that of the security guard to herself. This is left to the reader.

When she accuses Bubble of throwing everything away in order to 'live out some dumb escapist fantasy',[33] Mayfly is reinforcing Bryan Appleyard's theory that a deep conservatism and a longing for stability is what motivates the present generation of young people.[34] But she is also condemning the revolution of the 1960s without questioning why it happened. She points to what she sees as the self-indulgence, weakness and cowardice of the hippies but she refuses to consider any explanation. In fact, the causes of the Cultural Revolution of the 1960s were to be found in the profiteering of the 1950s. O'Sullivan draws attention to this by the fact that selling arms to the apartheid regime in South Africa is what has generated Mayfly's grandfather, Sir Gordon Blenthyne's, wealth. Mayfly has not considered that her father's generation was seeking to make a difference in the fight against racism, war and social injustice and was among the first to organize the civil rights movement and student protests against South African apartheid. Her mother, Andy, says: 'So we didn't solve the problems of the world? We did our bit, Fly, and we picked up a few words of wisdom along the way and tried to live them, tried to pass them on to you. What the hell else do you expect of us?'[35] The truth of Andy's words can be seen in Mayfly's attitude to the racist prejudice of the security guard and also in her use of herbal medicines. She also has an aversion to violence and tells Robby: 'Thou shalt not kill. Didn't anyone ever teach you that?'[36] These are things she has learned from her parents and are *her* interpretation of their principles. The hippie generation's legacy to the world is also evident, for example, in the forces of democratic individualism that brought about the fall of communism in the 1980s and in figures such as Vaclav Havel who has straddled both revolutions. The 1999 Nobel Peace Prize was won by a group of French doctors, Médecins Sans Frontières (MSF); an organization that was formed in 1971 by a group of young doctors who had participated in the May 1968 student revolt. So, far from being a failure, they were, in the words of Jacques Chirac, 'men and women who embody the progress of universal conscience'.[37]

There are other situations where Mayfly's perceptions do not match the reality. She had always believed that her father hadn't made it in the music world 'because he didn't have the guts to try'.[38] Also she doesn't understand his reasons for leaving his father's home. She believes that 'life had given him every chance, but he'd gone his own foolish way – and dragged Andy and Mayfly with him'.[39] Bubble spoke of his wealthy father as 'capitalist scum' and 'one of the rotten rich', but Mayfly had never met him and knew nothing about him. She just felt that at least Bubble had had a choice, whereas she 'would never have the opportunity to spit the silver spoon from her mouth'.[40]

The perceptions of parents don't always match reality either. Bubble admits he should have explained his reasons for leaving home earlier but he'd forgotten how quickly she had grown up. We get a glimpse of his fallibility when Bubble is replying to Mayfly's question as to why he had chosen to come to Ireland.

> 'It's a wonderful place, man', Bubble had said. 'Went there when I was a boy. Good people, you know? They take the time to talk

to each other and –'
'And kill each other', was Mayfly's withering reply.[41]

It is only when Andy finally loses patience with Mayfly's rebellious behaviour that she tells her the truth about why Bubble had used his musical talent to make the bubble-gum advertisement that had earned him his nickname and lost him the respect of other musicians. She explains that 'he didn't take the bubble-gum money because he was hungry, he took it because *I* needed it … I was a junkie'.[42] Andy's revelation of Bubble's selflessness leaves Mayfly embarrassed and ashamed. She protests that they should have told her, but Andy says: 'You should have known Fly, you should have known he was one of the good guys.'[43]

Just as Sean Wade and Liam O'Neill had done what seemed right at the time, so too what Bubble and Andy have done with their lives was constructed from their situation. Mayfly's situation is different from both her parents and her grandparents and her choices will be different, even though she may share many of their character traits. Although he has distanced himself from his family, Bubble tells her: 'I'll always be a Blenthyne. One arms dealer in the family doesn't mean I can't be proud of the name.' He lists the achievements of some of his other ancestors:

> My great-grandfather, for one. Came from nothing, built up a steel company, never forgot where he came from. My grandfather and his two younger brothers, all killed in the Great War. Three Victoria Crosses in one family. Their sister, Maud, spent her entire life as a Christian missionary in China. I don't have to agree with what they did to admire them. Brave people, Fly. You've got that Blenthyne spirit too.[44]

And indeed Bubble too has been brave, though his bravery has taken a different form from that of his ancestors. Qualities in themselves are not what make the subject. It is the way in which they are put to use that is individual. The idea that there is a variety of subject positions available, even to those who share the same character traits, is symbolized in the game that Mayfly plays. 'Rainbow Shades' is a game that includes both sameness and difference by recognizing that there are many different hues of the same colour: 'Think of a colour; think of every shade of that colour you can remember. Take blue. Navy, royal, sky, azure, indigo, ultramarine.'[45]

Unlike Eamon and McCabe, for whom 'the past often serves to promote both inflated self-esteem and self-pity, and distant events are employed to justify hate and violence towards others',[46] for O'Neill, and for Mayfly's parents as well, the revolution has not been wasted; has not failed. They have learned something about human imperfections and inadequacies and also about human goodness. They have allowed their children's generation the insight not to repeat their mistakes. They have helped to create more ethical beings who 'remember past misfortunes and are therefore less sure of themselves, less prone to implement their grand political projects'.[47] For both Robby and Mayfly, a major part of their growth as a subject is shown by their gradual awareness of the complexity of others and the realization that the choices and decisions of previous generations have to be viewed in the context of their lives as a whole.

Eyal Chowers in his paper 'The Marriage of Time and Identity' has explored the role played by concepts of temporality in shaping identity. Speaking of Walter Benjamin's theory of the integration of our temporal experience, whereby 'life without integrated memory is doomed to repeat the same cycle of violence, exploitation and injustice that is conspicuous in human history',[48] Chowers says: 'Every life contains a "story", and every story is the site of wisdom – of lessons to be learned, of things to be emulated and avoided. Thus it is only by looking backwards that the meaning of one's existence is revealed to oneself as well as to others.'[49] We make judgements according to our situation and in doing so we create new meanings which go beyond those we have inherited. This is what freedom is. For both Robby and Mayfly, this gives them a perspective other than their own limited one and allows them to move from the narcissism of their own fears and worries to a wider realization.

A comparison between their self-imposed isolation at the beginning of the novel and their inclusiveness in the community shown in the epilogue illustrates the growth of the two main characters in the space of one year. In the early chapters they are both lonely and angry and overwhelmed by the situations they find themselves in. In the epilogue, although Mayfly and Bubble still find that 'in their hearts, pangs of loss and hopes for the future vied for ascendancy like a moon and sun in the one sky',[50] still, she has survived her mother's death and is doing what she wanted. Robby too accepts that 'He'd had a lot to learn; he still had. But, with Bubble's help and that of an organic farmer Liam knew, they'd put together a plan and were working hard to make a success of it.'[51] He still hasn't made up his mind what he wants to do with his life. Some days he thinks about knocking down the old house and building a new one, 'but there were days, too, when he looked up from his work in the fields and thought, *Maybe not, maybe not*'.[52] The important thing is his awareness that the potential is there and the choice is his.

If Robby and Mayfly find it necessary to confront and struggle with their parents in order to assert their own subjectivity, the characters in *Angels Without Wings* must confront and struggle with their author before they can be free to pursue their own ends. This time the notion of subjectivity is explored as a dialogue or interconnectedness between author and character. The central protagonist in this novel is a character in a novel and its central action is how to stop the novel within the novel from being finished, because, as the narrator of Flann O'Brien's *At Swim-Two-Birds* says, 'death is a full stop'.[53]

Siegfried, Greta, Anna and Dieter are the four characters who make up the Lingen Gang. Their creator is Axel Hoffen, a popular adventure-story writer in the style of Enid Blyton, who has had huge success with his adventure series. Hoffen had reluctantly begun writing the adventure stories so that the profits from them could finance his poetry writing, but gradually his affection for his created characters grew. The true and trusting Siegfried, the thoughtful and serious Greta, Anna, the dreamer and lover of nature and Dieter the joker. But in 1934 in Berlin, the Nazis want him to write a story that shows the Jewish Anna and the one-armed Dieter in a way that gives credence to Nazi propaganda on Jews and the disabled. They want a book that shows 'the treachery of the Jew and the uselessness of the cripple, for these facts to be made clear in the young readers' minds'.[54] Axel must either write a new book twisting the gang to fit the Nazi ideals or face torture and death. When he refuses, the Nazis find 'a more willing writer' who is forced by the circumstances he finds himself in to write the story as the Nazis want him to. It is up to the characters, Siegfried, Greta, Anna and Dieter to put a stop to this alternative Lingen Gang book and at the same time save themselves from being stranded in the fantasy world of Leiningen forever.

The device of a narrative in which invented characters gradually begin to take control of their own thoughts and actions and also to take responsibility for them is a good fusion of form and content. There is an obvious relationship between the artefact of an author as the father of characters whom later take on a life of their own and the theme of the construction of subjectivity in the world outside the novel. Once again, O'Sullivan is concerned with finding a way between the egocentric subject and the deconstructed subject.

In 1968 Roland Barthes announced 'The Death of the Author', whereby 'every text is eternally written *here and now*'.[55] In opposition to the idea of the author as the sole originator of meaning, he denied that there could be any authorial intention. He declared that 'the true place of writing is reading ... the birth of the reader must be at the cost of the author'. In Mark O'Sullivan's novel we do not have to choose between a text whose entire meaning is that which the author intended and a text with no authorial intention whatever. Even though the two authors in the story do indeed die, in this novel the idea of the author is 'reborn', though not as the sole originator of meaning. Author and character have a dialogic relationship whereby the eventual construction of meaning is a joint activity based on communication, understanding and cooperation. There is a tension between the individuals who wish to progress from being a character in someone else's story, and the author or parent who brought these characters into being and gave them the potential to forge an identity for themselves. This tension reasserts O'Sullivan's belief that, although there are certain things given, we can change the script and assert an identity outside of it.

David Lodge explains it well when he says:

> It is of the nature of texts, especially fictional ones, that they have gaps and indeterminacies which may be filled in by different readers in different ways, and it is of the nature of codes that, once brought into play, they may generate patterns of significance which were not consciously intended by the author who activated them, and which do not require his 'authorization' to be accepted as valid interpretations of the text.[56]

In this case, time has moved on and circumstances have changed and this in itself has generated patterns of significance which could not have been consciously intended by the author. The new Leiningen was not the same place where Axel had set his stories. Siegfried 'had drifted back to Leiningen knowing little or nothing of the new Germany and returned with the terrible knowledge that everything had changed. A new god reigned there, a god of prejudice and suspicion: Adolf Hitler ... How much more innocent the adventures of the past had been!'[57] Now the mild-mannered had become revengeful, the good-humoured had become bitter. Siegfried thought about the story that had last brought him to Leiningen. 'Like all the Lingen Gang stories, it had a good and timely moral to offer – that is, like all the stories until now.'[58] Now the social and historical framework has changed.

Hoffen is a father figure who is proud of his created children. When Siegfried first becomes visible to him he exclaims: 'You're just as I imagined you', before adding: 'But what am I saying – of course you are. I made you.'[59] Axel may have provided the raw materials but the characters have not always fashioned them in the style he might have expected. There are several examples where they differ from Hoffen's assumptions and expectations. Although he looks exactly as his author expected, Siegfried is not always comfortable in the role of leader assigned to him by Axel. When he thinks that he may have killed Herr Gott he is afraid to go back into the room. Anna has to go instead. 'The once brave hero of the Lingen Gang was unable to muster the courage of his supposedly weaker companion.'[60] Later on in the story Dieter says: 'but then Siegfried never asked to be made into a leader. Axel did that'.[61] In fact, if there is a leader, it is Anna. She is the one who checks and finds that Gott is still alive. She takes the initiative when they hear Axel's screams:

> 'We'll have to help him, Siegfried.'
> 'I've tried but it's no good. I ... we can't do anything for him.'
> 'We'll see about that.'[62]

This surprises Siegfried because 'in the Lingen Gang books ... the girls were always portrayed as softer and weaker than the boys and not up to the tougher challenge'.[63] Dieter says: 'I'm not blaming Axel ... He wrote the Gang books in the same way that kind of book has always been written. You have a leader, a joker and a couple of none-too-bright girls and the rest is easy.'[64] Dieter's words draw attention to the way in which ideologies, which are presented as real, are often artificially constructed and themselves a fiction.

If life is about fashioning the raw material given to us to our own choosing, Frank Farrell points out that it can sometimes be the other way round:

> Autobiographies will sometimes assert that a certain life chose the one living it as much as the other way round, that an unconscious shaping of choices worked out a destiny ... that was poorly understood at, and may even have run counter to, the level of the individual's reflective deliberations. Yet that process may be seen as having given depth and worth to the life.[65]

This describes exactly what has happened to Axel. When Axel's publisher first suggested that Axel should write adventure stories to finance the publishing of his poetry, he was horrified: 'You want me to write adventures! I'm a poet, for heaven's sake!'[66] Even when the success of the stories was far greater than he or his publisher had anticipated and brought prosperity, still Axel felt a sense of failure because he hadn't become the respected poet he had once dreamed of being. 'He cursed the Gang, raged against their strange hold over him, blamed them for destroying the poetry in his mind.'[67] Eventually, however, Axel began to enjoy writing his stories and they did indeed bring depth and worth to his life – as well as being the inspiration for his best poems.

Patricia Waugh in *Metafiction: The Theory and Practice of Self-Conscious Fiction*, suggests that 'the imaginary world generated by the words of a novel is not less real than, but an *alternative* to, the everyday world'.[68] This idea is brought home in several ways in *Angels Without Wings*. At the beginning of the book, before the prologue, there is an epigram that underlines the importance of both writer and reader in the creation of meaning:

> Just as God creates angels, the writer creates characters. But these are angels without wings. Only the reader, by the power of imagination, can give them wings to fly.
>
> *Axel Hoffen.*

In the novel, Axel Hoffen scrawled this poem on a rough piece of brown paper when he was in hiding from the Nazis. Now it has escaped the boundaries of the novel. At the end of the book, following the epilogue, again outside the boundaries of the novel, there are four poems under the heading 'The Prison Poems of Axel Hoffen'. As well as using the epigram to set out a pre-text for the theme of the story, this device of framing the entire book with the work of the fictional author draws attention to the idea of inventing and constructing both in the real world and the fictional one. More importantly, it blurs the boundaries between the two. In an inversion of many metafictional novels, where very often the real author steps into the fictional world, here, the fictional author has stepped into the real world.

Hoffen also spills over into his own fiction. At one point Siegfried suggests that they should concentrate on saving Axel and saving themselves and forget about trying to stop the book. He says: 'there'll be hundreds of other books written anyway, won't there? What difference will one less book make?' In response Anna quotes a poem:

> And when the river's high
> One single drop of water is enough
> To make a flood.
> And when the leaves are dry
> One single careless spark's enough
> To set alight the wood.[69]

Siegfried looks at her in amazement. 'If this poem had been in one of the Lingen Gang books he would have remembered it. But there was no poetry in those books.'[70] In fact, although Axel's poetry writing is quite separate from his adventure novels, Anna is quoting from one of his poems. As well as pointing out that the imaginary world is no less authentic than the 'real' world, this also puts author and character on a more equal footing because neither author nor character is less real than the other.

In Jean-Paul Sartre's phenomenological analysis of existence, the authentic person cannot avoid the anguish and responsibility of freely choosing how to exist by presuming that the existential choice has been made for us.[71] Rather it is the realization that we create our own world, and that we bear responsibility for its meaning, that brings authenticity. An authentic existence is not easy. Anna says: 'It's wonderful. We can live our own lives.' When Siegfried tells her 'It won't be easy, Anna.' She replies 'Of course it won't – but nothing worthwhile ever comes easily.'[72]

Patricia Waugh asks why it is that metafictional novelists so frequently concern themselves with the problems of human freedom. The answer, she decides, is that 'it is a concern with the idea of being trapped within someone else's order'.[73] All through the book, Gott's story threatens to become the reality for the four characters written into it. The longer it goes on the more Siegfried begins to confuse role with self as he struggles against the fictional character created for him. At unguarded moments he begins to think and feel like Herr Gott's creation. Once, surprising a look of violence on his face Anna stared at him:

> 'What are you gawking at?'
> 'I've seen that look before', Anna said.
> 'I don't know what you're talking about', he snapped. 'And neither do you.'
> 'Just now, in the book. When you called me a Jewish swine, you had that look.'[74]

Although he protests that these are not his words but have been put into his mouth by Gott, the way that Siegfried has begun to slip into the role created for him by Herr Gott frightens all of them, including Siegfried himself:

> Seigfried seemed to crumble then. He fell against the wall and slid down to the grimy floor, bowing his head in shame and fear. 'What's happening to me? I didn't mean to say...' Dieter and

Anna were frightened too. A silence very like the silence of their long hibernation spread through the Grey Room.[75]

They begin to realize that freedom comes with a price. It brings choices and responsibilities. Siegfried, Dieter and Anna begin to think that 'real life was too difficult. It was so much easier to be a character in a book. When the story pauses you can rest and there is nothing to bother you. And when the book ends you can sleep a sleep without nightmares for months, perhaps years – even, if you're lucky, for all of eternity.'[76] But, in Sartre's philosophy, even the choice to have no choice is a choice. Being a character in someone else's story can be no excuse. We cannot deflect responsibility for our actions on to anyone else.

The alternating chapters, between the story within the story – 'The Last Of The Lingen Gang' – and the struggle of the characters to prevent this story being finished, are differentiated by a different typeface and also by being written in a different tense. Those chapters where the characters have control over their own thoughts and actions are written in the third person, while the chapters of Herr Gott's creation are written in the continuous present, a form of perception devoid of any active consciousness. This alternative Lingen Gang story which Herr Gott is being forced to write, again serves to make us aware that there is more than one possibility of self-identity from which we can choose. Siegfried and his friends self-consciously participate in two plots – one of their own making and one over which they have to struggle for control. At one point Siegfried reads his own story:

> Close by the bed was a richly carved writing desk. At its centre stood a typewriter flanked by a pile of crisp white pages. Siegfried peered at the top page.
> 'The Last of the Lingen Gang: Part 1', it read. 'Siegfried Geistengel stands on the tumbledown parapet above the ruins of Leiningen Castle'.[77]

In another scene two of the characters actually discuss how Axel should rewrite Herr Gott's plot, changing the ending in their favour: 'What if Axel were to write the next chapter and make Hempel the villain instead of your father. Then we could switch Axel's chapter with Gott's'.[78]

In his attempt to stop Gott from finishing the book, one of the solutions or choices which offers itself to Siegfried is for him to bring about 'the death of the author':

> Siegfried's blood ran cold. Was he prepared to go as far as Teufel,

perhaps further, to keep Herr Gott from the typewriter? Siegfried refused to answer his own question, refused to listen to his own protests. Even as he did, he knew that this was all it took to become one of 'them', one of the black or brown-uniformed ones he so despised.[79]

Siegfried is discovering that one of the reasons for the anguish, which comes with choosing, is that we do not choose just for ourselves but for all men. We should act in such a way that our actions are universalizable. They must try to persuade Gott to see things their way rather than assuming total authoritarian control by force, because total authoritarian control was, after all, one of the main reasons for the rise of fascism.

In the end, Gott, with their help, sees that his actions not only take away their freedom, but destroy his own integrity as well. He realizes that he himself is responsible for what he has become and that things could be otherwise. In a note which he leaves for the four characters he writes:

> A greater writer than I could ever be once said, 'For evil to prevail, it only takes good men to remain silent.' Perhaps I'm not a good man. But my silence is over. I must make my protest against Hitler and all those lackeys who will do anything, anything, in his name ... I can't stop them, but I can raise my voice; and if I can touch the heart of even one of these firebrands then it will have been worthwhile. And even if I don't, I must take this course for the sake of my own peace of mind.[80]

When it comes to the question of intersubjectivity, O'Sullivan's position owes more to the Hegelian synthesis of self and other than to Sartre. Sartre maintained that intersubjective relations were impossible because one of the subjects in a human relationship is obliged to become an object for the other. This led him to the conclusion that 'Hell is other people' because of the conflict as each struggles to assert his own subjectivity. For Hegel, on the other hand, self-consciousness arises out of the intersubjective relation.[81] For O'Sullivan too, the interrelation between author and character is crucial to the development of subjectivity in both author and character. It is not only Gott who benefits from the interaction with the four characters. Hoffen too is aware that he now feels good about his writing and his life and 'it's all thanks to you lot'.[82] It seems that it is through intersubjectivity that the subject comes into its own. In this case, the anguish of the authentic subject instead of reducing the other to object is what brings it to life as a subject. This is articulated in the first instance by the way in which each of the four fictional characters comes to life. Siegfried, the first of the characters to come to life, was 'born of the fear' from the despairing mind of his creator, Axel Hoffen. Next is Anna, and 'if Siegfried had been born to this new life through Axel Hoffen's fear, Anna had gained her life through Herr Gott's fear of an invisible tormentor'.[83] Dieter in his turn was 'woken from his slumber by Siegfried's fear',[84] and Greta, the last of the four characters to wake, did so in response to the fear of the other three. When Greta woke 'they were electrified, all three. A new energy, an energy that would have seemed impossible only moments before, charged through them ... their earlier hopelessness and despair had given way to a new sense of purpose.'[85] This seems to be the pattern. Each subject who wakes in response to the anguish of the others brings 'a new energy', giving them the strength to keep going. The first time that Herr Gott utters the despairing Beckettian phrase, 'I can't go on. I must go on',[86] he is alone and afraid and his only recourse is to alcohol. The next time he mutters the words 'I can't go on', Greta is there to encourag him. '"You must go on," Greta whispered. "For Romi and Chaim and the girls – and for Siegfried".'[87] This is existentialism, not as solipsism but as intersubjectivity, not as isolation but as interaction.

At the end of the story when the characters have all gone their separate ways, Anna buries Gott's unfinished book and his notes for a suggested ending along with Axel's poems. As she places the casket in the earth and begins to cover it with clay, all her memories vanish. At the same moment the other three characters also lose every last memory they had. 'It was the end. It was the beginning.'[88] The epilogue, in keeping with the rest of the book, blurs the distinction between the real and the fictional. It begins with a short summary of the events which followed on from 1934, including the building of the Berlin Wall in 1962, and its eventual demolition in October 1989. Immediately afterwards there is an item from a German newspaper which states that:

> An extraordinary literary find has been made by workers engaged in the dismantling of the Berlin wall on the southern side of the city. A home-made lead casket, bearing the inscription 'Read this book. 1934', was found to contain the typescript of an unfinished novel for young people entitled *The Last of the Lingen Gang*. Explanatory notes for a suggested ending were also included ... The mystery deepened when a set of poems by Axel Hoffman was

discovered among the pages of the typescript.[89]

The remainder of the epilogue brings us up to date on what has happened to Siegfried, Greta, Dieter and Anna since the night when Anna buried the history of their beginning. Although all the characters had become writers of stories and had found purpose and fulfilment in their new lives, there was always a feeling of emptiness arising from the eternal mystery of an unremembered childhood hanging over them. They could never be whole with no knowledge of their early history; with no access to the origins of their consciousness. When the account of the finding of the book and the poems appears in the newspapers, inexplicably, the three characters who are still alive experience a sense of peace. Seigfried, who has died three months earlier still regretting the loss of his childhood memories is given his peace when his grandson finds a dog-eared old paperback book called *The Adventures of the Lingen Gang*. There is a picture of four happy faces on the cover, one remarkably like that old photo of his granddad as a young man. The implication of the ending is that the knowledge of their beginning makes their lives complete:

> In Hurley, New York, it is ten o'clock at night and the snow is bright under the moon.
> In Holycross it is three in the morning and the wind stirs the trees.
> In Tel Aviv it is seven and the sky is red with the glow of dawn.
> Three writers, thousands of miles apart, share the same dream. They are in Leiningen. Young again, they lie in the long grass of a sloping field. Above them is Lingen Peak; below the ruins of an old Castle. The Lingen Gang is meeting again ... They move, all four, through eternal fields, telling each other the stories of their lives, the stories they have each written and read and heard and imagined.[90]

Mark O'Sullivan's novels set up situations useful for discussing a range of issues concerning subjectivity and intersubjectivity. He encourages young people to think about subjectivity in a way that avoids the extremes of both the omnipotent 'I' and the demise of the subject; to realize that no one is fully the author of themselves, but neither should they be simply passive victims of an external determining power. If we agree with Frank Farrell that 'autonomy is an achievement, not a metaphysical given',[91] we will realize that even though we may not be entirely unrestricted, we can, by our own efforts, achieve a satisfying degree of self-differentiation and self-development. Since the intended audience of these books – perhaps age thirteen or fourteen – is likely to be grappling with the idea of its own autonomy, O'Sullivan tries to give these readers an awareness of how the values of their world have been constructed and therefore the means to see how they can be challenged or changed.

NOTES

1. John Stephens, *Language and Ideology in Children's Fiction* (London: Longman, 1992), p.47.
2. Mark Lilla, 'A Tale of Two Reactions', *The New York Review of Books*, XLV, 8 (14 May 1998), p.4.
3. Stephens, *Language and Ideology in Children's Fiction*, p.218.
4. Mark O'Sullivan, *Silent Stones* (Dublin: Wolfhound Press, 1999), p.56.
5. Ibid., p.111.
6. Ibid., p.7.
7. Ibid.
8. Ibid., p.24.
9. Ibid., p.157.
10. Ibid., p.172.
11. Ibid., p.156.
12. Ibid., 25.
13. Vaclav Havel, 'Kosovo and the End of the Nation-State', *The New York Review of Books*, 46, 10 (1999), p.4.
14. O'Sullivan, *Silent Stones*, p.24.
15. Ibid., p.5.
16. Ibid.
17. Ibid., p.8.
18. Ibid., p.13.
19. Ibid., p.36.
20. Ibid.
21. Ibid., p.54.
22. Ibid., p.24.
23. Ibid.
24. Havel, 'Kosovo and the End of the Nation-State', p.4.
25. O'Sullivan, *Silent Stones*, p.90.
26. Ibid., p.130.
27. Ibid., p.14.
28. Ibid., p.102.
29. Ibid., p.10.
30. Ibid., p.15.
31. Ibid., p.148.
32. Ibid., p.40.
33. Ibid., p.84.
34. See Chapter 1.
35. O'Sullivan, *Silent Stones*, p.150.
36. Ibid., p.44.
37. 'Nobel Body Recognises Change in World Aid', *The Irish Times*, 16 October 1999.
38. O'Sullivan, *Silent Stones*, p.101.
39. Ibid., p.38.
40. Ibid., p.15.
41. Ibid., p.14.
42. Ibid., p.149.
43. Ibid.
44. Ibid., p.126.
45. Ibid., p.17.
46. Eyal Chowers, 'The Marriage of Time and Identity', *Philosophy and Social Criticism*, 25, 3

(1999), p.66.

47. Ibid.
48. Ibid.
49. Ibid., p.70.
50. O'Sullivan, *Silent Stones*, p.189.
51. Ibid., p.192.
52. Ibid.
53. Flann O'Brien, *At Swim-Two-Birds* (London: Penguin, 1967), p.216.
54. Mark O'Sullivan, *Angels Without Wings* (Dublin: Wolfhound Press, 1997), p.21.
55. Roland Barthes, 'The Death of the Author', in *Image-Music-Text*, trans. Stephen Heath (London: Fontana Press, 1977), p.145.
56. David Lodge, 'Milan Kundera and the Idea of the Author in Modern Fiction', in *After Bakhtin* (London: Routledge, 1990), p.159.
57. O'Sullivan, *Angels Without Wings*, p.36.
58. Ibid., p.37.
59. Ibid., p.106.
60. Ibid., p.75.
61. Ibid., p.136.
62. Ibid., p.76.
63. Ibid., p.74.
64. Ibid., p.136.
65. Frank Farrell, *Subjectivity, Realism, and Postmodernism* (New York: Cambridge University Press, 1994), p.243.
66. O'Sullivan, *Angels Without Wings*, p.9.
67. Ibid., p.10.
68. Patricia Waugh, *Metafiction: The Theory and Practice of Self-Conscious Fiction* (London: Routledge, 1988), p.112.
69. O'Sullivan, *Angels Without Wings*, p.92.
70. Ibid.
71. Jean-Paul Sartre, *Being and Nothingness: Essay on Phenomenological Ontology,* trans. Hazel E. Barnes (London: Routledge, 1993).
72. O'Sullivan, *Angels Without Wings*, p.75.
73. Waugh, *Metafiction*, p.119.
74. O'Sullivan, *Angels Without Wings*, p.124.
75. Ibid.
76. Ibid., p.125.
77. Ibid., p.39.
78. Ibid., p.91.
79. Ibid., p.114.
80. Ibid., p.149.
81. G.W.F. Hegel, *Phenomenology of Spirit*, trans. A.V. Miller (Oxford: Oxford University Press, 1977).
82. O'Sullivan, *Angels Without Wings*, p.128.
83. Ibid., p.74.
84. Ibid., p.95.
85. Ibid., p.125.
86. Ibid., p.40.
87. Ibid., p.140.
88. Ibid., p.161.
89. Ibid., p.165.
90. Ibid., p.171.
91. Farrell, *Subjectivity, Realism, and Postmodernism*, p.243.

The Dynamics of Narrative Exchange: Siobhán Parkinson

The storyteller takes what he tells from experience ... and he in turn makes it the experience of those who are listening to his tale.

'The Storyteller', W. Benjamin[1]

Internal storytelling is the way we constantly make sense of our experience. Without the ability to tell ourselves stories we would be unable to exercise any control in relation to the world, either as a way of making sense of past experience, or of shaping our hopes and plans for the future. However, we not only need to make up stories, we also need to tell them because 'The willingness to tell, the ability to judge the moment and the capacity to learn from telling are crucial maturational achievements.'[2] The idea of narrative exchange implies that there must be a dialogue, a give and take, a sharing. Walter Benjamin maintained that the ability or power to exchange experiences was what storytelling was all about, but, as far back as 1936, he believed that the community-centred interaction of a narrator who was known and who told his story directly, face to face, was becoming a thing of the past.[3] This is even more true today. In the daily life of the average person there is generally little time for telling stories. Also, nobody has the time to relax and listen, so that the art of listening has also declined. This, combined with the success of the novel and the dominance of television, means that we are losing the ability to communicate experience through story and to share it with others.

Happily, here in Ireland, the ancient art of the Seanchaí, the storyteller of the past, is experiencing a revival. Storytellers of Ireland, Aos Scéal Éireann, was established in 2003 to promote and foster the oral tradition of storytelling throughout Ireland and, together with The Verbal Arts Centre, they have established an Irish Storytelling Centre to promote and develop storytelling as a contemporary art.

Throughout the preceding chapters, I have been critically assessing narratives by looking at their content, but, as Ross Chambers points out, 'meaningfulness is not exhausted (and indeed it may be completely missed) by analysis of narratives in terms of their supposed internal relationships alone'.[4] There are other phenomena independent of the verbal text, which also merit consideration. In this chapter I want to look at two novels by Siobhan Parkinson which pay attention to the *act* of storytelling. They do this by shifting the focus on to the act of communication rather than the story told, thereby highlighting the notion that the significance of the stories may be determined much less by content than by the actual function of storytelling and the relationships thus mediated. The stories told in these two novels express something independent of their content and are a feature of the developing relationship between teller and listener. Narrative content is not of course irrelevant, but essentially it is the dynamic of exchange that gives meaning to the stories and has the power to change relationships. 'The storyteller, as Benjamin insists – although he distinguishes in this respect between storyteller and novelist – is one who has "experience" to impart.'[5] All of the storytellers in these two novels are traditional storytellers in the sense referred to by Benjamin in that they are communicating experience – their own experience – in such a way that it cannot be separated from the intention of the teller, nor from its specific listeners. The moment and the situation are important so that the act of communication becomes an experience itself and not simply a way of talking about experience.

In *Four Kids, Three Cats, Two Cows, One Witch (maybe)*, Parkinson begins by creating an appropriate frame for a storytelling journey. A quarrelling assembly of four children, from different social classes and with diverse personalities, sets out from the small seaside village of Tranarone on what Beverley calls an expedition to Lady Island. The island, only a short distance offshore, could be reached by wading out at low tide. Gerard's beloved fat cat – Fat for short, accompanies them. While there, they meet the eccentric Dympna who lives on the island – the 'witch' (maybe) of the title. One of the four, Elizabeth, draws attention to the fact that this is a storytelling journey by her reference to Chaucer's *The Canterbury Tales* and her insistence that they are on a pilgrimage, rather than an expedition:

'I think this is just like *The Canterbury Tales*', Elizabeth went on. 'We're like pilgrims, aren't we?'

'Wha-at?' asked Kevin, who'd never heard of Canterbury or its tales.

'You know, the pilgrims in *The Canterbury Tales* – they all tell
each other stories. This is just like that, a pilgrimage with stories.'[6]

Chaucer's pilgrims had a religious purpose and so were on a spiritual
journey but Parkinson's motley 'compaignye of sondry folk' are on a
different kind of journey. They are on a journey from childhood to
young adulthood. Again, this is evoked by the connection to *The
Canterbury Tales* where April, the start of spring fertility and growth,
is linked to the idea that 'Thanne longen folk to go on pilgrimages'.
Despite their social diversity, Chaucer's pilgrims enter a closed world
once they set out on their journey and so it is with the children in this
story. Almost as soon as they set out on their adventure to Lady Island
they leave their different lives behind and become a separate group – a
pilgrim company. Like Chaucer's pilgrims, they often quarrel but are
unified by their common goal or destination. The fact that they are all
on the same journey makes them appropriate listeners to each other's
stories because it ensures that they are non-distanced and empathetic
and so can understand the point of the story in a way that would be
difficult for a more distanced listener. There is, in other words, an
interdependence between the event that is narrated and the event of
narration, and the listener is a participant in the latter.

The children's transition from childhood to young adulthood is
accentuated in the opening story, or 'General Prologue' told by
Elizabeth, who, like the pilgrim narrator of Chaucer's General
Prologue, is a friendly and casual observer who is also involved in the
action. Walter Benjamin thought that the first true storyteller is the
teller of fairy tales: 'whenever good council was at a premium the fairy-
tale had it, and where the need was greatest, its aid was nearest'.[7]
According to Bruno Bettelheim, one of the fairy tales that offers most
good council to children who are learning individuation and independence is 'Hansel and Gretel', two characters who are reluctantly
forced into independence. The story that Elizabeth chooses to begin
with, although elements of it differ from the standard version, is
unmistakably that of 'Hansel and Gretel'. In this way the narrative situation is defined. Despite her variations on the pretext, there are certain elements which remain constant: siblings who are walking through
the woods together when they get into difficulties and of course the
tempting gingerbread house that contains both danger *and* the solution
to their problems.

Elizabeth's tale begins when the children are relaxed and drowsy
after cooking and eating in the open air. Beverley who is practical and
logical and who likes things to be clear-cut and self-evident, is not

impressed at the idea of telling or listening to stories. When Elizabeth begins, 'Once there were four children, two boys and two girls', and announces that she is telling a story, Beverley's reaction is one of impatience or perhaps embarrassment: 'A story! Good grief, Elizabeth, what do you think this is? Jackanory time at playschool?'[8] Storytelling, she thinks, is a diversion for small children and something that she has long grown out of. Her reaction is an indication of how little prized the art of storytelling has become. As Benjamin has said: 'More and more often there is embarrassment all around when the wish to hear a story is expressed. It is as if something that seemed inalienable to us, the securest among our possessions, were taken from us: the ability to exchange experiences.'[9]

In spite of Beverley's disapproval, Elizabeth continues and, in spite of herself, Beverley is drawn into a story about four children who one day went for a walk in the woods. Woods or forests are often used as referential signs. Bettelheim sees them as symbolizing 'the place in which inner darkness is confronted and worked through; where uncertainty is resolved about who one is; and where one begins to understand who one wants to be'. He goes on to say that 'If we … have entered this wilderness with an as yet undeveloped personality, when we succeed in finding our way out we shall emerge with a much more highly developed humanity'.[10] The children in Elizabeth's story were going happily on their way through the woods, eating the enchanted berries that they found there, when the magic berries caused them to change shape. Each metamorphosed into an animal that reflected both the physical appearance and the personality of Elizabeth herself and her three listeners, although it wasn't until much later that they recognized themselves or the fact that this story had personal meaning for all of them. For example, the boy in the story who corresponded with the tall, good-looking Kevin was 'turned into a very tall and beautiful black heron, with very long spindly legs and a long, black neck and wonderful glowing coal black feathers'. The fussy Beverley's story counterpart became 'a small, dainty sort of pig with an extremely curly tail and dumpy, stumpy little legs which she had to move very quickly in order to make any kind of progress over the ground at all'. Elizabeth herself was represented by a fawn and Gerard, the youngest, who was timid and asthmatic is recognizable in the 'furry little hamster' who 'went snuffling along at a great rate, wearing his little heart out with the effort of keeping up with the others'.[11]

When disaster struck in the shape of the fawn's hoof being caught in a trap, the animal-children were all wondering what to do when they spied 'the sweetest little gingerbread house they ever saw'.[12] The two older siblings, the heron and the pig, decided to go for help. At this point in the story Elizabeth insists on putting her own stamp on it. The existence of the pretext has led Beverley to expect a witch in the gingerbread house, but Elizabeth insists that it is not a witch but a wolf in grandmother's clothing. This inclusion of the 'Little Red Riding Hood' story further emphasizes the inner transformation that the children are undergoing. Again, according to Bettleheim, this is a story, which is of particular interest to children who are moving to another level of development. The threat of being devoured is the central theme of both 'Hansel and Gretel' and 'Little Red Riding Hood', but while Hansel and Gretel are forced to leave home against their wish, the more mature Little Red Riding Hood does so willingly. She is not afraid and just needs to learn to be more cautious. By the time Red Riding Hood is cut out of the wolf's belly, 'she is reborn on a higher plane of existence; relating positively to both her parents, no longer a child, she returns to life a young maiden',[13] having benefited from her experience and successfully made the transition from childhood to young adulthood. The animal-children in Elizabeth's story deal with the wolf by threatening him with the woodcutter. Unlike the children in the Hansel and Gretel story, only when the danger has passed do they help themselves to the candy door handles, clove rock bath taps and other good things that make up the gingerbread house. They find the necessary spells and ointments they need to rescue the fawn and in no time at all their problems are solved and they are continuing on their way through the woods as Elizabeth's story comes to an end.

When Gerard asked whether the animals eventually turned back into children, Elizabeth simply answered, 'No'. Just as it proved to be better for Hansel and Gretel not to find their way directly back home but rather to risk facing the dangers of the world, so too there is no turning back for the children in Elizabeth's story. Their metamorphosis is complete and they must continue on rather than return to their former state. But, if they continue to plan and act intelligently and cooperate in helping each other, they will be well equipped to solve life's problems. By refusing to turn the animals back into children, Elizabeth is unconsciously warning against regression and encouraging growth towards the next stage of development. In telling her story, she has defined the theme and indicated the situation which will bestow relevance on the stories which follow.

Michael Hanne has stated that: 'Frequently in societies I am familiar with (and my guess is that this is a very nearly universal practice), the telling of one story will trigger the telling of other stories by other members of a group, which illustrate the same theme or respond to the same question.'[14] This is what happens in *Four Kids, Three Cats, Two Cows, One Witch (maybe)* where Elizabeth's tale triggers a string of stories all broadly linked to the same theme. As in *The Canterbury Tales*, there is no sense of authoritative organization. The children themselves are given control over the ordering and the content of a series of stories, which appear to be without any unifying principle beyond the fact that they are all vaguely familiar fairy tales or legends. However, Elizabeth's story, having provided both the framework and the prompt, seems to have opened a door that allows the others, for the first time, to tell the story of their own experiences, all of which are, in different ways, products of their transition from childhood to the next stage. In this way, a new solidarity and sense of empowerment is created in a group which had previously felt isolated and powerless. In each storytelling performance there is a relationship between personal narrative and related events (although this is not recognized until later), so that the fairy tale structure is shaped by the unique circumstances of the teller. There is, however, a coherence that comes from the common narrative situation of teller and listener in that they are all reaching a new stage of development. This enables them to perceive the relevance of each other's communication. For all of them, the process enables the teller to communicate his or her experience and to lead it on so that they are enabled to work out their own feelings and to make judgements which are based on the new and emerging sense of authority that storytelling gives.

The next episode of linked storytelling comes from Kevin, with encouragement from Beverley. Kevin and Beverley have reluctantly split from the other two so that they can explore different parts of the island. This is the only story in the book where there is a one-to-one situation rather than a group telling and as such it highlights the developing relationship between them and the fact that the situation of the storytelling episode is, at the very least, as important as the story told. Up until now, Beverley, who likes to be in control of every situation, has been unimpressed with Kevin. The new sense of companionship has come about because of Kevin's sympathetic handling of Beverley's fear of heights. His tact and diplomacy following her hysterical outburst of screaming and sobbing and her subsequent embarrassment after climbing down 'a piddling little cliff', coupled with his efforts to find a solution that would allow her to save face, led her to the idea that he 'wasn't all that bad really'. When they arrive back on the beach, sodden with water from having waded through the sea, they sit back to back on a rock drying themselves in the sun and when Kevin tells her that the local people have lots of stories about seals she invites him to tell her one. There is a new sense of comradeship and 'all Beverley wanted to do for now was sit still on this rock and listen to Kevin talking and feeling the words running down her back. She didn't much care what he said.'[15]

According to Ross Chambers:

> To tell a story is to exercise power … and 'authorship' is cognate with 'authority'. But, in this instance as in all others, authority is not an absolute, something inherent in a specific individual or in that individual's discourse; it is relational, the result of an act of authorization on the part of those subject to the power, and hence something to be earned.[16]

Kevin has earned this authority. By his sympathetic response to Beverley's vertigo attack, she is now prepared to see him as someone who, like Benjamin's storyteller, may have interesting 'experiences' to share with her. Without this consent and encouragement the story would not be told. Alida Gersie says that: 'Each told story, therefore, articulates, in encoded or explicit form, the teller-listener's respective involvement with the dilemmas of their world. It simultaneously provides containment for their concerns.'[17]

Kevin's story, when he is finally persuaded to tell it despite his protestations that he can't tell stories, is a reversal of the seal wife legend; a legend that John Stephens identifies as dealing with initiative and power within marriage. However the children, who took part in Stephen's experiment by rewriting the ending, focussed more on 'the process of letting go of something which is an object of strong desire'.[18] In Kevin's story, contrary to the standard version where the seal wife leaves husband and children to return to the sea, the merman leaves wife and children to live with his new family on dry land. On a rare visit to his old family he explains that 'because he had married an earth-woman he had lost his merman's tail and grown human legs. He said he only had his tail now between dusk and dawn, and during the day he had to live on the land and breathe the air, like humans.'[19]

'In the process of storytelling a perspective must be selected as well as presented',[20] and although Kevin says at the end of the story that he doesn't know where it came from, the perspective unwittingly chosen by him, whereby he looks at events from the merman's point of view rather than that of the family left behind, adds to his way of interpreting what has happened in his life. When he begins to do this, Kevin realizes that the story isn't working out the way he wanted or expected it to and he protests that he can't tell it because he 'just can't make it come out right'. He is persuaded by Beverley to continue and the resultant re-telling of the seal legend increases his knowledge of an emotionally upsetting event in his life and allows him to reflect on the present position. The authority to tell his story has given him the power needed to decide how to work through the complexities of his parents' separation and it has also enabled him to work through the process of letting go for himself. It has allowed him to consider events and relationships in a new light and 'this newness in itself reinforces a recognition of the inevitability of change'.[21] The fact that Beverley has shared this experience with him by listening makes her an active participant in this accomplishment and changes the way they relate to each other. On his part, his story has been given value by her reception of it, and on her side, she realizes that 'she had obviously completely underestimated this boy'.[22] The shared experience of telling and listening has promoted a growth of trust between them. As Ross Chambers has said, 'to tell a story is an act, an event, one that has the power to produce change, and first and foremost to change the relationship between narrator and narratee'.[23]

The next time a story is suggested there are no objections. Beverley has by now 'got over her inhibitions about stories'.[24] She is as happy as the others to listen to a story and to postpone worrying about the problem of what to do about Elizabeth, who has sprained her ankle and is unable to walk. This time Gerard is invited to tell and his face lights up with pleasure because it is not often that people bother to listen to his side of the story. Gerard is the youngest of the group and is described as 'a small, pale, underweight, asthmatic eleven-year-old whose ears stuck out and who wore glasses that looked too big for him'.[25] He is the child of a single mother and has already discovered that there are two sorts of people in the world, 'the ones who despised you because your mother wasn't married, and the ones who bent over backwards to show that they didn't disapprove one little bit, in fact they hadn't even noticed that you hadn't got a father, though now you came to mention it, right enough, there didn't seem to be an adult male in your household'.[26] His story tells of a sheltered young woman from a good family, who is herself in transition from childhood to adulthood when she becomes pregnant out of wedlock. This was seen as a terrible disgrace, 'as young girls without husbands were not supposed to have babies in that country and at that time'.[27] In a story that would be familiar to everyone in Ireland a few years ago, it seemed that although the girl herself was 'happy enough' about the baby, she was given no choice. Her family wanted to keep the scandal hidden and so she was kept out of sight until the baby was born and could be taken away from her. Despite the fact that she married her sweetheart, the story concludes with the death of the young woman who, 'knowing … that her child was alive and well, but living among the beasts of the stall, never had a day's happiness, and she died soon afterwards of a broken heart'.[28]

When Elizabeth, speaking for all three of Gerard's listeners, declares that she doesn't like the ending and suggests that he change it, Gerard becomes unusually assertive and insists on maintaining the authority of the narrator because it is the lived experience of the teller which gives authority. Having being authorized to articulate his experience in story, he has reversed the situation whereby he is usually the weaker one, and he is now speaking from a place of strength and control. Not only has his story become an instrument of self-assertion, but it has also involved his listeners in a way that requires them to extend their way of thinking to take in different opinions, different life experiences and different assumptions; to be able to see a reality that may differ from their expectations. He is adamant that he cannot change the ending because 'it doesn't *work* like that. I made it up, but *that's* the way I made it up, with that ending. So that's the way it is. If you want to change the ending for yourself, well, I suppose you can, but then it's a different story.'[29] The ending is part of the whole narrative form and development and as such it helps determine the significance of the story. It also demands from the listeners that they are willing and able to explore other ideas, beliefs and experiences. Their desire for a cosy alternative ending that they feel more comfortable with would change the whole point of the story.

With a storm approaching and Elizabeth's sprained ankle posing a problem, there is a parallel with the children in Elizabeth's earlier story and that worries her a little. She has a notion that if you are not careful about how you tell it, 'you might get stuck inside a story',[30] a remark that underlines the importance of poetics. In a further reminder of Elizabeth's original story, Gerard tells them that he has seen a house on his way back to the beach that they hadn't noticed on their outward journey. '"It's made of gingerbread, I suppose!" Elizabeth tried to inject scorn into her voice, but she was half afraid that Gerard was going to reply that now she mentioned it, yes, it was actually made of gingerbread.'[31] But this is a real house not a 'magic' one and their failure to see it before is easily explained. '"It's at a funny angle", Gerard explained, as he thought harder about the house. "Yes, that's it. And it's well hidden by trees. It wouldn't be visible from the other direction".[32] Kevin, as the only one of the group who lives locally, has already guessed that the house probably belongs to the woman who lives alone on the island and who avoids all social contact with the people of Tranarone. Consequently, she is considered by the locals to be 'not the full shilling'. He is reluctant to go to the house for help though he can't say exactly why he is afraid of the mystery woman. However, in the face of being caught out in a rain storm with a patient who can't move, no lunch and no way of getting home, there isn't much choice and a decision is taken to throw themselves on the mercy of 'the witch, the madwoman whatever she was'.[33]

By now it is evident that a change has come over Beverley. She has 'a sudden fit of democracy', waiting for everyone's agreement when they are deciding whether or not to go to the house for help. This is in marked contrast to the 'old Bossy-Boots Beverley' who had earlier been annoyed at anyone who disagreed with her: 'first Elizabeth and now that Kevin. Taking over *her* expedition on *her* island'.[34] She is so concerned and sympathetic when Gerard realizes that his beloved cat is missing that Elizabeth wonders 'What had come over her?' When she offers to come back and help Gerard look for Fat after she and Kevin have carried Elizabeth to the house, he too is surprised. 'He didn't know what to make of all this unexpected tenderness from Beverley but he was grateful for it all the same.'[35] Alida Gersie believes that:

> stories told in a group generate both confluence and divergence. Groups thrive on the constructive exploration of difference. The largest possible tolerable variety is the material upon which democracy and well-functioning organisational or interest groups are built ... alternative understandings and interpretations grant group members ample opportunity to explore other ideas, beliefs and experiences.[36]

Certainly, the stories that Beverley has listened to seem to be having a softening effect on the 'Miss High-an' Mighty' who had begun this expedition. She appears to be less self-centred, although, as we see when she tells her own story, the old challenging Beverley is still there. When the 'whole pantomime camel' of the four children, hot, sticky and tired, reach the house it is empty, but there are several clues that the occupant isn't very far away. There is a fresh sticky ring on the oil cloth cover on the kitchen table and a mug with tea in the bottom sitting in the sink. They wait nervously for their strange hostess to return.

The 'madwoman of Lady Island' turns out to be called Dympna. She seems a surprisingly ordinary woman, if a little eccentric, 'a stoutish woman in a beige raincoat tied round the middle with blue twine, and with a funny squashed-looking, battered brown velvet hat on her head'.[37] She doesn't seem at all surprised to see three strange children and one local boy whom she recognizes in her kitchen and produces a sort of nervous, hysterical laughter from them when she continues the fairy-tale theme by asking in a high-pitched, stagey voice: '*Who's* been sitting in *my* chair?'

As soon as the kettle has boiled and the preparations made for tea, Dympna surprises the children by asking, 'Who's going first with the story?'[38] Suddenly Elizabeth remembers the sneeze on the beach that had come from none of the four children, she remembers a snort she had heard earlier and thought it had come from a sheep, she also remembers the feeling she has had all day of someone watching them. It seems that Dympna has been following them around and listening to their stories and now she wants to hear more. As the only one of the children who has not yet told a story, Beverley volunteers to be next. Although, first she has to impose her authority on the irrepressible Dympna, who doesn't think Beverley's opening description of a beautiful young girl with long, slim legs and long golden hair quite fits the bill. Dympna thinks that if Beverley is telling her *own* story 'stumpy little legs and wiry black hair' would be a more accurate description.

However, as soon as she begins her story Beverley feels in charge of things again. The familiar fairy-tale motifs of a beautiful girl imprisoned in a dense forest leads into a story where a fairy predicted at the girl's birth that her son would one day slay her father. In the context of the story, it does not take much imagination to translate this into a prediction that she will one day bear a son who will have little in common with her patriarchal father and who will effectively slay him by bringing an end to his power. In an effort to prevent this, the girl's father hides her away in a dense forest and sets an impossible task for any prospective husband who might be brave enough to enter the forest. There are obvious similarities with the story of 'Sleeping Beauty' where, despite all attempts to prevent the sexual awakening of the child, it takes place anyway. In this case, despite her father's attempts to retain patriarchal power, feminism prevails. One day a handsome young prince comes along who manages against all the odds to accomplish the task and carry the princess off to his own kingdom.

This is where the story usually ends happily ever after, but Beverley has realised that this is *her* story and it is possible to change the ending. The princess in Beverley's story asks to be taken to 'a school for young ladies, or to a convent perhaps, or to a family where there is a mother who longs for a daughter as I have longed all my life for a mother'.[39] She is looking for a female institution or role model that she can relate to. It is generally a characteristic of fairy tales that once the damsel in distress is freed from her captivity she marries her knight in shining armour and they live happily ever after. This princess has other ideas. When the prince begins to talk about preparations for the wedding, she asks innocently, 'Is somebody getting married?'[40] Once he has got over the shock of having his proposal refused and listened to her reasoned argument that she had not been consulted and that whatever contract he had with her father had nothing to do with her, the prince 'knew he had met his match for sure in this one. She was as clever as he, and as quick witted, and more than ever he desired to marry her. But he saw that this princess was not to be won by trickery, nor by gallantry, nor through contractual arrangements made with her father.'[41] In the end, he abides by her wishes, agrees to take her to his mother's house where she may live as long as she wishes without any more trouble from him and there the story ends.

The degree of additions and changes suggested by the other children is an indication of their engagement with the stories. Elizabeth is not happy with the abrupt ending of Beverley's story. She wants to hear more. She wants to have the loose ends tied up, but the only concession Beverley makes to Elizabeth's demand to know, 'But did she marry him or not?', was the reply: 'Perhaps. Perhaps not ... Maybe she will one day.'[42] She invites Elizabeth to add her own ending if she wishes but is not persuaded to change hers. Both Beverley's and Kevin's stories are about initiative and power within marriage. Having been enabled to impose their own predicaments and experiences onto the story, each has gained additional understanding of the other side and so the prospect of achieving harmony with a person of the other sex is increased.

The final story is told by Dympna. In the time that has elapsed since Beverley's story the children have been alarmed by Dympna's strange wailing, Kevin has rescued Gerard's cat despite his own fear of thunder, and Dympna has somehow miraculously cured Elizabeth's ankle. After all this activity they are having the farewell banquet suggested and presided over by Dympna, when Gerard invites her to tell *her* story. Dympna's story is reminiscent of Hans Christian Andersen's 'The Ugly Duckling' – a duckling who didn't like the water and who ran away to escape the derision of the other ducks. However, unlike the original story, the duckling in Dympna's story doesn't turn out to be a different breed and grow into a beautiful swan. It remains a duck who is fated to be 'unducklike' and eventually takes refuge in a cement mixer. The resulting 'duckling-shaped statue' sits in the garden of the building worker who found her and although it can sometimes be a lonely life, she is reasonably content to be left in peace. Gerard explains to the others:

> Well, that's really Dympna, you see. She's different, she's peculiar, she doesn't do the sort of things everyone else does and like the things other people like. She's like the duckling, and like the duckling, she ran away, looking for somewhere new to live, where she would be able to be different in peace … she needed us to understand how threatened she felt, how much she needed to be protected, and so she told us the story, like a sort of code so we'd understand.[43]

Before the storytelling 'pilgrimage' began the group members had not realized that others are also exposed each to their own particular pressures. When they began to tell, each story was born out of feelings that were not yet understood by the tellers themselves. Both Beverley and Kevin are surprised by their own stories and profess to have no idea where they have come from. And although they may have sensed the presence of a known referent behind each other's stories, this was not acknowledged until Gerard reminds them of what Dympna had said: 'When you tell a story, it's your story. Your telling it makes it yours. And every time you tell a story, you're telling people something about yourself.'[44]

The return journey to Tranarone brings us back to the story that started the ball rolling. Like Hansel and Gretel, the children are unable to return home after their adventures the same way that they came because they have missed the low tide which would have enabled them to walk back. In 'Hansel and Gretel' the children are helped by a duck who carries them safely across the water. In this case the children are helped by Dympna who lets them borrow her currach and who seems to personify the original kindly white duck who returned Hansel and Gretel to safety. Bettelheim, in *The Uses of Enchantment*, likens this to a new stage of development for Hansel and Gretel: 'The children do not encounter any expanse of water on their way in. Having to cross one on their return symbolises a transition, and a new beginning on a higher level of existence (as in baptism).'[45] This is also true of the children in Parkinson's story who seem to have reached a new beginning in their level of understanding of themselves and of others.

At the end of the book, in keeping with the fairy-tale world of their stories, the children are still wondering about the seemingly magical cure of Elizabeth's ankle with an ordinary bottle of pink baby lotion. The logical Beverley insists that it 'can't have been the Johnson's Baby Lotion' and 'she couldn't, simply couldn't, accept that it had been a miracle'.[46] Parkinson, however, like a good storyteller, leaves her audience wondering with Gerard's question: '"And what about my asthma? ... Has anyone noticed that I haven't had a single attack in three weeks, since the day on the island, in fact?" The others looked at Gerard in amazement. They hadn't noticed, but now that he said it, of course he was right.'[47]

If we do as Ross Chambers suggests, which is 'not simply to read texts in situation (which is inevitable) but also to read, in the texts, the situation that they *produce* as giving them their "point"',[48] then we will see that by the end of the novel, although nothing in the circumstances of the children has changed, inner attitudes have changed. In some cases change can mean a reinforced feeling, such as when Beverley's resolve is strengthened by her realization that she has control over the ending of her own story, although, as a listener, she has now also learnt how to negotiate different opinions or different life experiences. Change can also produce an alternative, as when Kevin learns to see things from his father's point of view. There is in each case, as Chambers puts it, 'a transformation *that itself has narrative structure*'.[49] Using the method of traditional fairy tales, they have developed a way of articulating their perceptions and a capacity to deal with emotional exploration and contradictory feelings. In other words, the fact that they have learned to tell and to listen means that they need not, as Elizabeth feared they might, get 'stuck inside a story'.

In *The Moon King*, Ricky is a young boy who is also crossing the threshold into the wider world, albeit in different circumstances. The children in *Four Kids, Three Cats, Two Cows, One Witch (maybe)*, once they had an interested and sympathetic audience, had no great difficulty in sharing their story with others. In *The Moon King*, Ricky comes from a violent home and is being placed in the care of foster parents. His inarticulacy and inability to tell his story is a symptom of the abuse he has suffered.

The subjection of Ricky by his circumstances is registered by the fact that he has difficulty in speaking at all, but especially by the fact that he cannot express subjective experience or perceptions of his own situation. This is evident from two exchanges which take place between himself and Rosheen, one of the children in his new foster home. The first of these exchanges takes place when Rosheen shows him his new room:

> He turned to Rosheen, his eyes shining. 'Yours?' he said, in a muffled tone, barely managing to get the word out.
> It was the first word she had ever heard him utter.
> 'No, yours', she said gently.
> 'Yes', he nodded, 'yours.'...
> 'No', giggled Rosheen, 'not mine, yours.'
> 'Yours', Ricky agreed and smiled at her.[50]

The second exchange takes place in the attic room where Rosheen finds Ricky asleep in the moon chair:

> 'You are the moon king, Ricky', she said again. 'You are the moon king.'
> 'You – are – the – moon – king', Ricky said carefully after her.
> 'No, no, Ricky, you always get that wrong. I can't be the moon king, I'm a girl. I can be a queen, but not a king. *You* are the moon king.'
> 'You are the moon king', Ricky repeated.
> 'No, no, oh Ricky, can't you get this right? Listen. Say it after me: I am the moon-king.'
> 'I?' said Ricky.
> 'Yes, yes, 'I', that's right', said Rosheen. 'I am the moon king.'
> 'You are the moon king!' said Ricky again. 'You are the moon king!'[51]

This absence of language renders him unable to share his story with others and thus unable to give shape and purpose to his individual subjectivity and so his stories are constructed in the silence of his mind. Gersie says that there may be many reasons why someone might be unable or unwilling to speak about their own experiences. One reason may be that, 'the ability to give voice to multitudinous perception is halted by the heart's commitment to some form of anonymity. In the inner world of people in this predicament, silence feels, and may well be, safer than speech.'[52] Ricky knew that his mam worried about him annoying Ed because then Ed hit him and this caused his mother to cry. 'Ricky didn't know which was worse, being hit or hearing his mam cry.'[53] The feeling that telling may be dangerous and that his story would not be received sympathetically by the more powerful Ed reduces him to a silence generated by the unwillingness or inability to tell. In order to survive he constructs first the Spiderboy image which helps him interpret events in his life, and then the storied image of the moon king which gives him the sense of being valued that he so passionately desires.

When the story opens Ricky is on his way to meet his new foster family accompanied by a well-meaning but remote social worker. In traditional stories, Ricky would fit into the type of character which Propp in *The Morphology of the Folktale* calls the victim hero. Gersie says that victim heroes are ambivalent about leaving their home even when they have been abused there, partly because the decision to leave was not their own. 'Instead of being relieved, they endlessly ponder what has gone wrong and how they are not even acceptable to bad people in a bad place.'[54] As he stands nervously outside the tall, sloping house waiting for some unknown person to answer the doorbell the thoughts running through Ricky's mind are contradictory. 'Don't like change. Want go home. No. Don't want. What then?'[55] He watches a spider on the wall. 'Want hide. Look at wall. Wall friendly. White, with cracks. Spider scuts out one crack, into another crack. All legs, spiders. Shoulders hunched. Busy, busy, busy.'[56] Looking at the spider, Ricky is envious and wishes he too had a crack to scuttle into. The character of 'Spiderboy' is thus created in Ricky's mind by the incident and he begins to use this figurehead as a way of both organizing the structure of events in his life and organizing the telling of them. In *Actual Minds, Possible Worlds*, Jerome Bruner states that: 'Discourse must make it possible for the reader to "write" his own virtual text.'[57] He goes on to list three features of discourse which he considers to be crucial in this process: a background in terms of which the stories may be interpreted, the depiction of reality through the eye of the story's protagonist, and multiple codes of meaning which allow for the creation of possibilities rather than certainties. The background in terms of which Ricky's stream of consciousness or 'stories' can be interpreted is provided by the spider who runs in and out of the cracks on the wall. The spider then conjures up the character of Spiderboy, who transforms the collection of impressions which make up Ricky's unworded narrative into a story, the telling of which helps to make his experiences comprehensible to himself. It also provides a stance to take towards that story. As the artifice of spiderboy distances him from his difficulties, it allows him sufficient space to grasp the meaning of it all and creates a fictional character who can deal with the real-life feelings he is experiencing.

Even though the self is disguised, Ricky is still telling his own story. His thoughts as Spiderboy are written in a different typeface which serves to emphasize not only the indirect nature of his voice, but also how the goings-on in his mind are isolated from the rest of the world. Bettelheim says that the only way a child can hope to get a hold over internal pressures is to externalize them. In the same manner as the characters of traditional fairy tales, Spiderboy offers a figure onto which Ricky can externalize what is going on in his mind and although he is as powerless as Ricky in many ways, Spiderboy can spin webs and scuttle into cracks when he sees trouble coming. Bettelheim goes on to explain that: 'when he experiences the emotional need to do so, the child ... may split himself into two people who, he wishes to believe, have nothing in common with each other ... the child externalises and projects onto a "somebody" all the bad things which are too scary to be recognised as part of oneself.'[58] As well as externalizing scary personality traits on to some other character, this same method can be used to deal with seemingly insurmountable problems. In this case, all the worrying events of Ricky's life are happening to Spiderboy, not to Ricky, and although he is still unable to share his experiences with others by storytelling, he has at least discovered a story *making* capacity; he has become a silent storyteller. This suffices for Mammy Kelly, her husband Tomo and the other children, especially Rosheen, all of whom, in the absence of spoken words, interpret Ricky's smiles, his paintings and his efforts to help with the family chores as a positive sign of his developing relationship with his foster family.

The one exception is Helen who doesn't want him to settle in. She is jealous and goes out of her way to get him into trouble and generally make life difficult for him. 'When we are upset, shocked or in pain, we become preoccupied with our inner world. This inner story is insufficiently checked to see that it actually matches the outer circumstances.'[59] This is precisely what happens when Helen tells Ricky that the social worker is coming to take him away. Despite Rosheen's assurances that Helen is just jealous and making the story up, and Fergal's derisive dismissal of the idea of Helen having any influence with the social worker, Ricky believes that he will be sent back to the violent Ed and so he runs away. He 'didn't have a clear idea any more what it was that he was afraid of, but his instinct was to run and run and run'.[60] Part of the reason for Ricky's fear is the thought that perhaps he is bad. Perhaps that is why Ed hits him and his mother doesn't make him stop. 'She must believe him if she went on letting him hit Ricky so often. She must think he needed to be beaten. Maybe he *was* a bad boy. Ed thought so. Helen thought so.'[61] In spite of Mammy Kelly and Tomo's efforts to make him feel secure and welcome, the memory of

potential violence and the absence of warmth and safety are ingrained in him and he doesn't understand what is happening. It is only
when he is cold, wet and scared and wants to find a safe sleeping
place for the night that he realizes that the place he has run away from
was 'the only place where most people were nice to him, where they
let him do his stuff and they didn't shout or make a fuss or tell him he
was bad'.[62] His decision to return, even though he is still worried
about the 'lipstick woman' coming to take him away, is based on the
hope that maybe Mammy Kelly wouldn't let her, or Tomo would tell
her to leave him be. It would seem that, due to the dynamics of his re-
ationship with his foster parents and the other children, Ricky is learning 'to re-animate the fictions of [his] inner world with more benign
possibilities and kindlier creatures'.[63] Their acceptance of his silent
state, encouragement of interactive behaviour and appreciation for
his contribution to family life have given him the ability to make the
right decision as to what the best course of action might be.

In traditional fairy tales when the hero sets out on his course of action a magical agent is needed. This object may be located in another
kingdom; it may be at the top of a mountain or the bottom of a lake.
Led by Rosheen, Ricky finds his particular magical aid at the top of the
dark, steep stairs leading to the attic. Usually, before he receives the
magical aid the hero is tested. Ricky's initial fear of climbing the stairs,
and his subsequent overcoming of this fear with Rosheen's help, eventually leads him to the attic room which contains the moon chair.
'Ricky gasped. He had never seen anything as magical as the moon
chair.'[64] For Ricky, the magic is contained in the chair's power to transport him to another place where he can experience things differently;
where his imagination can soar:

> Oh Froggo, look! It's great here, I think we must be on the moon.
> It's all shiny, look it's bright and light, there's oh! there's a rain-
> bow, only it's not a rainbow, it's filling the whole sky, the whole
> sky is a rainbow, it's like a roof, like a roof made of rainbow, all
> glittering with stars. A rainbow with stars! And, hey! I'm not
> walking under the rainbow, I'm flying, I'm gliding, I'm floating.
> Wheee! It's oh, it's like, what is it like, Froggo? I don't know, do
> you? It's like sailing, only it's in the air, it's air-sailing! It's like
> being a bird.[65]

He had been feeling rejected and longing for some sense of selfhood
and the moon chair allows a possible world where he can compen-
sate in fantasy. It provides him with a cathartic power. According to

Bettelheim: 'Every child at some time wishes that he were a prince or a princess – and at times, in his unconscious the child believes he is one, only temporarily degraded by circumstances. There are so many kings and queens in fairy tales because their rank signifies absolute power.'[66] When he is sitting in the moon chair Ricky becomes the moon king.

Every story needs both a teller and a listener because its meaning exists dialectically. Parallel with Ricky's inability to tell is Helen's inability or unwillingness to listen, which could be said to be due to a failure of narrative imagination. She doesn't like sharing her parents with so many other children and may feel that the content of other people's stories might challenge her position in the family. Whatever the reason, her refusal to listen means that she never allows herself to think herself into the place of the other person and consequently she is lacking in sympathetic imagination. Richard Kearney explains that: 'If we possess narrative sympathy – enabling us to see the world from the other's point of view – we cannot kill. If we do not, we cannot love.'[67]

It is Rosheen who sees that Helen's treatment of Ricky is a matter for moral reflection and change. She explains to her what it means to 'do the friendly thing': 'it's about thinking about the other person's point of view sometimes, instead of always about yourself. It's about noticing when someone is hurt, instead of just looking for notice yourself all the time.'[68] In other words, it is about listening to the other person's narrative and being able to use your imagination to empathize with them. Kearney illustrates his argument by quoting a passage from one of J.M. Coetzee's characters, Elizabeth Costello. The passage concludes by saying:

> There are people who have the capacity to imagine themselves as someone else, there are people who have no such capacity, and there are people who have the capacity and choose not to exercise it ... there is no limit to the extent to which we can think ourselves into the being of another. There are no bounds to the sympathetic imagination.[69]

Helen is one of those who has the capacity and chooses not to use it. She is initially unrepentant and professes that she doesn't 'get it' but Rosheen doesn't allow her to use this as an excuse. She tells her: 'You can *decide* to get it, Helen.'[70] The point is that, hand in hand with the importance of imagination, is that of ethical sensitivity. The connection can be seen when Helen decides to behave differently in future and her new-found sense of narrative sympathy leads her to suggest that going to the moon-chair room might 'inspire' them about where Ricky is.

Her personal triumph comes when she and Rosheen do indeed find Ricky there sitting in the moon-chair:

> 'It's him', whispered Rosheen excitedly. 'Oh, you were right, Helen.'
>
> Helen smiled in the darkness. She hadn't really been right. She hadn't expected they would actually *find* Ricky. But she had been sort of right. It *had* been her idea to come up here.[71]

She has been right because her idea and her action is connected to her empathy with Ricky, proving that storytelling is an intersubjective thing and that the dynamics of narrative exchange make possible 'the ethical sharing of a common world with others'.[72]

All fairy stories must offer consolation and have a happy ending. For Ricky, the knowledge that he will never again be deserted is the ultimate consolation. We seem to have the appropriate fairy-tale ending when Rosheen and a repentant Helen find Ricky asleep in the moon chair and realize that he has come home. When Helen admits that she lied about the social worker coming to take Ricky away, she tells him: 'I just made it up. She wouldn't take you away from here. Mam and Tomo are the best foster parents in the county. Everyone knows that. They never take people away from here, unless they're ready to go home. Honest to God, Ricky, cross my heart and hope to die.'[73] When Rosheen once again says, 'You are the moon king, Ricky', this time Ricky's small piping voice manages to answer: 'I – am – the moon king', and then more loudly 'I am the *moon* king', and finally with conviction, 'I *am* the moon king.'[74] It seems that Ricky's narrative ability has been jolted into action. He has found his voice because he has found sympathetic and willing listeners, and, as 'the effect of a tale rests not only with its content, but ... abides above all within the relationship between teller and listener',[75] we may confidently assume that Ricky will live happily ever after.

NOTES

1. Walter Benjamin, 'The Storyteller' in *Iluminations*, ed. Hannah Arendt, trans. Harry Zohn (London: Fontana/Collins, 1982 [1970]), p.87.
2. Alida Gersie, *Reflections on Therapeutic Storymaking* (London: Jessica Kingsley Publishers Ltd, 1997), p.2.
3. Benjamin, 'The Storyteller', pp.83–109.
4. Ross Chambers, *Story and Situation: Narrative Seduction and the Power of Fiction* (Manchester: Manchester University Press, 1984), p.8.
5. Ibid., p.50.
6. Siobhán Parkinson, *Four Kids, Three Cats, Two Cows, One Witch (maybe)* (Dublin: The O'Brien Press, 1997), pp.99–100.

7. Benjamin, 'The Storyteller', p.102.
8. Parkinson, *Four Kids, Three Cats, Two Cows, One Witch (maybe)*, p.40.
9. Benjamin, 'The Storyteller', p.83.
10. Bruno Bettelheim, *The Uses of Enchantment* (London: Penguin, 1991 [1976]), p.94.
11. Parkinson, *Four Kids, Three Cats, Two Cows, One Witch (maybe)*, p.45.
12. Ibid., p.47.
13. Bettelheim, *The Uses of Enchantment*, p.183.
14. Michael Hanne, *The Power of The Story* (Oxford: Berghahn Books, 1994), p.15.
15. Parkinson, *Four Kids, Three Cats, Two Cows, One Witch (maybe)*, p.81.
16. Chambers, *Story and Situation*, p.50.
17. Gersie, *Reflections on Therapeutic Storymaking*, p.8.
18. John Stephens, *Language and Ideology in Children's Fiction* (London: Longman, 1992), p.60.
19. Parkinson, *Four Kids, Three Cats, Two Cows, One Witch (maybe)*, p.88.
20. Gersie, *Reflections on Therapeutic Storymaking*, p.10.
21. Ibid., p.18.
22. Parkinson, *Four Kids, Three Cats, Two Cows, One Witch (maybe)*, p.90.
23. Chambers, *Story and Situation*, p.74.
24. Parkinson, *Four Kids, Three Cats, Two Cows, One Witch (maybe)*, p.100.
25. Ibid., p.20.
26. Ibid., p.19.
27. Ibid., p.104.
28. Ibid., p.106.
29. Ibid., p.108.
30. Ibid.
31. Ibid., p.110.
32. Ibid.
33. Ibid., p.123.
34. Ibid., p.57.
35. Ibid., p.115.
36. Gersie, *Reflections on Therapeutic Storymaking*, p.113.
37. Parkinson, *Four Kids, Three Cats, Two Cows, One Witch (maybe)*, p.127.
38. Ibid., p.139.
39. Ibid., p.140.
40. Ibid.
41. Ibid., p.141.
42. Ibid., p.142.
43. Ibid., pp.189–90.
44. Ibid., p.181.
45. Bettelheim, *The Uses of Enchantment*, p.164.
46. Parkinson, *Four Kids, Three Cats, Two Cows, One Witch (maybe)*, pp.186–7.
47. Ibid., p.187.
48. Chambers, *Story and Situation*, p.4.
49. Ibid., p.8.
50. Siobhán Parkinson, *The Moon King* (Dublin: O'Brien Press, 1999), p.43.
51. Ibid., p.76.
52. Gersie, *Reflections on Therapeutic Storymaking*, p.30.
53. Parkinson, *The Moon King*, p.141.
54. Gersie, *Reflections on Therapeutic Storymaking*, p.156.
55. Parkinson, *The Moon King*, p.15.
56. Ibid., p.10.
57. Jerome Bruner, *Actual Minds, Possible Worlds* (Cambridge, MA: Harvard University Press, 1986), p.25.
58. Bruno Bettelheim, *The Uses of Enchantment*, p.69-70.
59. J. Wigran, 'Narrative Completion in the Treatment of Trauma' quoted in Gersie, *Reflections on Therapeutic Storymaking*, p.33.
60. Parkinson, *The Moon King*, p.139.
61. Ibid., p.94.
62. Ibid., p.165.
63. Gersie, *Reflections on Therapeutic Storymaking*, p.167.

64. Parkinson, *The Moon King*, p.66.
65. Ibid., p.72.
66. Bettelheim, *The Uses of Enchantment*, p.205.
67. Richard Kearney, *On Stories* (London: Routledge, 2002), p.140.
68. Parkinson, *The Moon King*, p.151.
69. J.M. Coetzee, *The Lives of Animals* (Princeton, NJ: Princeton University Press, 1999), quoted in Kearney, *On Stories*, p.140.
70. Parkinson, *The Moon King*, p.152.
71. Ibid., p.170.
72. Kearney, *On Stories*, p.150.
73. Parkinson, *The Moon King*, p.172.
74. Ibid., p.173.
75. Alida Gersie and Nancy King, *Storymaking in Education and Therapy* (London: Jessica Kingsley Publishers Ltd, 1990), p.30.

'And nothing at all to do except wait to be eaten': Matthew Sweeney

Read it a hundred times ... It can never lose its sense of a meaning that once unfolded by surprise as it went.

Robert Frost[1]

In his essay, 'Education by Poetry',[2] Robert Frost makes the point that all thinking, except maybe mathematical thinking, is metaphorical, and it is true that all the novels discussed so far in this work can be read as metaphors for larger ideologies. Frost asks the question: how do we educate the young to judge contemporary literature; an editorial; a political campaign? Metaphor, he says, can be used for good purposes and bad. How can they tell the difference; how can they know when a metaphor is, in George Orwell's words, 'designed to make lies sound truthful and murder respectable, and to give an appearance of solidity to pure wind'?[3]

Orwell, in his essay 'Politics and the English Language', was disturbed by the worn-out metaphors of politicians and other public figures. He points out that the sole aim of metaphor is to call up visual images and if the images clash then it means that the writer or speaker is not seeing a mental image of what it is he is naming. In other words he is not really thinking. We are, Frost says, always talking about teaching young people to think, but we seldom tell them what thinking means; that 'it is just putting this and that together, it is just saying one thing in terms of another'.[4] It is, in fact, learning to be at home with metaphor so that you know where it is leading. Metaphor is, at its height, an attempt to 'say matter in terms of spirit or spirit in terms of matter, to make the final unity'.[5] Poetry, Frost says, is the place where it is done best and therefore the ideal place to learn to be at home with metaphor and to recognize its strengths and weaknesses. Much of the poetry that is aimed at children is unlikely to be of much help in recognizing the euphemistic jargon that is often used as a substitute for thinking, but one poet whose poems are capable of educating children in the way that Frost speaks of is Matthew Sweeney. In an interview with Lidia Viancy in July 2002, Sweeney describes his poetry saying: 'some of it strays beyond realism into the territory I call alternative realism ... and it often mixes humour and seriousness. Both these latter tendencies are common in the Irish Literary Tradition.'[6]

When Matthew Sweeney came to The Ark, the cultural centre for children in Dublin's Temple Bar, in March 1997, I went to hear him twice. Once in the afternoon when he gave a reading of his poetry to children, and again in the evening of the same day, when his audience consisted of adults. There was very little difference between the two occasions. Many of the poems read for the children were also read to the adult audience, and both audiences delighted in his quick imagination and surreal associations. Sweeney himself remarked on that occasion that he did not sit down with the intention of writing 'children's poetry'. He wrote a poem, he said, and then decided later whether it would go into a collection for children or for adults on the basis of whether it could be understood by a child as well as an adult. In his book, *Writing Poetry and Getting Published*, co-written with John Hartley Williams, Sweeney quotes W.H. Auden who said: 'While there are some good poems which are only for adults, because they presuppose adult experience in their readers, there are no good poems which are only for children.'[7]

'The Flying Spring Onion', the title poem of Sweeney's first collection for children, is the source of the title for this chapter:

> The flying spring onion
> flew through the air
> over to where
> the tomatoes grew in rows
> and he said to those
> seed filled creatures
> *My rooted days are done,*
> *so while you sit here*
> *sucking sun*
> *I'll be away and gone,*
> * to Greenland*
> *where they eat no green*
> * and I won't be seen*
> *in a salad bowl with you,*
> *stung by lemon,*
> * greased by oil,*

and nothing at all to do
except wait to be eaten.
With that he twirled
his green propellers
and rose above the rows
of red balls
who stared as he grew small
and disappeared.[8]

This poem is a foretaste of things to come and it serves well to illustrate what Sweeney has achieved both in this volume and the following one, *Fatso in the Red Suit*. It is a poem, which, even in its title, joins
the ordinary and the fantastic. The language is simple. It is aimed at a
lively imagination and it is no less well crafted because it is a poem for
children. The movement of the spring onion flying, suspended in the
air like a helicopter as it hovers over the tomatoes before soaring off
into the distance, is an example of the purely artistic achievement of
his poems. Each section of the poem is a combination of words whose
sound and movement seem to resemble the sound and movement they
denote. For example, in the final section, with the long run-on line
beginning, 'with that he twirled/his green propellers', the pace picks
up. The markedly audible consonant and internal vowel rhyme of
'rose' and 'rows' reflects the rise of the spring onion into the air, while
the lower pitch of 'stared as he grew small/and disappeared' produces
an effect of speeding off into the distance. I shall be referring to this
poem again later, but for now I want it to stand as a good example of
Sweeney's approach, which has been described by one critic as part
anarchy, part insouciance and part sheer wackiness.

What I propose to do in this chapter is to examine a number of
poems from two volumes of Sweeney's poetry for children in order to
witness a poet making a connection between what is happening in the
larger adult world and what is happening inside in the child's world.
Doing what he himself describes in *Writing Poetry* as seeing 'through
the eyes of a child while controlling these images and perceptions with
your adult mind ... [and] at the same time updating those images to fit
the modern world'.[9] I want to consider the poems in the light of a theory of absurdism, in the sense that his fantastic images often describe
the incomprehensible predicaments that are the reality of life more
accurately than any realistic descriptions could do. I shall also look at
the craftsmanship or technical means by which his aims are attained.

Sweeney acknowledges the impact of Franz Kafka on his work. He
says that when he first encountered Kafka's work he thought it was

fantasy but he later came to realize that, although Kafka appeared to be 'operating in non-realist territory', he was, in fact, applying the acute attention to detail that is the mark of realist writing.[10] Although the very concrete images of Kafka's stories initially seemed weird, for example Gregor Samsa's metamorphosis into a giant beetle, their point of departure was always to be found in the real, bureaucratic world in which he lived. They were his attempt to find a solution to the problem of expressing the preoccupations of his time and place in a new and interesting way. He did this by moving from the objective reality of the real world of outside to the subjective reality of inner states of consciousness; a place where obsessions and anxieties became concrete.

In that they attempt to externalise a psychic condition, Kafka's novels and short stories form part of a long tradition that uses the absurd as an expression of inner anxieties and preoccupations that are wholly contemporary. Theatre of the Absurd was a phrase coined by Martin Esslin to describe these trends in the new theatre produced by Ionesco, Beckett and Adamov in the early 1950s. In his book, *The Theatre of the Absurd*, Esslin describes a stage adaptation of Kafka's *The Trial* as being 'in the direct literary and stage lineage of the Theatre of the Absurd'.[11] In the sense that his poems show an awareness that any poetic representation of contemporary life that pretends that it can be explained simply and sensibly is in itself a fantasy, Sweeney makes his own contribution to this type of art.

There is no more contemporary a problem than that of a boy whose father leaves home, and this is the subject matter of the long title poem of *Fatso in the Red Suit*. In this poem Sweeney attempts to give expression to the boy's functioning of thought as events unfold. Like Kafka, he does this by moving from the happenings in the outside world to the happenings as reflected in the mind of the child and by mixing reality with irrational guilt and absurd dreams.

Just as theatre is always more than mere language, so too is poetry, but the performance and actions of the actors is replaced by the rhythm and structure of the poem. In 'Fatso in the Red Suit' Sweeney achieves his effects by shifts of form and tone. This is a poem in which all the parts, the rhyme, the rhythm, the shape, the narrative, work together to create the finished artefact. The composition of the poem is that of six movements appropriate to the unfolding situation; six movements of varying form, length and tone that together reproduce the changing feelings and emotions of the boy as he moves from a growing uneasiness, through feelings of guilt, desolation and bewilderment. It finally ends, with at least a temporary vindication of the boy's own belief in his inner imaginative world, when his father returns on Christmas Eve dressed in a red suit.

The first movement or section of the poem consists of two twenty-line stanzas, the first of which introduces the two worlds, outer and inner, that Dave lives in simultaneously; two hieroglyphs that are at the root of his biological and imaginative self: Dad and Santa Claus:

> It was October
> and already the fake Santas
> were filling the grottos
> in the big stores,
> and here was one on the telly
> in a false white beard,
> fat, like they always were,
> his red-covered belly
> bursting like he'd eaten a turkey
> by himself, his voice
> yo-ho-ho gruff,
> his grin showing in each eye.
> And Dave was on the sofa,
> watching, with Dad beside him
> sipping a glass of red wine
> then choking on a guffaw
> as he pointed at the screen,
> 'Would you look at him,
> that Fatso in the Red Suit',
> and Dave turned green.[12]

The alarm that Dave feels at the desecration of one of his heroes by another increases as his father continues his teasing, causing Dave to shout:

> He's good, and you're mean,
> and if you keep calling him
> Fatso in the Red Suit,
> he won't come here this year
> and he'll do you harm.[13]

The atmosphere in this first movement is one of mounting anxiety and apprehension. An apprehension which is explained and justified when the second movement of the poem establishes the context and gives the real reason behind Dad's sneering:

> ....It happened
> that Dad and Mum were fighting,
> not about Fatsos in Red Suits,
> about their own business. Every night
> as Dave sat in bed reading
> he'd hear them upstairs shouting
> at each other. Then one morning
> Dad packed his bag and left
> and Dave immediately blamed himself.[14]

Following the departure of Dave's dad, once again the narrative momentum and the poetic form changes. The third movement takes the form of seven couplets which, by means of varying rhyme patterns and a disrupting of the base rhythm, manage to illustrate the range of emotions felt by Dave in the aftermath of his father's leaving. The dullness and forlornness of the marking of time and space can be felt in the first three couplets:

> No word from dad for days,
> no luck ringing friends of his.
>
> Mum moping in her room,
> or saying he'd be back soon.
>
> Dave watching things on telly
> even he knew were silly.[15]

The repetition or echoing of the word 'No' at the beginning of the first two lines articulates the feeling of emptiness left behind by Dad's absence. The combination of off rhyme, (days/his, room/soon), and para rhyme, (telly/silly), brings home the resulting sense of confusion and loss felt by Dave. The irregularities of the final two couplets, where the rhythm and rhyme are temporarily disrupted, brings a momentary rush of hope and a falling back again:

> Then, a message on the ansaphone-
> Dad, for Dave, not Mum,
>
> saying, 'Miss you more each day.'
> To Dave he sounded far away.[16]

The quickening of hope brought by the telephone message fades quickly in the final words. With the coupling of continuing time and absence implicit in the rhyming of 'each day' and 'far away', the distance between Dave and his dad and the deepening sense of separation that Dave feels as time goes on is reinforced.

Martin Esslin describes Kafka's short stories and unfinished novels as essentially, 'meticulously exact descriptions of nightmares and obsessions – the anxieties and guilt feelings of a sensitive human being lost in a world of convention and routine'.[17] There is an analogy between a sensitive human being lost in a world of convention and routine and the sense of perplexity and bewilderment that a child feels when he has been deprived of the certainties of his world. The fourth movement of this poem is also the longest. It consists of twenty quatrains wherein Dave's fears and anxieties are presented in a series of dreams; dreams that contain his own personal intuition of the situation, not necessarily in a way that can be immediately recognized as true, but in the way that the situation presents itself to *him*. In a manner that is in keeping with absurdist principles, all the changing moods and inner thoughts that Dave is experiencing are shown by a series of poetic images that communicate to the reader the sense of guilt and loss he feels. Because they are a projection of the upheaval in his own personal world, nothing is as it should be in Dave's dreams; Santa has become a 'skinny', 'stubbled' and 'grumpy' man who 'didn't seem to like children'.

> Or that's how the first dream
> showed it. And Dave's dad
> didn't like children either,
> though Dave knew this was a lie.[18]

Also, the sense of guilt that Dave feels may seem irrational outside of the boy's inner world but this is his personal world and the dreams are not concerned with rationality, only with the way Dave feels. This sense of guilt is articulated in his sixth dream when Mr Christmas and Dave's dad are both peering into a book:

> The dream went in close-up.
> It was a notebook, with lists
> of the naughty children
> and Dave saw his name there.[19]

Dreams attend simultaneously to everthing that is in the mind, jumbling together memories, impressions, and feelings. In *The Field of Nonsense*, Elizabeth Sewell points out that dreams are essentially fluid and unreliable in that things happen simultaneously rather than in sequence. A thing may be two things, or a person two people at the same moment. The result is that dreams cannot be controlled because they cannot be broken down into distinct units. Sewell thinks that the mind can only control those things which can be broken down into small units capable of being looked at individually. She says:

> One cannot control hallucinations, nightmares, dreams or the more violent emotions. They are not capable of being broken down into distinct units which would make them controllable, and none of them, therefore can be played with ... Whatever form of activity the mind may indulge in, it has to have its material first in little bits. That is partly why language is so important to the mind, for language splits experience into small labelled units which the mind can then manipulate, and by the help of which it can mentally arrange experience.[20]

Although things do happen in Dave's dreams, for example the appearance of Mr Christmas keeps changing, and the toys keep mounting at the back of the factory, there is no linear story or plot, just impressions of Dave's state of mind. However, his simultaneous and contradictory feelings are understood by imposing his own distinct units of thought on the jumbled and strange dreams.

The essential distinguishing mark between order and disorder is the establishment of serial order. It may very well be an artificial system, but nevertheless it is the way we think logically. Although there is no sense of time in the dreams themselves, the poet shows a line of development by placing them in a time frame:

> Dave started to dream,
> he dreamed five nights in a row,
> then he stopped for two,
> and dreamed five nights more.[21]

The two dreamless nights are 'needed for resting'. The mention of days passing helps to express the totality of the images of Dave's mind by unfolding them in a sequence of changing but interacting scenes; a device that is reinforced by numbering the dreams and by the lines:

> Each of Dave's dreams
> led into the next, like chapters
> in a book, and in each
> was Dave's dad and the skinny man.[22]

The purpose of the numbers is merely to give the mind a sense of being in control of the situation. The disorder of dream and nightmare are ordered by number and logic in a way that enables Dave to mentally arrange his experience so that it becomes solid and controllable.

The last dreams all take place on Christmas Eve, although in reality Christmas is still weeks away. Christmas Eve is a time when anything can happen:

> ....when bees
> hummed psalms at midnight,
> and animals could talk
> and angels sang in pine trees,[23]

This is a magical time offering a view of the world where a solution may be found to any problem. The tone becomes more confident and Santa is now beginning to look more like himself: 'his beard white now/and him fat and wearing red'.[24] Martin Esslin likens the results of absurdist methods to the cathartic effect of Greek tragedy. It has, he says, a therapeutic effect. Speaking of the spectator of Theatre of the Absurd, he says, 'Stripped of illusions and vaguely felt fears and anxieties, he can face this situation consciously, rather than feeling it vaguely below the surface of euphemisms and optimistic illusions. By seeing his anxieties formulated he can liberate himself from them.'[25]
As the sole spectator of his own dreams, they seem to have had the same therapeutic effect on Dave.

There is, however, one point where Sweeney seems to deviate from absurdist methods. Esslin says that even the most pessimistic tragedies of the naturalistic or Expressionist theatres allow the audience to go home with some kind of message or philosophy in their minds: even if the solution is a sad one it will have had an intellectually or 'rationally formulated conclusion'.[26] However, because it does not deal with intellectual problems, Theatre of the Absurd generally does *not* provide clear-cut rational solutions. Dave's solution, when it comes in the fifth movement of the poem, may not be a rationally formulated one based on adult rules, but, as a purely subjective expression of Dave's vision of the world with its different dimensions of reality, it is both rational and practical.

> When the dreams stopped
> Dave wrote a letter,
> he addressed it 'Mr Christmas',
> made a photocopy,
> sent one to Greenland,
> the other to Iceland.
>
> He wrote 'Dear Mr Christmas,
> I don't want any toys,

> I want my Dad –
> the man you call Peter
> who dresses in black.
> I want him back.'[27]

For many of the child readers of this poem, for whom this would also be a rational and practical solution, it will come as no surprise when:

> ......on Christmas Eve
> as they made to leave
> for church
> he stood on the porch
> in his red suit
> looking *really* fat –
> Dave's Dad was home
> And Santa had still to come.[28]

There is no such magical solution or consolation for the boy in the poem 'Only the Wall'. Although, once again, the tone is effected and maintained by language and form, this time, in contrast to the many changes of mood and tone that go to make up 'Fatso in the Red Suit', 'Only the Wall' is almost monotone. The subject of the poem is bullying, and an evocation of the isolation and pain of 'the new boy' is contained in the short, clipped lines and bleak words of the five nine-line stanzas which tell the story in the most blunt and unembellished style.

> That first day
> only the wall saw
> the bully
> trip the new boy
> behind the shed,
> and only the wall heard
> the name he called,
> a name that would stick like toffee.[29]

The slant rhyme of wall/saw; bully/boy; shed/heard, coupled with the repetition of key words such as wall, bullies and new boy, which recur throughout the poem, serve to give a distinctly menacing intonation to the whole as it moves forward with a sense of inevitability. With each passing day as the same group of words is repeated, our mind thinks, along with 'the new boy', 'Here it comes again'. The only difference is that 'the bully' becomes 'three bullies' and then 'five bullies' and finally just 'the bullies'.

> The second day

the wall didn't see
the fight
because too many
boys stood around,
but the wall heard
their cheers,
and no one cheered for
the new boy.

The third day
the wall felt
three bullies
lean against it,
ready to ambush
the new boy,
then the wall heard
thumps and cries,
and saw blood.[30]

Part of the poem's force comes from the impersonal, objective voice that impassively relates the story. The only other observer is the inanimate and indifferent brick wall that is shown in the accompanying black and white illustration. This narrative strategy serves to dehumanize or depersonalize the victim who remains static as the nameless 'new boy', while the aggressiveness of the bullies seem to gather strength and power as the new boy is both physically and psychologically beaten. Eventually, they *need* a victim – any victim will do.

The fourth day
only the wall missed
the new boy
though five bullies
looked for him,
then picked another boy
instead. Next day
they had him back,
his face hit the wall.

The sixth day
only the wall knew
the bullies
would need that other boy
to savage.

The wall remembered
the new boy's face
going home,
saw he'd stay away.[31]

When you have read these two volumes of Sweeney's poetry for children you know what the world is like to a child. Both the above poems have an empathy, an emotional identification with their subject. Encouraged by the feel or rhythm of the poems, we know what it feels like to be a new boy bullied or a child whose home life is not as it should be. Sweeney's obvious remembrance of childhood emotions is surprising in its intensity and a reminder that childhood is not a separate state. For the adults among us it is proof that the child we were is still there and can be touched by poems such as these. For children, these keenly perceptive poems must surely make the adults they will become more politically aware.

Lisa Ede, in the introductory chapter to a PhD dissertation entitled 'The Nonsense Literature of Edward Lear and Lewis Carroll',[32] makes the point that, for Kant, the term 'nonsense' was not something that should be understood as being totally devoid of any sense. Rather, in his attempt to distinguish between sense and non-sense, Kant defined sense as what man can assert with certainty and non-sense as that which is beyond rational powers. Ede sees Kant's definition as 'an elevation of the imaginative faculty' and says that the continued questioning of what man can say with certainty that he knows has 'resulted in a general movement everywhere in modern philosophy from positive content and from the various dogmatisms'. A significant characteristic of Sweeney's poetry is an attempt to imagine new and different ways of living in an imaginary world that is light years away from the mundane world that we live in every day. There is an effort to shake off the constraints of reason that often cannot be shaken off in reality. According to Martin Esslin, the absence of logic that this requires is a feature of the literature of verbal nonsense made familiar by writers such as Lewis Carroll and Edward Lear and it is identified by Esslin as being influential on the Theatre of the Absurd. Esslin quotes Freud who says: 'Delight in nonsense has its root in the feeling of freedom we enjoy when we are able to abandon the strait jacket of logic.'[33] Elizabeth Sewell would disagree with the notion that nonsense verse 'abandons the strait jacket of logic'. Instead, she believes that the aim of nonsense is to set before the mind a possible universe in which everything goes along serially. Pointing out that one of England's two great nonsense writers (Edward Lear), said of himself in his self-portrait in verse 'His mind is concrete and fastidious',[34] while the other (Lewis Carroll), was a professional logician himself, she asserts that:

> Nonsense as practised by Lear and Carroll does not, even on a slight acquaintance, give the impression of being something without laws and subject to chance, or something without limits, tending towards infinity ... Nonsense is not merely the denial of sense, a random reversal of ordinary experience and an escape from the limitations of everyday life into a haphazard infinity, but it is on the contrary a carefully limited world, controlled and directed by reason, a construction subject to its own laws.[35]

Either way, Sweeney achieves a feeling of freedom in poems such as 'The Flying Spring Onion' mentioned earlier, with images that expand possibilities beyond the limits of reason. The anarchic image of a spring onion that decides one day to uproot itself and take off, rather than just sit around and 'wait to be eaten', goes delightfully beyond the limits of the world and its usual standards of reference. So too does the idea of a party in a rented air balloon at which you may arrive by hitching a ride on a helicopter and where your fellow guests may be angels wearing spacesuit evening wear. As for the food, well,

> .... There'll be larks' eggs
> and flying fish, and roast crow.
> (Horrible? How do you know?)
> And specially imported moon figs.[26]

At least as good as the mince and slices of quince enjoyed by the owl and the pussycat, and infinitely better than the standard fare of

> ....an Old Person of Ewell,
> Who chiefly subsisted on gruel;
> But to make it more nice, he inserted some mice,
> Which refreshed that Old Person of Ewell.[37]

There is, of course, also a cruel or brutal streak in many of Lear's limericks. Examples abound:

> There was a Young Person of Smyrna,
> Whose Grandmother threatened to burn her;
> But she seized on the Cat, and said, 'Granny, burn that!
> You incongruous Old Woman of Smyrna!'

Or

> There was an Old Person of Buda,

Whose conduct grew ruder and ruder;
Till at last, with a hammer, they silenced his clamour,
By smashing that Person of Buda.[38]

In spite of the violent images, these rhymes evoke no horror, probably because they are so far removed from reality. Sewell likens it to a game the rules of which require an absence of feeling and points out that the 'same robust carelessness over its objects' is also a feature of nursery rhymes. The people have become playthings in the power of the player who is free to treat them exactly as he pleases. She says: 'To children and to the mind in play, the people have become things; no contact of feeling or sympathy with them is permissible, and so it does not matter if they meet with dreadful fates, in great variety.'[39] This type of detachment and indifference to cruelty that is typical of the tradition of nonsense is echoed in Sweeney's poems 'Into the Mixer' and 'Johnjoe's Snowman' – both from *The Flying Spring Onion*.

Into the mixer he went,
the nosy boy,
into the mess of wet cement,
round and round
with a glugging sound
and a boyish screamed complaint.

Out of the mixer he came,
the concrete boy,
onto the road made of the same
quick-setting stuff.
He looked rough
and he'd only himself to blame.[40]

This is not a million miles away from the dreadful and variable fates of many of Lear's characters:

There was an Old Man of Nepaul,
From his horse had a terrible fall;
But, though split quite in two, by some very strong glue
They mended that man of Nepaul.

Or

There was an Old Man of Peru,
Who watched his wife making a stew;
But once by mistake, in a stove she did bake,
That unfortunate man of Peru.[41]

As Sewell says: 'If anyone is inclined to take that "by mistake" too seriously, they have only to look at the picture accompanying the rhyme'.[42] The picture in question shows the woman striding purposefully towards the oven, her finger pointing at her husband who is struggling in the long handled pan used to put the bread into the hot oven. As Lear did all his own drawings, it is clear that he intended the reader to know that the wife of the Old Man of Peru knew perfectly well what she was doing. However, the image is too far removed from reality to be really horrifying. This is an imaginary world the existence of which is clearly distinct from society and which offers a safety valve from the trials and irritations of the real world.

Sweeney thinks that 'because of their innocence maybe, the sinister is not as real or as threatening for children (in their games or literature at least) as it is for us'.[43] He reminds us of the violence of many children's cartoons, such as *Roadrunner* or *Tom and Jerry*, and also the elements of dark surrealism in the books of Roald Dahl – both forms of art that are hugely popular with children. The black humour in Sweeney's poetry does however seem to worry some adults. Sweeney tells a story about the poem 'Johnjoe's Snowman'. This poem was once removed from a radio programme because of the offending lines:

> Johnjoe built a snowman
> shaped like a wigwam
> and postbox-sized.
>
> What he didn't tell
> was that inside the snowman
> he'd stuffed the cat[44]

The rest of the poem has Johnjoe building the snowman to his own specifications rather than the generally accepted idea of what a snowman should be. Finally, because

> What the world didn't need
> (apart from frozen cats)
> was another white snowman.
>
> In memory of the cat
> he took the snowman
> and sprayed it black.[45]

Apparently, the BBC producer of the radio programme feared that after hearing the poem children throughout the land would be stuffing cats into black snowmen. Sweeney replied that if he could find a cat that would sit there quietly and allow itself to be immersed into a snowman, then he would grant that the producer had a point. In any case, the producer was adamant and the poem stayed out.

George Orwell tells us that 'Aldous Huxley, in praising Lear's fantasies as a sort of assertion of freedom, has pointed out that the "They" of the limericks represent common sense, legality and the duller virtues generally. "They" are the realists, the practical men, the sober citizens in bowler hats who are always anxious to stop you doing anything worth doing.'[46] Esslin thinks that 'verbal nonsense is in the truest sense a metaphysical endeavour, a striving to enlarge and to transcend the limits of the material universe and its logic'.[47] His inability to understand this makes the BBC producer in question a good example of the 'They' of Lear's limericks.

Eugene Ionesco talked about the need to break down the language of society, which he says is:

> nothing but clichés, empty formulas and slogans ... If anything needs demystifying it is our ideologies which offer ready-made solutions (which history quickly overtakes and refutes) and a language that congeals *as soon as it is formulated*. It is these ideologies which must be continually re-examined in the light of our anxieties and dreams, and their congealed language must be relentlessly split apart in order to find the living sap beneath.[48]

Sweeney examines language in this way in 'The Money Tree'.[49] By taking a fresh look at an old truism he challenges our acceptance of an aphorism that may have outlived its usefulness, showing that prevailing economic forces may need a new perception of reality that cannot be conveyed adequately by hackneyed expressions. The poem is structured round the idea, that, contrary to what we have always believed, money *does* grow on trees. However, the tree is not available to everyone. The first line of the poem sets up a tension between the old expression, 'money doesn't grow on trees', and the alienating effects of capitalist economies: 'Listen, there *is* a money tree'. This tree is watered everyday and 'It's not just water – there's sweat/and blood mixed in'.[50] There is also hatred and jealousy, and a sense of danger and intrigue. The intrigue is emphasized by the fact that the information comes to the narrator via the brother of his friend Bill's mate Joe. Joe is a money-gardener.

> There's another works with him,
> another money-gardener
> and they hate each other,

watch each other like dogs –
that's part of the job.

The tree is in a courtyard
surrounded by blank walls
with slits for rifles,
and a ceiling of perspex
that can slide open.

Where is this courtyard?
Joe's brother doesn't know.
Every morning he has to go
to a rooftop in the city
where a copter lands.

They put on a blindfold
and no-one speaks. They whirr
Joe's brother somewhere
in the city, he can't say.
It's best he can't.[51]

The direct question at the beginning of the seventh stanza, 'Why is
there only one tree?', forces the reader to consider the answer and so
take an active part in the discussion. The reader might agree with the
speaker that: 'You'd think they'd grow/plantations of the stuff', but
Joe's brother laughs. He knows better:

He sees the look
on the faces that come
every weekday at noon
to collect the picked leaves.
They wouldn't share.[52]

The newly invented metaphor of the above poem forces us to look in
a critical way at our capitalist society. It evokes a visual image; has an
evocative power that the worn-out original has lost. We began this
chapter by considering the matter of judgement and how it might be
arrived at. To be a good judge of the use of metaphors, our own and
other people's, we need to be sure that the metaphors that do our
thinking for us are not clichéd or too easy interpretations of meaning.
A meaningless cliché can start a whole chain of illogical argument that
appears to hold up. This is the concern that Frost had when he said of
college students that: 'They don't know when they are being fooled by
a metaphor, an analogy, a parable'.[53] This is because even 'the devil can

quote Scripture, which simply means that the good words you have lying around the devil can use for his purposes as well as anybody else'.[54] We must be constantly on guard and ready to question the meaning of what is said rather than take it at face value. We must learn how to know and manage metaphor. The readers of Matthew Sweeney's poetry will have made a beginning. They will have had their feet set 'on the first rung of a ladder the top of which sticks through the sky'.[55]

NOTES

1. Robert Frost, 'The Figure a Poem Makes', in Edward Connery Lathem and Lawrence Thompson (eds), *Robert Frost Poetry and Prose* (New York: Henry Holt & Co., 1972), p.396.
2. Robert Frost, 'Education by Poetry', in Lathem and Thompson (eds), *Robert Frost Poetry and Prose*.
3. George Orwell, 'Politics and the English Language', in Sonia Orwell and Ian Angus (eds), *The Collected Essays, Journalism, and Letters of George Orwell* (London: Secker & Warburg, 1968), Vol.IV, p.139.
4. Frost, 'Education by Poetry', p.336.
5. Ibid.
6. In *L.V. Desperado Essay – Interviews,* Editura Universiti din Bucuresti, 2006. http://lidia-vianu.scriptmania.com/Matthew%20Sweeney.htm.
7. Matthew Sweeney and John Hartley Williams, *Writing Poetry and Getting Published* (London: Hodder Headline Plc, 1997), p.141.
8. Matthew Sweeney, 'The Flying Spring Onion', in *The Flying Spring Onion*, illustr. David Austin (London: Faber & Faber, 1992), p.1.
9. Sweeney and Williams, *Writing Poetry and Getting Published*, p.145.
10. Ibid., p.12.
11. Martin Esslin, *The Theatre of The Absurd* (London: Penguin Books, 1983), p.356.
12. 1995), p.3.
13. Ibid., p.4.
14. Ibid., p.5.
15. Ibid.
16. Ibid.
17. Esslin, *The Theatre of The Absurd*, p.354.
18. Sweeney, 'Fatso in the Red Suit', p.6.
19. Ibid., p.8.
20. Elizabeth Sewell, *The Field of Nonsense* (London: Chatto and Windus, 1952), p.29.
21. Sweeney, 'Fatso in the Red Suit', p.6.
22. Ibid.
23. Ibid., p.9.
24. Ibid.
25. Esslin, *The Theatre of The Absurd*, p.414.
26. Ibid., p.415.
27. Sweeney, 'Fatso in the Red Suit', p.10.
28. Ibid., p.11.
29. Sweeney, 'Only the Wall', in *Fatso in the Red Suit*, p.28.
30. Ibid., p.29.
31. Ibid., pp.29–30.
32. Lisa Ede, 'An Introduction to the Nonsense Literature of Edward Lear and Lewis Carroll', in Wim Tigges (ed.), *Explorations in the Field of Nonsense* (Amsterdam: Rodopi BV, 1987), pp.49–50.
33. Quoted in Esslin, *The Theatre of the Absurd*, p.340.
34. From Holbrook Jackson (ed.), *The Complete Nonsense of Edward Lear* (London: Faber & Faber, 1947), p.vii.
35. Sewell, *The Field of Nonsense*, p.5.

36. Sweeney, 'My Party', in *Fatso in the Red Suit*, p.12.
37. From Jackson (ed.), *The Complete Nonsense of Edward Lear*, p.56.
38. Ibid., pp.5 and 14.
39. Sewell, *The Field of Nonsense*, p.138.
40. Sweeney, 'Into the Mixer', in *The Flying Spring Onion*, p.13.
41. From Jackson (ed.), *The Complete Nonsense of Edward Lear*, pp.27 and 28.
42. Sewell, *The Field of Nonsense*, p.141.
43. Sweeney and Williams, *Writing Poetry and Getting Published*, p.144.
44. Sweeney, 'Johnjoe's Snowman', in *The Flying Spring Onion*, p.14.
45. Ibid.
46. Orwell, 'Politics and the English Language', p.46.
47. Esslin, *The Theatre of The Absurd*, pp.341–2.
48. Eugene Ionesco. 'The Playwright's Role', in *Notes and Counter Notes*, trans. Donald Watson (London: John Calder, 1964 [1962)]), p.93.
49. Sweeney, 'The Money Tree', in *The Flying Spring Onion*, p.66.
50. Ibid.
51. Ibid., p.67.
52. Ibid., p.68.
53. Frost, 'Education by Poetry', p.331.
54. Ibid., p.335.
55. Ibid., p.336.

Conclusion:
Rethinking the Past;
Imagining the Future

For literature to happen, the reader is quite as vital as the author.

Terry Eagleton[1]

We are accustomed to think of a subversive literature as one that disrupts or challenges tradition. But, as Luke Gibbons, quoting C. Litton Falkiner, has pointed out in *Transformations of Irish Culture*, the notion of tradition as it is formulated in imperial nations which have a consistent and uninterrupted past is quite different from that on the other side of the imperial divide. Here 'tradition itself speaks in confused and scarce intelligible accents'.[2] It follows then, that the task of a subversive Irish literature is not to disrupt tradition but to restore it in a radical rethinking of our past that will transform how we perceive ourselves in the future. In the past, this restoration of tradition has been very successfully employed as a means of promoting national identity. Exponents of the Literary Revival were convinced that it was only by restoring the traditions of a pre-colonial past that the Irish race could regain their national identity. To this end they set about creating a national literature with an indefinable Irish quality of rhythm and style by translating old stories and legends 'in which the ancient heart of Ireland still lives, into a shape at once harmonious and characteristic'.[3] And it was indeed largely due to the cultural and social activities of the revivalists that the new Irish state owed its existence. However, this 'regressive nostalgia' eventually became disabling because it took no account of the continuity of life. It is not possible to restore a historically continuous and allegedly pure pre-colonial heritage. There must be an effort to relate the meanings that attach themselves to tradition to the different context of the present or future.

Walter Benjamin believed that in the context of subsequent changing events, it was possible to find new meanings in the values of tradition.

He believed that the 'redemptive' power of remembrance was inexhaustible and that there was a latent energy in things which could not be known in advance.[4] This idea is exemplified in Mark O'Sullivan's *Angels Without Wings* where the characters created by Axel Hoffman in pre-war Germany eventually separate themselves from their author and his expectations of them. Although they had come into being in a more innocent time, in the different context of Hitler's Germany their personal identity and character evolve in response to the different demands of their own time and place. The characters subsequently grow in directions that could not have been anticipated by their creator and go on to lead independent lives. Even though Hoffman had created them, they contained a potentiality that even he could not have predicted.

Following on from Benjamin, Luke Gibbons has remarked that 'preserving a national heritage is not an act of embalming: it is often a matter of revitalising a moribund tradition, opening it up to new cultural energies and influence'.[5] Preserving national traditions is still the goal, but not as a fixed image of the past grafted onto the present. Rather it should be sought in the potentiality which lies dormant in our past and which is activated by the new context. Benjamin thought that it was important that we use traditions in this way because, unless they can be rescued or rediscovered in a way that renders them of contemporary relevance, the most prized elements of tradition are in danger of falling into oblivion.

On the evidence of the previous six chapters, I want to suggest that, over the past half century, this 'revitalising' of Irish identity which could signal the end of our colonial history has been achieved most successfully in children's literature. There are several reasons why this might be so, all of which relate to the part played by the young readers and their response to the social and political issues raised. Consequently, this chapter sets out to examine and question the assumption that adult perceptual strategies are of more value than those of an 'immature' reader.

We have always taken for granted that an informed adult point of view is the better one; that the child reader's innocence or lack of knowledge forces a simplicity on children's texts that precludes any debate on complex matters. However, as the texts discussed above show, simple language and a reduction in the type of knowledge available to adult readers does not necessarily rule out complex debate. In fact, these texts show that knowledge can sometimes be a negative and limiting thing that encourages recognition and repetition rather than imagination and development. On the other hand, a reader's lack of, or limited, knowledge allows the writer to express another possible view and thus to forge the means for a new way of thinking.

For example, the self-defeating consequences of previous linear readings of Irish history, particularly the famine, are illustrated by the impasses to which it has brought us. While the story of mass suffering needed to be told, in most famine stories, as Celia Keenan points out, famine people have been identified in formulaic ways, 'there is a tendency for the hungry to become indistinguishable from each other, to become mere objects of pity and horror'.[6] Marita Conlon-McKenna avoids this trap. Early on in her trilogy she restores their original and living individuality by naming the people and giving details of their occupations:

> Poor father Doyle is very bad and hasn't stirred at all in weeks – his housekeeper Annie died a few days back. The few men that are left were sitting by the fire in Mercy Farrell's, and not even one was having a sup of porter. I met Corney Egan – that man is nothing but a bag of bones. They wouldn't take him for the road-works, so there is nothing for him now.[7]

From the standpoint or perspective of a given time and space the story of victimization and horror may be the right one. But this is a different time and place. We can go back and start again and make the story different. In fact this is what we must do if there is to be any progress. There are other 'lost energies' in the story which are of more value in our efforts to redeem the present.

While a revision of national history may be necessary, it can be fraught with difficulties for those who go down the well worn nationalistic or reactively revisionist paths. A popular image of revisionism is one that denies all past suffering. Desmond Fennell claims that it 'seeks to show that British rule of Ireland was not, as we have believed, a *bad* thing, but a mixture of necessity, good intentions and bungling; and that Irish resistance to it was not, as we have believed, a *good* thing, but a mixture of wrong-headed idealism and unnecessary, often cruel violence'.[8] Brendan Bradshaw too, has accused revisionists of evading the traumas of Irish history.[9] Roy Foster, on the other hand, sees revisionism as 'an ability to appreciate half-tones, to be sceptical about imputing praise or blame, to separate contemporary intentions from historical effects'.[10] But, if life in the present is part of an evolving historical process, then in order to foster a sense of wholeness we must somehow confront the past. Somewhere in this debate there must be a way that is less 'narrowly political in its focus' and will thus avoid the previous stalemate.

Bradshaw says that the key to an alternative interpretative procedure can be summed up in two words:

> The first is empathy – a notion for long familiar in the social sciences to where it migrated, ironically from the humanities. The second is imagination – a quality much suspected by rational scientists of earlier generations but now generally acknowledged as equally crucial to rational investigation as to the creativity of the artist.[11]

As Marita Conlon-McKenna's treatment of history shows, this idea of an imaginative and empathic approach can relate the facts of Irish history without filtering out the trauma, while at the same time move away from the politics of blame. She does this, not by reminding her young readers of a victimized past, but by reminding them of the courage and resilience of their ancestors; not by replicating old divisions of history, but by finding a *different subject position* which allows for a different view. This combination of politics and poetics allows her to give a truly revisionist account; one that can help to foster a relationship between past and present and allow us to move forward to the future.

The notion of finding a different subject position is crucial to the success of Conlon-McKenna's treatment of history. Literature for children, like literature for adults, is written by adults, so, what defines its generic distinction is the reader, and, as Peter Rabinowitz points out, a reader 'can read as the author intended only by being in the right place to begin with'.[12] For adults, this can be very difficult. The time and space from which they view things has different values attached to it. This difference of time and space has less to do with actual physical distance from historical events and more to do with a different mental space and time. Children who are in the process of growing and maturing are always in the 'becoming' stage and thus avoid the trap of subjectivity. Their view is generally more flexible and forward thinking than that of an adult, which is more likely to be static and fixed. This enables the child reader to break with the idea of historical determination or sequence as the primary explanatory context for the present. I believe that the writers discussed in this book have identified in the different location of their child readers 'the right place' to open up a liberating zone for a critique of both traditional Irish dichotomies and contemporary Irish problems. Without changing the facts, these writers have offered a perspective that allows us to see our unquestioned cultural assumptions with new eyes because our adult assumptions may not form any significant part of a child reader's experience.

This is not to say that children are a blank sheet and that they have completely dislodged the past. Young readers will have absorbed enough of their parents' experience to ensure that they are not entirely remote from the personal and emotional response of a previous generation. A look back at Chapter Five will remind us how the concept of reaction can inhibit the progression of both parents and children while the process of interrelation or intersubjectivity which puts different forms of experience in dialogue with each other can promote a new understanding. So too can a dialogical relationship between past and present. It is not a question of rejecting adult theories or discussions but of opening up new lines of thought that make these theories irrelevant. While the facts themselves do not change, a different perspective makes for a different story and events that were previously seen as peripheral may become central while those that were previously central may now be irrelevant. For example, in Conlon-McKenna's version of Irish history, the children's different perspective places the emphasis on courage and survival rather than the feeling of victimization which had previously lasted long past the time of victory. When the famine story is stripped right back to the moment rather than recalled through the light of subsequent happenings, what becomes in Benjamin's terms its 'truth value' is courage and survival. According to Benjamin's theory, we are doing the people who lived and died in that historical moment a disservice if we allow that to be forgotten. He says, 'Only that historian will have the gift of fanning the spark of hope in the past who is firmly convinced that *even the dead* will not be safe from the enemy if he wins.'[13]

This rejection of a feeling of being hard done by in favour of a celebration of the 'great people' of the famine times is a repudiation of the constant backward look that characterizes much adult Irish writing and a retrieval of the positive elements of this era of our history. By focusing on the points of courage and survival the rest fades into the background and becomes less important and so history is transformed. Consequently, Eily and her siblings emerge triumphant at the end of this trilogy offering a way out of the impasses of Irish history where adult theories had found none.

During the-nineteenth century the children's literature scene in Ireland appeared to be vibrant. As Janette Condon tells us in an article entitled, 'Children's Books in Nineteenth-Century Ireland', there was an interest in child readers from, on the one hand, imperialist writers attempting to civilize the Irish by catching them early on in order to improve their minds and their morals, and, on the other hand, nationalist writers reacting against the Anglicization of Irish children.[14] Throughout the nineteenth century authors and critics from both sides competed to instil their ideas into the minds of Irish children. Condon quotes 'A Child's Hymn of Praise' by Ann Taylor as an example of the cultural imperialism that typified the school text books of the period which were supplied by the administrators of the national school system set up in 1831.

> Thank the goodness and the grace,
> Which on my birth had smiled,
> And made me in these Christian days
> *A Happy English child.* (Condon's emphasis)

She goes on to say that: 'The Board's aim of creating "happy English children" in Ireland was not, however, allowed to proceed without challenge from prominent nationalists of the day.'[15] The Christian Brothers in particular 'tried to instil in their pupils the sense that they had a country of their own and a separate cultural identity different and apart from England'. However, as Condon argues, this literature was best understood in relation to imperialist ideas of control. She says: 'Central to this discourse of tutoring "young Ireland" is the nineteenth-century concept of the child's mind as a *tabula rasa* onto which adults could write their social values and political ideals.'[16] This of course means that there was no space left for the readers themselves to bring anything to the text; nothing left for the reader to do. It was more about actively sending adults to passively receiving children. Much more comparable to today's truly vibrant children's literature was the adult Irish literature that flourished from the end of the nineteenth-century up to the middle of the twentieth-century; a time when Ireland was moving rapidly from being a province of the United Kingdom to political independence. This literary output shared many of the characteristics that contribute to the subversive nature of children's literature.

In *Kafka: Towards A Minor Literature* Giles Deleuze and Felix Guattari describe what constitutes a minor literature. They say: 'A minor literature doesn't come from a minor language; it is rather that which a minority constructs within a major language.'[17] This is something that can be applied both to the writers of children's literature and any minority writer within a major language, such as black American writers or the Irish writers of the Literary Revival who were writing in the English language. The literature of the revivalists falls into the category of minor literature as described by Deleuze and Guattari for two reasons. First of all, as it was written in the English language, it came in the form of a language that was not their own and whose literary tradition did not reflect Irish experience. Secondly, it came at a time when the Irish, as colonized subjects, were a marginalized people who were treated as children: innocent and lacking in 'adult' knowledge. In the same way that a colonized people has no fixed idea of its own identity, so child readers do not begin with fixed ideas which they wish to express. They read the story anew and then formulate their impressions.

According to Deleuze and Guattari, minor literature has three characteristics. The first of these they describe as deterritorialization. Deterritorialization means that the literature is outside of the mainstream. The Anglo-Irish writers of the late nineteenth and early twentieth-century used the English language with an incorrect syntax and a vocabulary that was heavily influenced by Irish. The development of a literature in this appropriation of the language of the colonial power was a significant factor in the development of a national identity and also allowed for a new mode of expression and a new flexibility. Because they were not restrained by rules, not weighed down by old expectations of some pre-existent category or literary genre, the old forms were broken. When a form is broken the content is too and is free to be reorganized and restructured in a different way. All the elements can be fused together in a new unity which gives a new look to the event, thus giving the writer similar advantages to that of the child reader. After a period of time, Anglo-Irish literature began to acquire its own rules and become 'reterritorialized' which may explain why, when the expectations of the Anglo-Irish tradition began to weigh heavily on him, Samuel Beckett switched to writing in French.

The second characteristic of minor literature put forward by Deleuze and Guattari, and one which the literary revivalists shared with the best writing for children, is that it is always political. In the second chapter of this book, Eilís Dillon's stories of Ireland set in the 1940s, 1950s and 1960s show how an internalized subjection, that comes from the way we read Irish history, has in the past affected many aspects of the way we live: economic, bureaucratic and juridical. How we read history affects all our present and future choices because we tell ourselves stories about how things have been and draw from this conclusions about how they will remain. In *The Sea Wall* for example, the defensive attitude of the people of Inisharcain affects their ability to make decisions and almost brings about the destruction of their island. But, if we can change the way we read history then we have the power to change our direction and it is the ability of minor literature to reorganize and restructure the facts of history that make it political. The third characteristic of minor literature is that it is always collective. This means that it lacks the linear or subjective nature of much mainstream literature. Instead it has the ability to start again from the beginning and rediscover 'the truth value' of an event. The truth value is never something that is purely subjective. Rather it can be described as the essence or the spirit of a thing. Yeats, for example, had this ability to take the spirit or essence of the past and adjust it to modern conditions. In the chapter entitled 'W.B. Yeats – Building Amid Ruins', in *Irish Classics*, Declan Kiberd argues that Yeats' creative energy came from an invisible life of earlier times. It takes, he says, the form of 'trapped energy, saved from earlier generations'.

> Amidst the ruins of the modern world, Yeats felt himself able to tap into the images and energies of a collective past long erased from official memory. The greatest sin would be to bring the work of dead predecessors to nothing: for those predecessors expected the later generations to press on their behalf a claim to a restored divinity.[18]

This bears great similarity to Marita Conlon-McKenna's achievement in her famine stories.

The gap in Irish children's literature during the first few decades of the twentieth century has been well documented. Robert Dunbar has remarked that, compared with English and American books of the same period, 'Those children's books from the late nineteenth and early twentieth century which can, with varying degrees of legitimacy, be considered "Irish" books, today have only an antiquarian or academic interest'.[19] This period has failed to produce any classics of children's literature. The gap is usually explained by the fact that Ireland was a branch of the British book market rather than having its own publishing industry. The combination of a small population and a lack of money meant that there was no market for children's books in Ireland and so the literature was produced mainly for the British and American markets. Emer O'Sullivan asks the question: 'What does a literature look like which is produced predominantly for a foreign market?'[20] In answer she quotes from Kenneth Reddin's 1946 article 'Children's books in Ireland':

> What is the matter with the Irish writers of children's stories? They are completely stage-Irish. Pigs in the kitchen and little red hens and tinkers splitting skulls down bohereens, and ass carts

> and clamps of turf and heaps of muck, cabins, sleans, Seans, illiteracy, bad whiskey and general 'divilment'. All the things we have blamed England for in her attitude to Paddy the Irishman; all the things which America loves to think make the 'rale' Irish scene.[21]

In order to find a market for their books, Irish children's writers were forced to write about themselves in a way that confirmed the expectations of the British or American markets.

Undoubtedly there is a large measure of truth in the notion that there was no market for children's books in Ireland and that this is a contributory factor in the lack of classic children's literature in this period. But I do not believe this to be the only reason for the dearth of children's literature. It seems equally likely that the gap can be explained by the fact that there was no *need* for the subversiveness of children's literature when this quality was being supplied by the adult literature of the time. It is certainly worthy of note that after political independence when adult literature was less vibrant was the time when Irish children's literature began to come into its own. Eilís Dillon began writing children's books in the 1950s. Her subsequent criticism of the provincialism and stagnation of the new Irish state had begun long before any changes in the conditions of production for children's literature in Ireland. Indeed, it is arguable that her influence spawned a new generation of children's writers who precipitated the founding of the new publishing houses and children's imprints that came at the beginning of the 1980s rather than the other way around.

Academic theory, even if it has not until recently concerned itself much with children's literature, has undoubtedly contributed much to our understanding of it and may perhaps be the thin end of the wedge that will eventually allow it to penetrate the inner sanctum of mainstream criticism. But, the idea that the different perspective of child readers can change the way we perceive and respond to old narratives would suggest that this is a two way thing and that child readers have something important to contribute to academic theory. It would seem that the reason why the best children's literature has always been seen as subversive is that it serves as a radical questioning of adult texts and theories. The disquieting connections between imperialism and culture, pointed out in many of Eilís Dillon's children's stories, are proof that without continuous questioning theories can imitate the very state they set out to subvert. If events mediated through the particular intersection of time and place of a child reader can highlight, or even lead to, a solution to problems, then it follows that the response of young readers may be seen as an active or revolutionary force in the shaping of future theories. The value of children's literature is that it can, and does, become 'the revolutionary conditions for every literature within the heart of what is called great (or established) literature'.[22] It has repercussions, not only for the children's writers that follow on, but also for the adult writers of later generations. This was the central thesis of Juliet Dusinberre's book, *Alice to the Lighthouse,* in which she connects children's books of the late nineteenth century to developments in education and psychology culminating in the modernism of the early twentieth century.

Dusinberre's theory is that, 'radical experiments in the arts in the early modern period began in the books which Lewis Carroll and his successors wrote for children'.[23] In her study of the relation between children's literature and writing for adults, she shows how Carroll's *Alice's Adventures in Wonderland* (1865) and *Through The Looking Glass* (1871), mark the beginning of a revolution in aspects of language, structure, vision, morals, characters and readers:

> The absence of a deliberately pointed moral, and of linear direction in narrative, the abdication of the author as preacher, and the use of words as play, all of which were pioneered in children's books in the latter half of the nineteenth century, feed into the work of Virginia Woolf and her generation of writers.[24]

Dusinberre shows very convincingly how Carroll's *Alice* books are the precursors, not just of children's books such as E. Nesbit's *The Phoenix and The Carpet* (1904), Kenneth Graham's *The Wind in the Willows* (1908) and R.L. Stevenson's *Treasure Island* (1883), but of adult books too. They provide, she argues, the impetus for the modernism of writers such as Lawrence, Proust, Joyce and Virginia Woolf.

One of the many ways in which Dusinberre shows the *Alice* books as setting the scene for changes later mirrored in adult fiction is in the relation of author and reader. Maria Louisa Charlesworth's *Ministering Children* published in 1854, eleven years before *Alice in Wonderland,* seems a fair example of what was available and what the mid-Victorian generation of parents expected their children to read. The children in the story are 'paragons of piety and philanthropy, distributing tracts, prayers and packets of tea with abundant sweetness'.xxv The author's right to dispense morals and dictate to the reader, especially the child reader, had been taken for granted in Victorian fiction, until that is, Lewis Carroll declared that he was content for his books to mean whatever his readers wanted them to mean. He dispenses with the pretensions of moralistic authors in Alice's encounter with the Duchess:

'The game's going on rather better now', she said, by way of keeping up the conversation a little.

'Tis so', said the Duchess: 'and the moral of that is – Oh, 'tis
love, 'tis love, that makes the world go round.'

'Somebody said', Alice whispered, 'that it's done by everybody
minding their own business!'

'Ah, well! It means much the same thing', said the Duchess, dig-
ging her sharp little chin into Alice's shoulder as she added, 'and
the moral of *that* is – Take care of the sense, and the sounds will
take care of themselves.'

'How fond she is of finding morals in things!' Alice thought to
herself.[26]

According to Dusinberre, Carroll set a precedent for a challenge to
authority and an irreverence that initiated a movement away from the
writer as a dictatorial figure and which influenced the next generation
of writers. She gives as one example Virginia Woolf's *To The
Lighthouse*, where writer and reader struggle together to interpret and
understand the world, causing Erich Auerbach to say of its author: 'She
does not seem to bear in mind that she is the author and hence ought
to know how matters stand with her characters.'[27] Dusinberre quotes
the following passage from *To The Lighthouse* to illustrate the point:

> Was she crying then for Mrs Ramsey, without being aware of any
> unhappiness? She addressed old Mr Carmichael again. What was
> it then? What did it mean? Could things thrust their hands up and
> grip one; could the blade cut; the fist grasp? Was there no safety?
> No learning by heart of the ways of the world? No guide, no shel-
> ter, but all was miracle, and leaping from the pinnacle of a tower
> into the air?[28]

Dusinberre points out that Woolf was rebelling against 'the "privileged
discourse" through which the author commands his own creatures'.
She adds that this 'form of insurrection by the author on behalf of the
reader had begun much earlier in the children's book'[29] and has lead on
to 'the death of the author' in modern critical theory. She thus relates
Alice not only to a whole generation of children but to the thinking and
writing of those children when they grew to adulthood so that the child
becomes 'not just a mirror ... but also the creator of culture'.[30]

The child reader as 'the creator of culture' is exemplified in many
of the books discussed in the previous six chapters. For example, in
Silent Stones O'Sullivan's young adult characters finally manage, with
the aid of the more enlightened members of the older generation, to

construct their own vision of the future. The idealism and hope necessary for a new image of the future needs the energy and optimism of youth. In *Angels Without Wings,* another of O'Sullivan's stories, the young protagonists literally share with the author the burden of writing the story. Unlike Pirandello's *Six Characters in Search of an Author,* in which the characters of an unfinished play are dependent on their author to complete their story, the characters in *Angels Without Wings* want to have some control over the completion of their own story. If Lewis Carroll has made Alice the initiator of the modernist movement away from authorial control, then Mark O'Sullivan's characters could be said to be correcting the overreach of postmodernism by finding a middle way between the omnipotence of the author and the death of the author.

All this is a far cry from Samuel Pickering's assertion that, 'unlike the novels of Faulkner and Joyce or the poetry of Stevens and Eliot, the matter of much children's literature is understandable at first reading and does not lend itself to multiple close readings or interpretations'.[31] He goes on to say that 'because the texts are usually straightforward, children's literature is not a good field of study for the "creative" new critic'.[32] Pickering's remarks were made in 1982, only five years before the first publication of Dusinberre's *Alice to the Lighthouse*. Although things have improved much in the recent past, it remains true, with the odd exception, that children's books are *still* not seen as a good field of study for the creative new critic. This is largely because, in spite of books like Dusinberre's, children's books 'are perceived by the critical establishment as belonging to a separate sub-culture which has never been allowed a place in the discussion of high culture'.[33]

It is one thing to look back and trace the links between innovations in children's literature and new trends or theories in main stream literature a generation later. It is quite another thing to predict absolutely the political currents of the future that might have their roots in today's children's literature. We can see and appreciate the difference and distance between previous and current thoughts but we cannot see ahead. Having been disorganized both in form and content, the themes of the novels discussed in this work are, to use a phrase from Deleuze and Guattari, 'caught in a becoming'. This means that although the political, ethical and ideological themes that run through them may contain the seeds of a radical redirection of Irish identity, and should certainly have a place in the history of Irish literature, we can only guess at what might follow on. What is obvious is that past insecurities and failures are becoming irrelevant. Whether this will eventually lead to increased confidence, a better society, and a state which plays an important leadership role in Europe, or, on the other hand, an arrogant, materialistic and hedonistic society, is difficult to predict with certainty. What *is* certain is that, even if we cannot recognize it at the present time, there is a procedure in action, a continuous process going on which is quite likely to be found to have its genesis in these books.

Of course, as has been mentioned before, children's literature is the product of adult craftsmanship. All of the writers discussed in this work play an important part in the evolution of individual consciousness in the minds of their readers. They do so by showing that there are other points of view, other ways of seeing, and by challenging their young readers to grasp the complexity and multiplicity of the world. The potential of the child's different view has been implemented in these texts through the poetics of metaphors, analogies and strategies used by the writers concerned and which motivate the child to become fully engaged with the text. For example, the task for Eilís Dillon is to present the tension between past and progress and offer explanations and solutions. The aesthetic problem she sets herself is how to use the language and folklore of tradition to enrich the present. To this end, her stories are woven through with the stories and traditions of her childhood in such a way that she gives to the future the voice and experiences of the past. Without this passing on of our cultural inheritance her message would be greatly diminished.

But her sense of Irishness is not just an aesthetic one. She also engages with the political issues that have shaped modern Ireland, most obvi-ously colonialism and its legacy of oppression, in a way that demands of her readers that they recognize the difficulties and seek to under-stand. The different perspective represented by the child protagonists demonstrates the negative aspects of their elders' way of seeing, while the children themselves are shown the reasoning behind the different attitude of the older generation. In *The Cruise of the Santa Maria* when the children and Tomas capture Morgan McDonagh, the man who had tried to steal Colman Flaherty's land from him, they are torn between pity and anger:

> We jerked him to his feet. Tomas said in a kindly tone:
> 'Breathe deeply several times. It will make you feel better.'
> I guessed that like myself he had begun to feel pity for Morgan – he looked so helpless and his story was so miserable. But it struck me then, as it often did later in my life, that it was a strange thing for a man who had suffered oppression himself to have treated someone else as badly. One would have thought he would have learned from his own sad life to be charitable and generous

in his dealings. With him as with many another it seemed to have worked the other way: he had become sour, and jealous of the good fortune of everyone else...

Morgan gave a kind of low snarl, like a dog that was defending himself from others. He had seemed so submissive that I was astonished.[34]

Although the children may not immediately understand it, they recognize in both Colman Flaherty and in Morgan McDonagh the paradoxical mixture of aggression, defensiveness and submission that characterizes a colonized people. While their critical view certainly undermines the old way of seeing things and shows the way forward, they also learn that the views of Colman and Morgan are connected to historical and social issues and should be understood in this way. In *The Island of Ghosts* Dara says of Bardal:

He spoke so sadly and sounded so sincere that I felt my bitterness towards him lessen. His dream, Hy Brasil, filled his mind so completely, leaving no room for anything else. It was as if his genius had him in its power, so that he no longer cared about the needs of anyone outside of himself. When I understood this, I felt a pang of pity for him, though I knew it was dangerous to soften in any way.[35]

In these stories, children, for whom by their very nature the norm is future orientated and hopeful, represent the principal perspective and draw attention to the outmoded views of their elders. However, Dillon inhibits any straightforward drawing of easy moral or political conclusions by encouraging her readers to fill in gaps, recognize ambiguities and seek to understand.

In Mark O'Sullivan's novels, the theme of intersubjectivity is mirrored in the way the text itself functions. In this case the structure of perspectives is less hierarchical and all the characters learn from each other. The narrative presentation of both of the novels discussed in Chapter Five is segmented in such a way as to open up a view on other perspectives apart from that of the main protagonists. This has the effect of giving a stronger account of the different historical moments in which other people may be located. In *Angels Without Wings*, when Siegfried in desperation is prepared to murder Herr Gott rather than allow him to finish the story, Anna insists that he read the letter which Gott had dropped on the floor earlier. The letter goes some way towards explaining why Gott is prepared to write the story for money.

> Dearest daughter Romi, the letter began, I hope this note finds you safe and well. Don't worry yourself on my account. Why, I've never been so healthy in all my life. Every evening I walk along Unter Den Linden and meet my old friends at the Blue Note Café … Better still, I've found a way, at last to get the money to help you and Chaim to escape this sad country … I can't tell you how much I regret the pain I've put you through since you married Chaim. Did I see in him a man, loving and kind? Did I see the doctor working among the poor? No, I looked at Chaim and saw only a Jew … Perhaps now I can undo some of the harm I've done.
>
> I ask you to accept this money when it comes, as I swear it will. This time I will not fail you, my daughter. I will send you the money if it is the last thing I do.[36]

The fact that Gott is trying to make up for his earlier mistakes and save his daughter and her family from the Nazis, goes some way to explaining his present actions, even if we cannot agree with them. Once they know the circumstances the characters are more sympathetic and turn their energies to helping him find another more honourable way of obtaining the money. The way the reader makes sense of the text is dictated by the switching of perspectives which encourages him or her to see the other person's view in context. In this way author and reader work together to produce a realization of the continual process of change and the continual need to reassess.

It seems amazing that, in spite of all this effort, writing for children is often perceived as requiring less literary skills than writing for adults. But, the evidence would seem to show that it is not true that it is more difficult to write for adults. In fact it is arguably more difficult to see through the eyes of a child because, to do this successfully, it is necessary for the writer to bridge the gap between childhood and adulthood in order to implement the potential of the child reader's different perspective. All of the writers discussed in this book have managed to do that and along the way they have demonstrated that by putting the different experience of child readers and adult writers in dialogue with each other, the best writing for children can contribute greatly to the development and understanding of modern and contemporary Ireland.

NOTES

1.   Terry Eagleton, *Literary Theory: An Introduction* (Oxford: Blackwell Publishers, 1992), p.74.
2.   C. Litton Falkiner quoted in Luke Gibbons, *Transformations in Irish Culture* (Cork: Cork University Press, 1996), p.5.

3. W.B. Yeats, Preface, in Lady Augusta Gregory, *Cuchulain of Muirhemne* (New York: Gramercy Books, 1986 [1902]), p.334.
4. Richard Wolin, *Walter Benjamin: An Aesthetic of Redemption* (New York: Colombia University Press, 1982).
5. Luke Gibbons, 'Challenging the Canon: Revisionism and Cultural Criticism', in *The Field Day Anthology* Vol.III (Derry: Field Day Publications, 1991), p.565.
6. Celia Keenan, 'The Famine Told to Children', in Valerie Coghlan and Celia Keenan (eds), *The Big Guide 2: Irish Children's Books* (Dublin: Children's Books Ireland, 2000), p.69.
7. Marita Conlon-McKenna, *Under the Hawthorn Tree* (Dublin: O'Brien Press, 1990), p.37.
8. Desmond Fennell, 'Against Revisionism', in Ciaran Brady (ed.), *Interpreting Irish History: the Debate on Revisionism* (Dublin: Irish Academic Press, 1994), pp.184–5.
9. Brendan Bradshaw, 'Nationalism and Historical Scholarship in Modern Ireland', in Brady (ed.), *Interpreting Irish History: the Debate on Revisionism*, p.215.
10. Roy Foster, 'We Are all Revisionists Now', *The Irish Review*, 1 (1986), p.1.
11. Bradshaw, 'Nationalism and Historical Scholarship in Modern Ireland', p.215.
12. Peter J. Rabinowitz, *Before Reading* (Columbus, OH: Ohio State University Press, 1998), p.26.
13. Walter Benjamin, *Illuminations*, ed. Hannah Arendt, trans. Harry Zohn (London: Fontana/Collins, 1982 [1970]), p.257.
14. Janette Condon, 'Children's Books in Nineteenth-Century Ireland', in Valerie Coghlan and Celia Keenan (eds), *The Big Guide 2: Irish Children's Books* (Dublin: Children's Books Ireland, 2000), p.54.
15. Ibid.
16. Ibid.
17. Gilles Deleuze and Felix Guattari, *Kafka: Towards a Minor Literature* (Minneapolis, MN: University of Minesota Press, 1986), p.16.
18. Declan Kiberd, 'W.B. Yeats – Building Amid Ruins', in *Irish Classics* (London: Granta Books, 2000), p.447.
19. Robert Dunbar, 'Classic Irish Children's Books', in Valerie Coghlan and Celia Keenan (eds), *The Big Guide 2: Irish Children's Books* (Dublin: Children's Books Ireland, 2000), p.60.
20. Emer O'Sullivan, 'The Development of Modern Children's Literature in Twentieth Century Ireland', *Signal*, 81 (1996), p.193.
21. Kenneth Reddin, 'Children's Books in Ireland', *Irish Library Bulletin*, 7 (1946), p.74.
22. Deleuze and Guattari, *Kafka: Towards a Minor Literature*, p.18.
23. Juliet Dusinberre, *Alice to the Lighthouse: Children's Books and Radical Experiments in Art* (London: MacMillan Press, 1999), p.5.
24. Ibid., p.xxi.
25. Ibid., p.43.
26. Quoted in Dusinberre, *Alice to the Lighthouse*, p.59.
27 Ibid., p.41.
28. Ibid.
29. Ibid.
30. Ibid., p.68.
31. Samuel Pickering Jr., 'The Function of Criticism in Children's Literature', *Children's Literature in Education*, 13, 1 (1982), p.15.
32. Ibid., p.16.
33. Dusinberre, *Alice to the Lighthouse*, p.xvii.
34. Eilís Dillon, *The Cruise of The Santa Maria* (Dublin: O'Brien Press, 1991), p.155.
35. Eilís Dillon, *The Island of Ghosts* (London: Faber & Faber, 1990), p.66.
36. Mark O'Sullivan, *Angels Without Wings* (Dublin: Wolfhound Press, 1997), pp.115-16.

Bibliography

PRIMARY SOURCES

Conlon-McKenna, Marita. *Under the Hawthorn Tree* (Dublin: O'Brien Press, 1990).
—— *The Blue Horse* (Dublin: O'Brien Press, 1992).
—— *Wildflower Girl* (Dublin: O'Brien Press, 1992).
—— *Fields of Home* (Dublin: O'Brien Press, 1996).
Dillon, Eilís. *A Herd of Deer* (London: Faber & Faber, 1969).
—— *Inside Ireland* (London: Hodder & Stoughton, 1982).
—— *The Island of Ghosts* (London: Faber & Faber, 1990).
—— *The Cruise of the Santa Maria* (Dublin: O'Brien Press, 1991).
—— *The Singing Cave* (Dublin: Poolbeg, 1992).
—— *The Sea Wall* (Dublin: Poolbeg, 1994).
Jackson, Holbrook (ed.). *The Complete Nonsense of Edward Lear* (London: Faber & Faber, 1947).
Joyce, James. *Portrait of the Artist as a Young Man* (London: Paladin, 1990 [1916]).
Lewis, C.S. *The Last Battle* (London: Harper Collins, 1998 [1956]).
MacRaois, Cormac. *The Battle Below Giltspur* (Dublin: Wolfhound Press, 1988).
—— *Dance of the Midnight Fire* (Dublin: Wolfhound Press, 1989).
—— *Lightning Over Giltspur* (Dublin: Wolfhound Press, 1991).
Ní Dhuibhne, Eilís. *The Dancers Dancing* (Belfast: The Blackstaff Press, 1999).
O'Brien, Flann. *At-Swim-Two-Birds* (London: Penguin, 1967).
O'Sullivan, Mark. *Angels Without Wings* (Dublin: Wolfhound Press, 1997).
—— *Silent Stones* (Dublin: Wolfhound Press, 1999).
Parkinson, Siobhan. *Four Kids, Three Cats, Two Cows, One Witch (maybe)* (Dublin: O'Brien Press, 1997).
—— *The Moon King* (Dublin: O'Brien Press, 1999).

Pirandello, Luigi. *Six Characters in Search of an Author* (Milton Keynes: Open University Press, 1977).

Sweeney, Matthew. *The Flying Spring Onion* (London: Faber & Faber, 1992).

—— *Fatso in the Red Suit* (London: Faber & Faber, 1995).

Swift, Graham. *Waterland* (London: Heinemann, 1983).

Yeats, W.B. *Autobiographies* (Dublin: Gill & Macmillan, 1955).

SECONDARY SOURCES

Appiah, K. Anthony. 'The Multiculturist Misunderstanding', *New York Review of Books*, XLIV, 15 (9 October 1997), pp.30–6.

Barthes, Roland. *Image-Music-Text*, trans. Stephen Heath (London: Fontana, 1977).

Baudrillard, Jean. *The Illusion of the End*, trans. Chris Turner (Cambridge: Polity Press, 1994).

Bell, Daniel. 'The Return of the Sacred', in *The Winding Passage. Essays and Sociological Journeys 1960–1980* (Cambridge: ABT Books, 1980).

Benjamin, Walter. *Illuminations*, ed. Hannah Arendt, trans. Harry Zohn (London: Fontana/Collins, 1982 [1970]).

Bensmaia, Reda. Foreword, in Gilles Deleuze and Felix Guattari, *Kafka: Towards a Minor Literature* (Minneapolis, MN: University of Minnesota Press, 1986).

Berger, John and Jean Mohr. *Another Way of Telling* (New York: Pantheon, 1982).

Bettelheim, Bruno. *The Uses of Enchantment* (London: Penguin Books, 1991 [1976]).

Bew, Paul. *The Making of Modern Irish History* (London: Routledge, 1996).

Boland, Eavan. 'The Emigrant Irish', in *The Journey and other Poems* (Manchester: Carcanet, 1987).

—— *A Kind of Scar: The Woman Poet in a National Tradition* (Dublin: Attic Press, 1989).

Boyce, D. George and Alan O'Day, (eds). *The Making of Modern Irish History* (London: Routledge, 1996).

Bradshaw, Brendan. 'Nationalism and Historical Scholarship in Modern Ireland', in Ciaran Brady (ed.), *Interpreting Irish History: the Debate on Revisionism* (Dublin: Irish Academic Press, 1994).

Bruner, J. *Actual Minds, Possible Worlds* (Cambridge, MA: Harvard University Press, 1986).

Bullock, Marcus and Michael Jennings (eds). *Walter Benjamin. Selected Writings.* Vol.1. 1913–1926 (Cambridge, MA: Harvard University Press, 1996).

Butler, Hubert. *The Children of Drancy* (Mullingar: Lilliput Press, 1988).

Chambers, Ross. *Story and Situation: Narrative Seduction and the Power of Fiction* (Manchester: Manchester University Press, 1984).

Chowers, Eyal. 'The Marriage of Time and Identity', *Philosophy and Social Criticism*, 25, 3 (1999), pp.57–80.

Coe, Richard. *When The Grass was Taller* (New Haven, CT: Yale University Press, 1984).

Condon, Janette. 'Children's Books in Nineteenth-Century Ireland', in Valerie Coghlan and Celia Keenan (eds), *The Big Guide 2: Irish Children's Books* (Dublin: Children's Books Ireland, 2000).

Conlon-McKenna, Marita. Interview with Robert Dunbar, *Children's Books in Ireland*, 3 (December 1990).

Conrad, Peter. *Modern Times Modern Places: Life and Art in the 20th Century* (London: Thames & Hudson, 1998).

Cook, Guy. *Discourse* (Oxford: Oxford University Press, 1989).

Deane, Seamus. *Celtic Revivals* (North Carolina: Wake Forest University Press, 1985).

—— *Strange Country. Modernity and Nationhood in Irish Writing since 1790* (Oxford: Clarendon Press, 1997).

Deleuze, Gilles and Felix Guattari. *Kafka: Towards a Minor Literature* (Minneapolis, MN: University of Minnesota Press, 1986).

Dienstag, Joshua Foa. 'The Pessimistic Spirit', *Philosophy and Social Criticism*, 25, 1 (1999), pp.71–95.

Dillon, Eilís. 'Literature in a Rural Background'. Paper given at Loughborough Conference on Children's Literature, Trinity College Dublin, 1981.

Diner, Hasia R. *Erin's Daughters in America* (Baltimore, MD: John Hopkins University Press, 1986 [1983]).

Dunbar, Robert. 'Classic Irish children's Books', in Valerie Coghlan and Celia Keenan (eds), *The Big Guide 2: Irish Children's Books* (Dublin: Children's Books Ireland, 2000).

Dusinberre, Juliet. *Alice to the Lighthouse: Children's Books and Radical Experiments in Art* (London: Macmillan Press, 1999).

Ede, Lisa. 'An Introduction to the Nonsense Literature of Edward Lear and Lewis Carroll', in Wim Tigges (ed.), *Explorations in the Field of Nonsense* (Amsterdam: Rodopi BV, 1987).

Ellmann, Richard. *Yeats: The Man and The Masks* (London: Penguin Books, 1987 [1948]).

—— *James Joyce* (Oxford: Oxford University Press, 1982).

Esslin, Martin. *The Theatre of the Absurd* (London: Penguin Books, 1983).

Fanon, Frantz. *The Wretched of the Earth* (Harmonsworth: Penguin, 1990 [1961]).

Farrell, Frank. *Subjectivity, Realism and Postmodernism* (New York: Cambridge University Press, 1994).

Fennell, Desmond. 'Against Revisionism', in Ciaran Brady (ed.), *Interpreting Irish History: the Debate on Revisionism* (Dublin: Irish Academic Press, 1994).

Foster, R.F. *The Irish Story: Telling Tales and Making it up in Ireland* (London: Penguin, 2001).

—— 'We Are All Revisionists Now', *The Irish Review*, 1 (1986), pp.1–5.

Frost, Robert. 'Education by Poetry', in Edward Connery Lathem and Lawrence Thompson (eds), *Robert Frost Poetry and Prose* (New York: Henry Holt & Co., 1972).

Fukuyama, Francis. *The Great Disruption* (New York: Touchstone, 2000).

Gersie, Alida. *Reflections on Therapeutic Storymaking* (London: Jessica Kingsley Publishers Ltd, 1997).

Gersie, Alida and Nancy King. *Storymaking in Education and Therapy* (London: Jessica Kingsley Publishers, 1990).

Gibbons, Luke. 'Challenging the Canon: Revisionism and Cultural Criticism', in *The Field Day Anthology* Vol.III (Derry: Field day Publications, 1991).

—— *Transformations in Irish Culture* (Cork: Cork University Press, 1996).

Goldring, Maurice. Foreword, in *Pleasant the Scholar's Life: Irish Intellectuals and the Construction of the Nation State* (London: Serif, 1993).

Hanne, Michael. *The Power of the Story* (Oxford: Berghahn Books, 1994).

Havel, Vaclav. 'The State of the Republic', trans. Paul Wilson, *The New York Book Review of Books*, 45, 4 (5 March 1998), pp.42–6.

—— 'Kosovo and the End of The Nation State', *The New York Review of Books*, 46, 10 (1999), pp.4–7.

Hegel, G.W.F. *Phenomenology of Spirit*, trans. A.V. Miller (Oxford: Oxford University Press, 1977).

Held, David. *Introduction to Critical Theory: Horkheimer to Habermas* (Berkeley, CA: University of California Press, 1980).

Holbrook, David. 'The Problem of C.S. Lewis', *Children's Literature in Education*, 10 (March 1973), pp.3–25.

Hughes, Ted. 'Myth and Education', in Geoff Fox and Graham Hammond (eds), *Writers, Critics and Children* (London: Heinemann Educational Press, 1976).

Hunt, Peter (ed). *Literature for Children* (London: Routledge, 1992).

Ionesco, Eugene. *Notes and Counter-Notes*, trans. Donald Watson (London: John Calder, 1964 [1962)]).

Jackson, Rosemary. *Fantasy: The Literature of Subversion* (London: Methuen, 1981).

Jameson, Fredric. 'Postmodernism, or the Cultural Logic of Late Capitalism', *New Left Review*, 145 (1984), pp.53–92.

Kearney, Richard. *The Wake of Imagination* (London: Century Hutchinson Ltd, 1988).

——— *Poetics of Modernity* (New Jersey: Humanities Press, 1995).

——— *On Stories* (London: Routledge, 2002).

Keenan, Celia. 'The Famine Told to Children', in Valerie Coghlan and Celia Keenan (eds), *The Big Guide 2: Irish Children's Books* (Dublin: Children's Books Ireland, 2000).

Kennelly, Brendan. 'A Soft Amen', in *Cromwell* (Dublin: Beaver Row Press, 1983).

Kenny, Vincent. 'The Post Colonial Personality', *Crane Bag*, 9 (1985), pp.70–8.

Kiberd, Declan. *Synge and the Irish Language* (London: MacMillan Press Ltd, 1979).

——— *Irish Classics* (London: Granta Books, 2000).

Kristeva, Julia. *Revolution in Poetic Language*, trans. Margaret Waller (New York: Columbia University Press, 1984).

——— *Nations Without Nationalism* (New York: Columbia University Press, 1993).

——— *Hannah Arendt: Life Is a Narrative*, trans. Frank Collins (Toronto, Buffalo, London: University of Toronto Press, 2001).

Kundera, Milan. *Testaments Betrayed* (London: Faber & Faber, 1996 [1995]).

Levi Strauss, Claude. *The Savage Mind* (London: Weidenfeld and Nicolson, 1962).

Lilla, Mark. 'A Tale of Two Reactions', *New York Review of Books*, XLV, 8 (14 May 1998), pp.4–7.

Locherbie-Cameron, M.A.L. 'Journeys Through the Amulet: Time Travel in Children's Fiction', *Signal*, 79 (January 1996), pp.45–61.

Lodge, David. 'Milan Kundera and the Idea of the Author in Modern Fiction', in *After Bakhtin* (London: Routledge, 1990).

Lurie, Alison. *Don't Tell The Grown-ups: Subversive Children's Literature* (London: Bloomsbury Publishing, 1990).

Lyons, F.S.L. *Ireland Since the Famine* (London : Fontana, 1989 [1971]).

MacRaois, Cormac. 'Old Tales for New People: Irish Mythology Retold for Children', *The Lion and The Unicorn*, 21, 3 (1997), pp.330–40.

Miller, J. Hillis. *Tropes, Parables, Performatives: Essays on Twentieth-Century Literature* (London: Harvester Wheatsheaf, 1990).

Moore, Jacqueline. 'Gender, Representation and Ireland' (Unpublished Essay, 1994).

Moynihan, Maurice (ed.). *Speeches and Statements by Eamon de Valera 1917–1972* (Dublin: Gill & Macmillan, 1980).

O'Carroll, J.P. and J.A. Murphy (eds). *De Valera and His Times* (Cork: Cork University Press, 1986).

O'Driscoll, Robert. 'Return to the Heartstone: Ideals of the Celtic Literary Revival', in *Place, Personality and the Irish Writer*, ed. Andrew Carpenter (Buckinghamshire: Colin Smythe Ltd, 1977), pp.41–68.

O'Faolain, Sean. *The Irish* (London: Penguin Books, 1969).

O'Neill, John. *The Poverty of Post Modernism* (London: Routledge, 1995).

O'Sullivan, Emer. 'The Development of Modern Children's Literature in Late Twentieth Century Ireland', *Signal*, 81 (1996), pp.189–211.

O'Sullivan, Patrick (ed.). *Irish Women and Irish Migration*, in *The Irish World Wide. History, Heritage, Identity* Vol. 4 (London: Leicester University Press, 1995).

O'Sullivan, Sean. *The Folklore of Ireland* (London: B.T. Balsford Ltd, 1974).

O'Tuathaigh, M.A.G. 'Irish Historical "Revisionism": State of the Art or Ideological Project?', in Ciaran Brady (ed.), *Interpreting Irish History: the Debate on Revisionism* (Dublin: Irish Academic Press, 1994).

Opie, Peter and Iona. *The Singing Game* (Oxford: Oxford University Press, 1985).

Orwell, George. 'Politics and the English Language', in Sonia Orwell and Ian Angus (eds), *The Collected Essays, Journalism and Letters of George Orwell* (London: Secker & Warburg, 1968), Vol.IV.

Paul, Lissa. 'Imitations of Imitations', in Peter Hunt (ed.), *Literature for Children* (London: Routledge, 1992).

Pickering, Samuel Jr. 'The Function of Criticism in Children's Literature', *Children's Literature in Education*, 13, 1 (1982), pp.13–18.

Póirtéir, Cathal. *Famine Echoes* (Dublin: Gill & Macmillan, 1995).

Postman, Neil. *The Disappearance of Childhood* (New York: Vintage, 1994 [1983]).

Prentice, Chris. 'Problems of Response to Empire', in Chris Tiffin and Alan Lawson (eds), *De-Scribing Empire* (London: Routledge, 1994).

Propp, V. *The Morphology of the Folktale*, trans. L. Scott (Austin, TX: University of Texas Press, 1968).

Rabinowitz, Peter J. *Before Reading* (Columbus, OH: Ohio State University Press, 1998).

Reddin, Kenneth. 'Children's Books in Ireland', *Irish Library Bulletin*, 7 (1946), pp.74–6.

Rose, Jacqueline. *The Case of Peter Pan or The Impossibility of Children's Fiction* (London: Macmillan Press, 1984).

Ryan, Desmond. *Unique Dictator* (London: Arthur Baker Ltd, 1936).

Said, Edward. *Culture and Imperialism* (London: Vintage, 1994).

Schama, Simon. *Landscape and Memory* (London: Harper Collins, 1995).

Sewell, Elizabeth. *The Field of Nonsense* (London: Chatto and Windus, 1952).

Shils, Edward. *Tradition* (London: Faber & Faber, 1981).

Spufford, Francis. *The Child That Books Built* (London: Faber & Faber, 2002).

Steiner, George. *Errata: An Examined Life* (London: Weidenfeld & Nicolson, 1997).

Stephens, John. *Language and Ideology in Children's Fiction* (New York: Longman Publishing, 1992).

Sweeney, Matthew and John Hartley Williams. *Writing Poetry and Getting Published* (London: Hodder Headline Plc, 1997).

Synge, J.M. *Plays, Poems and Prose*, ed. Alison Smith (London: J.M. Dent & Sons Ltd, 1992).

Terdiman, Richard. *Present Past: Modernity and the Memory Crisis* (New York: Cornell University Press, 1993).

Thacker, Deborah. 'Disdain or Ignorance? Literary Theory and the Absence of Children's Literature', *The Lion and the Unicorn*, 24, 1 (January 2000), pp.1–17.

Thomas, Jenny A. 'The Language of Power. Towards a Dynamic Pragmatics', *Journal of Pragmatics* 9 (1985), pp.765–83.

Tiffin, Chris and Alan Lawson (eds). *De-scribing Empire* (London: Routledge, 1994).

Wade, Allan (ed.). *The Letters of W.B. Yeats* (London: Rupert Hart-Davies, 1954).

Walsh, Jill Paton. 'The Art of Realism', in Betsy Hearne and Marilyn Kaye (eds), *Celebrating Children's Books* (New York: Lothrop, Lee & Shepard, 1981).

Warner, Marina. *From The Beast to the Blonde* (London: Vintage, 1990).

Waugh, Patricia. *Metafiction: The Theory and Practice of Self-Conscious Fiction* (London: Routledge, 1988).

White, Hayden. *Metahistory: The Historical Imagination in Nineteenth Century Europe* (Baltimore, MD: John Hopkins University Press, 1993 [1973]).

White, Hayden. *Tropics of Discourse. Essays in Cultural Criticism* (Baltimore, MD: John Hopkins University Press, 1990 [1978]).

Wolin, Richard. *Walter Benjamin: An Aesthetic of Redemption* (New York: Colombia University Press, 1982).

Yeats, W.B. Preface, in Lady Augusta Gregory, *Cuchulain of Muirhemne* (New York: Gramercy Books, 1986 [1902]).

Index

Visions and Revisions Irish Writers in Their Time
John Banville

John Kenny

John Banville is an accessible yet detailed study that brings to the surface many of the hidden depths of one of the major writers of contemporary Irish and world fiction. It mediates between two existing kinds of critical work on Banville: novel-by-novel introductions, and specialised academic analyses. While it approaches some of Banville's works individually, its discussions are arranged thematically, thus demonstrating the overall patterns in his oeuvre and in his literary thinking. With a close eye on chronology, the book begins by establishing the intellectual and cultural contexts of the oeuvre and its reception, then provides readings of Banville's Irish themes, his crucial theories of the Imagination, his thematic preoccupation with morality and immorality, his idiosyncratic devotion to a self-reflexive art. Work of all Banville's periods is covered, from his first book, *Long Lankin* (1970) to his Man-Booker winning novel, *The Sea* (2005), and his recent popular fiction written under a pseudonym.

Rather than incorporating the frameworks of the existing Banville criticism, one of this book's major benefits is that it allows the author to speak for himself at all stages by referring to all his principal statements on his art and worldview. The discussions here are all attentive to those who may be in the early stages of familiarity with Banville, so that the general application of ideas and arguments can be understood without firsthand or detailed knowledge of the works under discussion. Those who are well acquainted with the Banville oeuvre will also find new aspects of emphasis and suggestion. A number of important items from Banville's career as a literary essayist and reviewer are used in the chapters, and the book is thus a good starting point for readers wishing to further develop their interest.

2008   224 pages
978 0 7165 2900 2 cloth €60.00/£45.00/$74.95
978 0 7165 2901 9 paper €19.95/£17.95/$32.95

Visions and Revisions Irish Writers in Their Time
Patrick Kavanagh
Stan Smith

This volume offers a comprehensive account by a range of established scholars of the richness and variety of Patrick Kavanagh's work both in prose and verse, and situates his writings in the social and cultural contexts of the workaday Ireland which emerged from the heroics of nationalist insurrection and civil war. The distinguished scholars who contribute to this account bring a diverse range of approaches and perspectives to offer a fuller understanding of his work. Patrick Kavanagh has for long represented an alternative vision of Irish poetry to the high melodrama and attitudinising of W. B. Yeats. Low key and apparently equable in tone, though often revealing a sly acerbic wit, Kavanagh's verse has represented a domestic, though not domesticated, alternative to the high-falutin' rhetoric of the Yeatsian mode, pitching itself to the quotidian world of de Valera's 'Catholic Republic', famously extolling the virtues of the 'parochial' in contrast to the siren call of the cosmopolitan and metropolitan, like Joyce finding its inspiration in the streets and alleys of a middle and lower class Dublin and the stony acres, literal and metaphoric, of a sparse rural economy, and, like Flann O'Brien, preferring the bicycle as a mode of poetic transport to the high horse of the 'last Romantics'. It confirms Seamus Heaney's claim that Kavanagh 'gave single-handed permission for Irish poets to trust and cultivate their native ground and experience.'

2008   224 pages
978 0 7165 2892 0 cloth €60.00/£45.00/$74.95
978 0 7165 2893 7 paper €19.95/£17.95/$32.95

Visions and Revisions Irish Writers in Their Time
Elizabeth Bowen
Eibhear Walshe
Foreword by Neil Corcoran

This edited collection, provides a complete academic account of the fictions of Elizabeth Bowen (1899–1973) the most important Anglo-Irish novelist of the 20th century. It covers Bowen's life, her family background and her writing career between London and North Cork. Of particular interest is her position as an Anglo-Irish writer and her centrality as a major novelist within the traditions of 20th century writing, within modernist literature and, in particular, within modern Irish writing. This book provides an overall cultural context for her novels and short stories. Each chapter explores Bowen's links with other 20th century novelists and her modernist deployment of the novel form, her representation of Ireland, of the Anglo-Irish and of the Irish War of Independence.

Also considered are the wide range of Bowen's short stories from 1929 up to 1967 and her experience of living in London during the Second World War. Other chapters discuss the changes in narrative form used in Bowen's last novels, novels of experimentation and increasing darkness. This book locates her writings within contemporary notions of the construction of gender in relation to fictive representations of sexuality and sexual identity. Bowen has been read as a modernist, a structuralist and also within feminist and post-colonial theories of fiction writing. Since her death in 1973, Bowen's novels have been constantly in print and many critics and biographers, like Victoria Glendinning, Patricia Craig, Neil Corcoran, Hermione Lee, Maud Ellmann, Roy Foster and many others have written on her. This book provides a comprehensive scholarly account of her creative life and that critical afterlife.

2008   240 pages
978 0 7165 2916 3   cloth €60.00/£45.00/$74.95
978 0 7165 2917 0   paper €19.95/£17.95/$34.95

This major book series demonstrates the growth, variety and achievement of Irish writing in the eighteenth and nineteenth centuries. Covering prose, poetry and drama, the volumes not only contain work by major authors but also includes less obvious material gleaned from sources such as letters, diaries, court reports, newspapers and journals.

Irish Literature
The Eighteenth Century

An Annotated Anthology

Edited and Introduced by
A. Norman Jeffares and
Peter van de Kamp

Foreword by Brendan Kennelly

424 pages 2005
978 0 7165 2799 2 cloth €65.00/£49.50/79.50
978 0 7165 2804 3 paper €29.95/£22.50/$37.50

Irish Literature
The Nineteenth Century
Volume I

An Annotated Anthology

Edited and Introduced by
A. Norman Jeffares and
Peter van de Kamp

Foreword by Terence Brown

424 pages 2005
978 0 7165 2800 5 cloth €65.00/£49.50/$79.50
978 0 7165 2805 0 paper €29.95/£22.50/$37.50

Irish Literature
The Nineteenth Century
Volume II

An Annotated Anthology

Edited and Introduced by
A. Norman Jeffares and
Peter van de Kamp

Foreword by Conor Cruise O'Brien

336 pages 2006
978 0 7165 3333 7 cloth €65.00/£49.50/$79.50
978 0 7165 3334 4 paper €29.95/£22.50/$37.50

Irish Literature
The Nineteenth Century
Volume III

An Annotated Anthology

Edited and Introduced by
A. Norman Jeffares and
Peter van de Kamp

336 pages 2006
978 0 7165 3357 3 cloth €65.00/£49.50/$79.50
978 0 7165 3358 0 paper €29.95/£22.50/$37.50

Oscar Wilde's Plagiarism
The Triumph of Art over Ego

Florina Tufescu

Oscar Wilde's plagiarism practices across genres are seen as part of a neo-classical tradition. His allegory of plagiarism in *An Ideal Husband* is compared to those created by fellow playwrights, including Ibsen and G. B. Shaw. Wilde's polemical imitation of Shakespeare's cut-and-paste method in *The Portrait of Mr. W.H.* inspires Joyce to experiment with the erasure of quotation marks in *Ulysses*. The blatant collage of Wilde's poetry anticipates T. S. Eliot's *The Waste Land*, just as it recalls Manet's paintings, which provocatively assert artistic status by drawing attention to their flatness. The mosaic-like structure of *The Picture of Dorian Gray* is akin to that of other anti-individualist masterpieces, notably Goethe's *Faust* and D. M. Thomas's *The White Hotel*.

The extent of sophisticated plagiarism in the canonical works and the impressive list of its apologists from Ackroyd to Zola indicate the need for new models of authorship and intellectual property, models that would benefit scholarly and artistic creativity and solve the paradox of plagiarism as simultaneously one of the most serious and most common of literary crimes.

2007   244 pages
978 0 7165 2904 0   cloth €45.00/£30.00/$55.00

Maurice Harmon
Selected Essays

Barbara Brown (Ed)
Foreword by Terence Brown

Maurice Harmon: *Selected Essays* assembles published articles with unpublished talks and lectures, all of which show Harmon's lively, readable style and draw upon a lifetime of study and contemplation. They provide authoritative readings of Irish writers and their work over three centuries, beginning with discussions of the origins and development of Irish literature in the nineteenth century and of the issues and contexts that determined the formation of an indigenous literature. They conclude with assessments of Modern Irish Literature in the work of such poets as John Montague, Thomas Kinsella, Seamus Heaney, and more recent figures.

Other essays concentrate on writers and topics in the post-colonial, post-revolutionary period – Patrick Kavanagh, Seán O'Faoláin, Mary Lavin and Francis Stuart – and show the variety and the vitality of their commitment to artistic freedom. With clarity, vigour, and good sense, Harmon considers their historical and cultural milieus. Editorials from *Poetry Ireland Review* and the influential *Advice for a Poet* engage with the current generation of Irish poets and reflect his critical values.

The originality of its perspective places *Selected Essays* in a class of its own. It complements rather than competes with other work in the field. Scholars, students, and the general reader will benefit from these accounts of significant Irish writers and their work by a distinguished specialist.

2006   248 pages
978 0 7165 3400 6 cloth   €65.00/£40.00/$75.00
978 0 7165 3401 3 paper €27.50/£20.00/$30.00